STORM IN MY SOUL, FLOWERS AT MY FEET

Sketches and Reflections from a Life across Borders

Sanjay Mathur

To my parents,
who entrusted me with freedom

Contents

Note to the Reader

Writing a memoir is a tricky business. How much is true? If true, is it the whole truth? Is it nothing but the truth? And what has been deliberately or subconsciously left out and why? What are the motives of the author?

It has been rightly said that "all life once lived is fiction" (anonymous), that we are not capable of telling the whole truth about the anything. But it has also been said, "Life is lived forwards but understood backwards" (Danish philosopher Soren Kierkegaard). That is one reason I purport to write something like a memoir, but really a series of sketches, vignettes, and reflections held together by a narrative here and there only.

My motives are several. It is to make sense of my own life. It is also to capture, in third person, those moments that stand out in my mind for their significance—physically, emotionally, mentally, spiritually. I also take to writing for enjoyment of writing and language—the love of description, the apt word, fleeting emotion, beauty of all types, and sought after meaning, or lack thereof. A writer must be in love with language and wish to tell a story reasonably well while, in the form of memoir, remaining fundamentally faithful to recollection of events. A devilishly tricky, devilishly fun proposition.

I cannot capture everything. I cannot write only of good things. I restrict myself therefore to what is my story to tell, and not someone else's story; and to tell it with the meaning I sensed or that escapes me, hidden in a nutshell still.

Finally, the past is the past and not meant to be clung to. While it strengthens one to look back now and then, there can be no dwelling in the past from the point of view of liberation. Freedom of the self requires unburdening from the past, which perhaps you can get a sense of by understanding your own conditioning and not reacting always to either the wounds or the supposed glory days of any time of life. It is my intent to use this form of writing and self-reflection to be free of the past in order to embrace the present. Alas, easier said than done.

Part I

Childhood

Well, this was not my fate, nor even that of the poet of British imperialism who wrote these lines, nor that of the many millions in history who have travelled far from home and found themselves grappling with cultures different from their own. The two have met and mixed and mingled and sometimes married, producing children like myself or whole societies like the Anglo-Indians of India or even the mestizo majority of Mexico. The intermingling of people has been a constant in human affairs since time immemorial and, however nested we are, we all have a part of the nomad and the wanderer in our heritage as human beings.

We are all mixed and mixed up. It's only more obvious with people like me. Marriage between people of different "races" or ethnicities or nationalities has become more common recently due to increased travel along with society's acceptance of such liaisons, offsetting what society once called "miscegenation" and what the United States and other countries attempted to circumscribe through "anti-miscegenation" laws. Many other societies in history, all over the world, have tried to stop such "mixing", and it has not been possible.

Being of mixed heritage and being a child of immigrants shaped my consciousness and my sensitivity in profound ways. ***What was it like growing up as the child of multi-cultural parents in a country that belonged to neither of them but was effectively the only country the child knew?***

Sketch: Infancy in Bombay

Mama, Daddy, and the Matterhorn, 1966

He had no conscious memory of the place. He was too young. There were only black and white photographs and the odd story or two. There he was, being pushed by his mother in a metal stroller on Juhu beach, according to the caption. Maybe they had swung by Crawford market where his mother used to go with a friend. In another photograph, he was standing in wavy hair, dappled sunlight over his face, his arm resting on the window sill after pulling the blinds. Maybe it was in the same room where his crib was said to have shifted from one side to another during an earthquake. Remarkably, his parents said, he never woke up.

Myself as an infant, Bombay 1968

But he had no memory of the monsoon that the city is famous for, of the tremendous downpours filling the potholes and opening up others, of rats headed to higher ground and suburban trains grinding to a halt. Pure liquid oblivion. And he had no memory of the markets and market people, of the many languages spoken around him, of the calls of the vegetable hawkers and the smells of the street stalls cooking up spicy snacks on portable stoves. Evenings would have been long and languid and resplendent under the lights on Marine Drive, that famed "necklace of pearls" on the shores of the Arabian Sea.

This was Bombay, later re-named Mumbai, and he had no memory of it except for whatever might have seeped into his bones and blood, his mind and heart. Yet it was the place of birth that he would fill out on every form that required it for the rest of his life. It was the place he told people he was born in when they asked him in that far-away land that awaited him because they were curious about his foreign name and copper skin tone and protruding nose. This port city of endless migration tied him, strangely, to an enormous country that his father liked to say he belonged to "by accident of birth."

On one momentous day he doesn't remember, his father would have come home with visas in their passports to emigrate to the United States. On another epic day, his mother would have scooped him out of that rickety metal stroller one last time and carried him into the airport's international departures terminal enroute to Switzerland, her country. On yet another day, some weeks later, his father would have followed, leaving behind his country and the family that nurtured him, not knowing when he would return. When his father reached them in Switzerland, the little boy might have felt the excitement and optimism and anticipation of his father, the willing emigrant, along with his mother's acquiescence and trepidation. But he cannot remember.

When the three of them arrived in New York City, it was June 1968. They were met by friends from India who lived in upstate New York. Two months later, following his father's job search, they found themselves in a hot and muggy southern city called Houston. Of that place, in the confines of a red brick apartment community full of trees and squirrels, he would have his first memories. It would be home.

Form-filling at time of emigration (April 1968)

Name: Sanjay Prem Mathur

Date of birth: July 6, 1966

Place of birth: Bombay, India

Citizenship: India

Father: Jamshed Mathur

Born: November 23, 1929

Place: Jamshedpur, India

Mother: Margrit Landerer

Born: January 31, 1929

Place: Winterthur, Switzerland

Siblings: Siblings: none
younger brother, younger sister

Citizenship: India   Citizenship: Switzerland

Date of marriage: November 24, 1964

Place of marriage: Calcutta, India

Other children: none

Date of arrival in the U.S.: 1 June 1968

Narrative: East and West Meet in Houston

After our soft landing with friends in Ithaca in New York in June, and after two months of looking elsewhere for a job, my father was offered work in Houston as a petro-chemical engineer in the burgeoning oil and gas industry of Texas. By August, we had reached there in sweltering Gulf of Mexico summer heat. To our everlasting contentment, we had the good fortune of moving into a place called Parkwood Apartments.

Here, East and West met frequently, casually, and comfortably. There were two other Indian families, one from north India like my father's family, who were also navigating this new world and society. Our neighbors downstairs were from Peru and became lifelong friends, inspiring my mother to learn Spanish. In my birthday party photos, one sees the troop of neighborhood friends in my age bracket, including Sonu and Anju from north India, Sandra and Ursula from Peru, Arup and Rita from east India, Raul and Joseph from Mexico, Donnie and Dodie from Minnesota (grandparents from Denmark) and Tommy, Katie, and Joseph from Texas (yet with a grandfather from Italy). And many others from the vastness of America, including a close African-American friend Wassel, and his sister Alicia and brother Brian, from north Texas as well as kids like Marcela and Pilar from Paraguay, Eduardo from Venezuela, Boon from Japan, Barak from Israel, and Ricardo from Guatemala—even another "mixed race" boy like me, Charles, whose father was Filipino and mother was Canadian.

This is not to forget that the majority of residents were Americans by birth. But for younger families like ours, whether of American or foreign origin, it was the location of Parkwood Apartments on the fringes of the Texas Medical Center, with world-renowned hospitals, that had drawn many of the immigrant families as medical students, doctors, and researchers.

Sketch: Apartment Home

Myself in front of our home on 1918 Brunson, top floor right side

His first memory is not an indoor memory, it is outdoors. He is standing at the top of the stairs, his left hand on the banister of the black stairwell leading down into the backyard of his apartment community home. A crepe myrtle tree with small reddish and pink flowers stretches up to nearly his height. He looks out over the interior of the complex and surveys the trees, the sidewalk circling around the trees and connecting each apartment building to the carport, the common clothes line where mothers would hang up clothes to dry, and a sandbox for the kids to play. In front of some apartment buildings are tricycles and "big wheels" for children to move about on the sidewalks. In his hand, he carries a plastic bucket and plastic spade as though he were going out for a bit of gardening but really he was intent on getting to the sandbox.

Besides the people, a mix of natives and immigrant families from different corners of the world, it was the many trees, mostly oaks, that made the place special and gave it its name, "Parkwood." They sheltered squirrels and birds and also offered a higher world of play to children. He could be high up in a tree he didn't know the name of and his friend might be on another branch and another friend further down and a fourth boy on another limb. Suddenly—and it wasn't unexpected—one boy might yell, "*Twiiiiiiiig fiiiiiiighting!*" Like monkeys springing to life, the boys broke off twigs on the branches around them and hurled them at each other with a fury and glee that was blissful mayhem—ducking twigs, flinging the same, delighting in near misses, and shouting with triumph at direct hits. The poor old trees, swaying with the weight and movement, would have to endure just such a commotion of boys from time to time.

If it were raining, on the other hand, he and his friends would wait in anticipation for the storm to be over. Then they would come out on the street and race twigs in the water running alongside the curb down to the drains. Each boy would follow his little twig in the water, removing impediments like leaves, stones, and sediment, especially where the tires of cars parked in the street came close up on the curb. The air was fresh and the excitement was high, nothing was on TV that mattered to them and there were no video games. As the twigs flowed down to the drain, evading all obstacles, the boys could be heard exclaiming to each other and no one in particular, "look at mine", "mine can really go", and "I'm in the lead". Such was the simplicity, spontaneity, and creativity of much outdoor play. One never knew what one might do when a friend came to the door, which was opened by the mother, and the friend asked innocently, "Can Sanj come out to play?"

Sketch: Going to the Zoo

Sunday mornings could find him sprawled on the carpet floor of their Houston apartment home, poring over the baseball box scores, feet dangling in the air. Then, with friends at church and the zoo due to open at 9:30 AM, he and his father would get into the old gray Ford Mustang Mach II and set out for the zoo. They navigated the potholes on Staffordshire road that ran through the apartment complex, made a left on Wyndale and drove past the old chicken farm, and then turned right onto Braeswood and crossed the bayou bridge before stopping at the light on Holcombe with the vastness of the Medical Center beginning on one side. They continued straight under enormously tall oak trees and past the golfers in their white carts, striped shirts, and corduroy caps. At Ben Taub hospital, they veered right and that was when he would catch the first glimpse of the fountain of water shooting high up into the air before collapsing on itself and the lake below. This was the thrill of being welcomed to the zoo at Hermann Park.

After his father paid a negligible entrance fee, the boy would run to the enclosure where the seals were swimming in circles around their little island. Feeding time was prompt and the keeper would get the seals to jump in the water and even dance on their flippers for a fish. On some days, the whooping sounds of howler monkeys could be heard echoing across the zoo grounds and beyond. After that first look at the seals, father and son would move back by a pond full of ducks to enjoy a drink, even an early Coca Cola, and a bag of peanuts. Then it was down the lane of grazers like the gazelles and springbok from South Africa and of course the nilgai from India. His father seemed to have a fondness for the nilgai, telling him with a smile that it translated to "blue bull." They then proceeded to a little island for small monkeys before moving on to the children's zoo where he could check in on a baby monkey named "Ugmo" or the next little monkey that was born. Then came the rhinos and elephants and condors. At each enclosure, he took in the signs and maps, learning where all the animals came from, an unexpected lesson in geography.

After an hour and a half or so, they left the zoo and drove by the park on one side of the amphitheater. There, at the bottom of Hippie Hill, amid the ever so tall pine trees, they would kick a soccer ball to one another for another half hour or so. This father-son Sunday routine went on for years, lending color and variety to an already sweet childhood.

Sketch: Ball Player

A brick wall. A ball. Imagining he is the pitcher on a major league team, the hometown Houston Astros. It is a tennis ball. The strike zone is visible. The wind up—he could be Larry Dierker, Joe Niekro, J.R. Richards—and he flings it across home plate. Strike! The ball bounces back and he scoops it up with his glove.

It is a red brick apartment complex and a red brick wall with no windows, just a bedroom behind it. Hopefully, they are not trying to sleep in the middle of the day.

He pretends now that he is the shortstop. He steps to the side, flanked by another apartment building, and throws the lime green tennis ball hard to one end and dashes to catch it after a bounce or two with the back of his glove and in one motion throws it back to home plate. Roger Metzger, Davey Concepción. Out!

He could play like this for hours. A world of imagination and practice. Alone. His friends were out. His arm grew in muscle tone, his back in flexibility, his mind in hand-eye coordination. And imagination. And endurance.

Sketch: A Summer Camp to Forget

He sat on the olive green camp cot, alone in the barracks-like building, hiding, with no lights on. Through the window's mesh screen, he was aware of the boys outside. Something wasn't right and he couldn't say what. He had escaped without being seen for now. Sitting on the edge of the cot, he did not know what to do, except to pass the time, another day or so, until camp would end and he could go home. This was not what it was supposed to be like at all. There were boys who were wild, rough, uncouth, violent, racist even. Everyone was white.

He had not expected this when invited by his friends, the two brothers in the apartment complex in Houston. But now they were all far away from the city and he was separated from them. It was completely rural here, remote, in the midst of towering trees. There was a swimming pool and he could not swim so well. His skin was a little darker than the rest, especially in summertime like this. His name was quite different and easy fodder for jokes. He thought of his parents and how different they were from everyone here, in outlook, in manners, in speech.

It was all this and more. He did not feel comfortable at all. When boys went around trying to hit each other in the groin—"the balls", "the nuts", they said—to force a person to cover up, he felt doubly uncomfortable. It was not something he would do. Or when a boy would seize an opportunity to twist a boy's arm behind his back and pull him around with pain until he screamed for mercy, it frightened him. He knew that pain. He himself could not and would not inflict it on anyone else. There was a looming violence here that was pinning him down and he felt an outright aversion to. Suddenly he could sense the shadow of a boy at the door, possibly coming to look for him. He ducked and lay down under the cot, his cheek cool against the cement floor. The boy did not see him and left.

He would stay here as long as he could. Let them play their games without him. Let them forget about him. It seemed like even the two brothers from the apartment complex, who were both his good friends, had forgotten about him already, what with the opportunity to make so many other friends here. He wanted out. He stopped talking to everybody. A few days later, when the bus came to take them back to the city, he sat in the very front seat. He can picture himself in that seat still, so safe. He was never so happy to be home as he was returning from that summer camp. He must have been about ten years old only.

Sketch: A House in Winterthur

Childhood Trips to the Old World	
Switzerland	June—December 1973
India	December 1976—January 1977
Switzerland	December 1977—January 1978

In the heart of western Europe, in the north of Switzerland, a house stood on a gentle slope walking distance from a small town center near the bahnhof (railway station). Painted white, it was a two-story A-frame with a clothesline and garden out back. The living room could barely fit a couch, table, and two armchairs on either side of a fireplace. The kitchen was equally tiny. The wooden stairs were narrow. The whole place seemed to creak with every footstep. It was new at one time, probably built after the Great War.

His mother grew up here as the only child of a Swiss homemaker and Austrian tailor who had escaped to Switzerland after what is now called World War I, rightfully leery of more war to come. When times were hard, he worked in a pastry shop and later in a factory. His name was Hans and he doted on his daughter Margrit, in contrast to his wife Lina, who enjoyed being "strict", as though it were her only means of self-assertion.

Therefore the boy's strongest early memory of Grossmama was of her sitting in the living room, piercing him with her narrow eyes and shushing him across the language barrier by saying "psssht, psssht" every time he spoke. Her very eyes seemed to drive home the message that children like him were to be seen and not heard. He may not have paid her much mind, since he responded to her in like terms, saying "psssht, psssht" with one finger across his mouth. His mother could only smile. She seemed to know all too well the ways of her own mother.

On the other hand, the memories of his Grosspapa were rich and varied. He was his helper when he worked in the garden. They would walk down into the town of Winterthur and he would introduce him to one and all as his "American grandson." Most of all, there was nothing better than relishing his homemade Christmas cookies glazed with sugar and shaped like a star or tree or bear.

Growing up here couldn't have been easy for his mother, but she didn't say much about it. He was too young and didn't need to know. He could not understand their conversations in Swiss-German, whether serious or light. But he could detect the friction between his grandmother and his mother. It could start on the first day and go on for three or four days. Then his mother would ask him to pack his suitcase and they would be gone the next day to stay with an old childhood friend of hers. It may have been only the blue Austrian eyes of his Grosspapa that expressed regret at these departures. He too must have suffered over the years.

Years later, his mother would receive an international call. It must have been Grossmama. It was about Grosspapa. His mother began to sob. He was aware of it and felt his mother's grief though he was not close enough to Grosspapa to cry himself. He had not really thought about where people went after they died. He can't remember if it was him or his mother who said it, but both agreed Grosspapa must now be "one with Nature." He, the grandson, carried his blue eyes.

Much later, when he was married and a year after his own mother's death, he received a letter from the son of a brother of his Grossmama that he didn't know even existed. He had never met any brother of Grossmama's on any of the trips they had made to Winterthur during his childhood. In the most cordial of terms, the letter writer requested his signature giving up any claims to that house on a hill. As the only child, his mother may have had a claim on it that neither he nor his father knew about and that now came to him. He did the needful, signed the paperwork, and received an appreciative email thank you from that individual who on paper was a cousin he never knew he had, had never met, and never would meet. As far as he was concerned, it was as though he had no relatives in Switzerland. That branch of the family tree was now bare.

Sketch: At the Bahnhof

The boy might have been holding his mother's hand. The pedestrians walked and stopped, walked and stopped. He thought he could make out the languages he heard them speaking: Swiss-German, French, Italian. And there was that one language that was harder to make out, nasal, the words ran together. Was it east European? Portuguese?

They crossed the iron rails in front of the tram stop. It was a mesmerizing synchronicity of multiple-bogey trams. This was in front of the main train station and there was shopping inside. He followed his mother. He waited outside the shop watching the passing of people rushing home at day's end, little briefcases and bags in their hand, dressed in suits and dresses, heels and hats. Faintly, he could hear the sounds of a large and long train coming to a stop, pushing and pulling air into the overhang of the station, its wheels grinding the rails, its air brakes hissing as the train ground to a halt.

Outside, the day's fading light was shining on Grossmünster Kirche. The light transformed the lichen green of its enormous stone walls into something softer, grander, serener. Its steep angular steeple, narrow like a sword's handle, stood out in black offset only by the white balconies of the apartments on the hill beyond. A line of ducks, olive green and tawny tan, suddenly flew up where the Limatt river flowed canal-like into Lake Zürich, dark and deep and cold. Lights slowly lit up on the opposing banks, far away, so distant, so enchanting under the enormous evening sky. The mountains watched it all. This scenery, these place names, the languages, this entire ambience—so unlike Houston—also became part of his mental make-up. It was his mother's home.

Zürich, Switzerland, 1973

Sketch: Boy on a Train

It was perhaps a privilege to be on the Trans European Express (TEE) train, Zürich to Brussels, with a stop in Strasbourg, France. He had heard his mother and friends speak of the so-called "TEE train" in what seemed like mystical admiration of its speed. The boy was anyways in love with trains and mountains in Switzerland. He loved to count the tunnels while passing through a mountain, from light to dark and light again, from wispy clouds to the specter of sun on the other end.

His mother had to speak swiftly at this stop in Strasbourg. The mountains were behind them. The migrations officer flipped through his passport, hunting for a visa. The officer was dressed in navy blue uniform and wore a cone of a hat, flat on top. His mother had told him it was going to be a short stop. She was speaking to the officer in a language he did not understand and seldom heard her speak. They had just crossed a border and this express train—how he thrilled to it—had only this one stop to make in this country they were merely passing through. If his mother could delay the officer long enough, the train would start moving. And maybe all this visa business would be forgotten. After all, he was only a boy and his mother had a passport that worked.

Fellow passengers sensed the cause of the delay and turned to look at him, eyeing him with curiosity that bordered on something new, suspicion. What was wrong with his passport? With the country he came from? But didn't he and his mother come from the same country? No, he knew his passport said "India", like his dad's, and no one here could be from India, no one looked like his dad, no one here had a name like his or a bronze skin like his or a nose like his. He himself was too young to dwell on these things but he was impressed with it now, in this moment, between countries.

Just then, the train lurched forward. The migration officer's voice rose as he held on to a rail in the compartment. But the officer spoke in that language of his, in the manner of a warning as far as the boy could make out, not as though a punishment were on the line. The officer had to jump off now and the train picked up speed. He looked at his mother's face. She maintained a stoic composure, though she could well feel the disapproving stares of the other passengers.

The boy looked out the window, lifted again by the beauty of the passing fields. And he saw his mother's reflection in the window. She too was looking out. Smiling brightly to herself.

Strasbourg, France, 1973

Sketch: Encounter in the Hills

He trotted ahead of his dad, galloping sprightly, energetically, joyfully, for they walked among the highest mountains of the world. The mountaineering institute was closed and they were descending a hillside road back to the town. That was when he saw the other boy. He could have been any one of a million, scarcely though did any one of them get noticed. He was his age, barefoot and dressed in torn clothing, pants ripped at the knee and smeared with dirt. He had seen them coming and had jumped up the embankment from the vicinity of numerous hovels of the kind that were lightly constructed, some with bricks and some with just corrugated tin or plastic sheets.

For a moment, they stood face to face, peering into each other's eyes. Then the other boy stretched out his hand and said something in a pleading manner that was perfectly expected and yet the exact words were lost in the air. He was shorter, stunted even, and his eyes looked up at the jaunty half-breed from a far-off world as though looking from behind a curtain, timidly and curiously.

He could hear his dad's footsteps approaching now and he came back to himself, feeling his blood pulsating under his skin and a strange apprehension and fear. Who was this boy? What right did he have to approach him in this manner and ask him for money? It felt too sudden, too direct, too unexpected, like a violation of some sort.

Later, at dinner in the comfort of the big hotel on the hill with its roaring fireplace and easy chairs and shelves full of books and puzzles for kids, he thought about it again. There was something not right about one boy begging another, one's own age even, a mere 10 years old. How often did that boy do it? Why? How did he live? Did he not go to school? It was not right. And he felt ashamed. Both of his own feelings and of the conditions that forced one boy to beg from another.

Darjeeling, India, 1976

Sketch: An Uncle in Asansol

I did not really know I had an uncle until I was already a lad of ten,

When first in my conscious recollection I met this rare gem of men.

He was my Ranjit chacha, posted in Asansol doing a job for the railway,

And I came with a passion for trains and train sets that set my mind astray.

He took me to the office right away, and introduced me to all the staff,

Though only a boy, I felt like the guest of honour ready to smile and laugh.

He traced for me our location amid the tangle of train routes on a map on the wall,

And moments later led me up the steep steps of a locomotive at the front of them all.

A train driver I was, a dream come true, pulling on the whistle and towing a carriage or two,

It was the first of many Indian rail journeys my Ranjit chacha would facilitate for me as I grew.

And symbolic it was of his fondness for children anywhere and everywhere and theirs for him,

This man of boundless sentiments, rich imagination, and a child's sense of play, wonder, and whim.

His would be the face I would look for in the crowd at the airport upon my arrival in this fabled land,

Though short in stature and you might think lost in a crowd, he proved always to be right at hand.

In his bugler's cap, tweed coat, and black rim glasses, his elfish smile always found you first,

As though his own needs were not the thing, whatever he sacrificed seemed not to be for the worst.

For his love for his family and fellows, nature and dogs, and the arts and mystery and beauty of life,

These things made up his core and led us to profoundly adore and love this man of yore.

In Asansol, the boy also met his dadiji. She exclaimed to his father, "But look how neatly he has packed his suitcase?" "That is credit to his Swiss mother!" replied his father. The house was set back from the road in what seemed like a small town then but today is a thriving city. The driveway was lined with tall trees in which roosted many large cawing black crows which the boy found fascinating, so riveting that he could not resist the boyish temptation to let fly stones attempting to strike them. His dadiji reprimanded him but couldn't quite keep up with him. There was the matter of chocolate in the refrigerator, or rather missing chocolate. This forced her to place a lock on the refrigerator. He felt hunger pangs for the same and, when servants were told not to let him fire stones at the crows, he had to read or play games of chess with Ranjit chacha. For reading, he was given a book by Jim Corbett titled "Maneaters of the Kumaon."

It is not as though he was insensitive to nature and animal life. His most impactful memory was not driving the locomotive, but rather of the bird that waited too long to cross the tracks in front of the locomotive. Why? When all the other birds had flown at the last second, as though a bird's game of daring and fun, why had this bird not flown? The bird struck the glass of the locomotive that he was conducting, making a sickening thudding sound, its wings and body flattened before falling below the tracks. It marred the engine ride for him, something he could not forget of that day.

Asansol, India, 1976

Reflection: More on My Immigrant Childhood

1968 was a turbulent year in a turbulent country marked already by the assassination of the Rev. Martin Luther King Jr. in April followed by the assassination of Robert F. Kennedy a few weeks after our arrival in June. Anti-war demonstrations and the bombing of Vietnam and Cambodia continued relentlessly. The American troop build-up in Vietnam would reach its peak of over 500,000 that year.

And there we were, "the new immigration." It was no coincidence that "we", as immigrants from Asia, were arriving then. Since the 1920s, immigration to the U.S. had been severely restricted as a whole and immigration from Asia, Africa and, to some degree, countries south of

Mexico had been all but cut off. It was the Immigration Act of 1965 that replaced the national origins system of quotas and prioritized "skills" that loosened immigration from non-European countries.

While Houston had its Mexican restaurants like Ninfa's and others, it was nothing like what it came to be later. Immigrants who came from further away like us were, relatively speaking, cut off from the Old World, like the bulk of past immigrants to the U.S. Air travel to and from countries as distant as India and Switzerland was expensive and rare for all but the wealthy. There was little reading the news of one's country of origin or watching its news on TV, not even of neighboring countries like Mexico. One kept in touch with the Old World by letters (dubbed "snail mail" later), the occasional expensive, inordinately loud, and too soon cut off or curtailed phone call, and the vastly more expensive and less frequent visit. A treasure trove of books, photo albums, and memories had to suffice. And one faced America. Besides the occasional article in a New York Times or Houston Chronicle or on the televised news, there soon came to be special publications directed towards the immigrant community.

My father subscribed to India Abroad, allowing him to keep up with both key events in India as well as the progress of the Indian community in the U.S. As a marker of how far the community had to go even in a major metropolitan area like Houston, there was no Indian Cultural Center, no Indian restaurant, and no Hindu temple when we arrived. They all came about over the next decade, in that order. I can still remember going to the opening of the Tandoor Indian restaurant (1978), because it was opened by my best friend Sonu's father, who was also a close friend of my father. Unbelievably to me when I found out later, my father served as secretary to the inaugural Indian Cultural Center (1974), writing the few speeches for the president, who was also Sonu's father and who later helped open the first Hindu temple in the Pearland suburbs. Other community leaders eventually got time on the public radio station on Saturday mornings to play bhajans, ghazals, and Hindi film hits and yet others got permission to show a Hindi film from time to time in a marquee cinema like Meyerland Cinema. I used to go with Sonu and his mom and others to see such classics, comprehending little but mesmerized nonetheless by the feverishly energetic dances and crooning singers even while counting time until intermission when warm samosas and mint and tamarind chutney and sweet milky chai would be served. Later, it might be a film in Tamil or Bengali and not even Sonu's mother, Manju Auntie, could comprehend it, but being a rare and cherished cultural event for the Indian community, we still went and still got samosas and chai.

For my mother's part, she subscribed to some type of newsletter from the Swiss Consulate in Houston, but it was flimsy and businesslike in comparison to India Abroad as a publication. While she tried to teach me some Swiss-German, I was good only at retaining words like "soybandi", or pig, which might be said my way if I didn't adhere to Swiss standards of order and cleanliness! I can remember my mother gabbing at length by phone in Swiss-German but I do not remember any Swiss-German friend she had other than a woman married to an American. There was one restaurant that served fondue but no proper Swiss restaurants. However, there was a fine Swiss bakery called Andre's, where we made it our routine to go practically every other Saturday morning. Besides fine quiches and bread like "zopf" and freshly baked cookies minted with chocolate frosting as well as Lindt chocolates, hazelnut being a favorite, I would be rewarded with about four "bunchcuglars" or rum balls that fit neatly in a square white carboard box to take away. They would hardly last the week in our refrigerator.

I would hear my parents speak of the United States in ways immigrants or people with significant experience elsewhere in the world are wont to do, making observations, drawing comparisons, both favorable and unfavorable. For my father, it was always "the U.S." and "this country" and "here", meaning not simply Houston or Texas but the country as a whole. He was an engineer yet learned and erudite in a way that, in all my wanderings and meetings with people, I have seldom found apart from himself and a few other members of my family in India. His was a rather exquisite rendering of the world and its nuances from the point of view of a family that counted three ambassadors in its ranks, and of a country like India, newly independent and yet with a long, complex, and fascinating history and presence—and set of pretensions—on the world stage. The uncles widened the horizons of the nephews and nieces and passed on the virtues of a classical education as evinced by a love of English literature, German classical music, a strong appreciation of one's own country and culture, and the apt quote or anecdote in history, Western perhaps but with an Eastern perspective.

My father, besides benefitting from a solid education in private schools and the tutelage of revered uncles, applied his own native intelligence and curiosity not only to science, chemistry, and engineering but to the full scope of the "liberal arts." On his bookshelf, I might browse any number of titles and authors, from Arnold Toynbee to Stokely Carmichael and Malcolm X to Dag Hammarsköld and D.T. Suzuki to Ernest Hemingway and Mark Twain, T.S. Eliot and Arthur Miller, William Faulkner and Rabindranath Tagore etc. With time, Indian historians and writers of fiction began to compete for space, along with the latest on the politics of oil and gas in the Middle East or the revolution in Iran or fresh and engaging new writers of fiction or magical realism like Gabriel Garcia Marquez. They were almost always male, with Daddy's interest in women writers coming only later.

Perhaps every two to three weeks, guests would come over or we would be invited to their homes, and I was aware, though not listening or comprehending, of my father's talent and delight in offering an anecdote or regaling them with a tale. He could not deadpan it or offer a wry, dry, or sarcastic sense of humor. Nor did he tell it pretentiously or scholarly, but rather with straightforward verve and gusto, like an engineer constructing something and then marveling at it with a smile and a laugh that he was barely able to contain, even before his listener's laughter joined in, which it always did.

It wasn't long before we arrived in Houston that we left the country on vacation, and this was to Mexico City, to which my mother responded instinctively, with its plazas, street-side cafes, cobblestone streets, and art in public space bearing a strong flavor of many European cities. As a good Swiss, she was already fluent in four languages, namely German, French, Italian, and English. Inspired by both Mexico and the preponderance of our apartment neighbors from Latin America, she added Spanish to her linguistic repertoire with the help of Berlitz tapes, lessons at Rice University, and self-study. She would also bring out the lawn chair to join "the Latin American" housewives in our apartment complex to gab under the trees in the afternoon, sharing the pleasures and novelties of life in the United States.

Every Friday, Daddy would take us out to eat, almost always to Michelangelo's, a favorite Italian restaurant off Westheimer. If not there, then to a Chinese restaurant further away. We never ate at a steakhouse, much less a McDonald's or Burger King, even for lunch or fast food. Instead, for the occasional hamburger, my mother would make small thick patties from scratch. These would be topped with Swiss cheese and served on toast with lettuce, mayonnaise and a dollop of ketchup or Dijon mustard. I was the lucky beneficiary of only the best and healthiest home-cooked food, with plenty of rice and occasional gourmet dishes like beef stroganoff. The processed frozen food that was newly flooding the markets, so-called "TV dinners", was out of the question unless it was Stouffer's pizza, macaroni and cheese, or tater tots. Cakes were even made from scratch. Perhaps three to four times per year only, Daddy would pick up Kentucky Fried Chicken but that was it for fast food. It was as if the more plebeian tastes of America, from a European perspective, were kept at a distance. I did enjoy hamburgers and hotdogs at a ballgame of the Astros or Oilers at the Astrodome. Otherwise, the nearest I got was Antone's sandwiches with a bag of chips on a Saturday morning.

All the way until 1982 and the debut showing of the film "Gandhi" starring Ben Kingsley, we never even went to a movie as a family. Instead,

I went more often with my friend Tommy to a "picture show", as his mom called it. It was a unique experience and I still remember the first title, a romp for kids called "The Apple Dumpling Gang." In our home, we had only a small black and white TV set on a small table with long antlike antennas balancing in front of the enormity of the long bookshelf. The only time it was turned on was for Daddy to watch the evening news with Walter Cronkite or for Mama and Daddy to watch Masterpiece Theater on Sunday evening or for me to watch cartoons on Saturday morning.

I would take the TV into my room on Sunday afternoons or Monday night to watch American football, a sport my father only learned the rules of in the 1980s when he moved to Chicago and the entire office on Monday morning would talk about the Bears. My childhood heroes were athletes in the American sports of baseball, basketball, and football, yet my parents understood none of the rules of these games and never watched these games, not even my own minor league baseball games when I would suit up and play first base and bat in 3rd or 4th place, evidence of my talent in a sport they knew nothing of. I would hit quite well and round the bases and they weren't there, except if my father arrived early to pick me up. My mother did make birthday cakes and birthday cards for me, which in one way or another highlighted my biggest hero and role model, Bob Watson, first baseman and clean-up hitter for the Houston Astros. And, for Christmas, I would receive a Houston Oilers jersey or jacket if that's what I wanted.

Our calendar at home was always sent from Switzerland, courtesy of my "Swiss god-mother" Madeleine. It was hung prominently, every month revealing sharp white-capped mountains, flower-filled valleys, wide green meadows, and pristine blue lakes. Meanwhile, on our bookshelf, a small statue of the Buddha sat on one end and a statue of Ganesh on the other, with a wooden elephant on one shelf and the portrait of Prem my grandfather on the other and a yellow ashtray somewhere in between. Ours was a small and elegantly but sparsely furnished home, the sort of flat that many Europeans and Indians might be accustomed to living in. There also hung a few paintings of abstract but colorful modern art. When I asked my father what such a design could possibly represent, he replied, "Whatever you may like it to be, that is the beauty of it, it can be whatever you like, whatever you see in it."

Is that not emblematic of life in America, or in a modern and globalized world in general today, where an individual is more and more able to "shape one's own destiny?" Certainly, my childhood and my parents set me up for that.

Part II

Adolescence

"Youth to itself doth rebel."
– Shakespeare (Hamlet, Act 1, Scene 3)

"A boy's will is the wind's will,
And the thoughts of youth are long, long thoughts."
– Henry Wadsworth Longfellow

When does childhood end and adolescence begin? When does adolescence end and adulthood begin? Adolescence then is that time period when we become less influenced by parents and more influenced by peers but also when we question the motives and actions of everyone, including ourselves, and begin consciously to shape our own identity, and we question that too. It is a time full of questions and doubts, vulnerability and volatility, dependence and budding independence. It is a time of dreams and illusion, of great movement of thought and emotion, of fear and fragility but also energy and power, strength of will, and the intoxication of possibility. A time of exploration and the beginning of self-knowledge.

List of Grade Schools Attended		
Roberts Elementary – on Greenbriar, central Houston	Kindergarten to 6th grade	1971 – 78

List of Grade Schools Attended		
Lanier Junior High – on Woodhead, close to Westheimer	7th grade to 9th grade	1978 – 81
Bellaire High School – by Meyerland Plaza, SW Houston	10th grade to 12th grade	1981 – 84

Sketch: A Fistfight

There had been another fight. From the safety of the yellow school bus in the parking lot, he could see the crowd of kids on the football field even now. The pack seemed to heave and surge, and he knew the fight was still on. It had proved unbearable for him to watch. He thought he saw it start, almost right after the last school bell, as if two boys were waiting for that moment. Maybe they had said words and made threats to each other during the day. It could have been anything—a wrong word, a bad look, an insult to one's mother, a girl, a bully, lunch money, drug money. Bad tempers, repressed energy, acting out what one saw at home or in the neighborhood, bravado, competition, machismo.

To the boy on the bus, in seventh grade and newly arrived in junior high school, where such boys who squabbled in elementary school now ranged up to ninth grade and could do more harm to one, violence felt inimical. So outside his skin, so not a part of himself. It was not fear but something else. It was as if he were allergic to it. It upset his stomach, it made his skin crawl, threw his mind. His heart would feel heavy, hurt by a pain he could not even see, the mere thought of a raging fistfight. It was the same with wrestling on TV—grown men with bulging biceps throwing one another around viciously, he thought, not realizing that it was all an act on soft canvas. He could not bear to watch. It almost gave him nightmares. It wasn't the same with American football and tackling, even with heavy contact. It was not same even with boxing—he loved

Muhammad Ali and the flair of "float like a butterfly" and "sting like a bee." They had gloves, it was refereed.

But fistfights at school ran against his blood in ways that it didn't seem to do for others. They ran to the fight, egged one another on, talked about it later with gusto and glee, revelled in what seemed to him like gratuitous brutality and violence that lay dangerously under the surface of otherwise brotherly human beings. He sat on the school bus, confused, hoping the driver would just start the bus, put it in gear, and head down the streets, home.

It was the Vietnamese kids who, though smaller, could defend themselves against anyone. You couldn't pick on them. He himself had found that out. Inexplicably in class, he had troubled a Vietnamese boy who did not resist or speak back to him, probably since he did not know English. So he troubled him some more, wanting to get a response. He might have said something, flicked his hair or jabbed him on the side or kicked him under the table. Until, from out of nowhere, the other boy with the shoulder-length black hair suddenly turned around and, with a rapidity he never would have expected, struck him on his shoulder with his open hand. It was a board-like blow but so controlled, an open hand that knew to strike forcefully but just enough to convey the message to think twice about harassing him. The boy looked at him and his eyes were all reluctant warning. He had not wanted to strike him but had been pushed to do it. He understood and stopped. A newfound respect had sprung up, and he could hear the teacher, unaware of what had happened, speaking again as she wrote on the chalkboard.

Here was the solution. Smaller and averse to violence, he too must learn self-defense. He asked his father about taking a karate class. His dad soon enrolled him in Kim Soo Karate, located on Clay Street in downtown Houston. He began learning tae kwon do on Tuesday and Thursday evenings and Saturday mornings. More than self-defense, he learned a self-discipline that most other boys his age lacked. "People think karate only physical, physical, physical", the ever cheerful and placid Master Kim Soo quipped, "but it is all mental, mental, mental." Noone had ever spoken to him like this before. Learning tae kwon do equipped him with a newfound self-confidence and ability to deal with the fact of fear, physically.

Sketch: Afraid to Speak

The teacher called on him. Even though he had his hand up, he could not answer. The words would not come. It was on the tip of his tongue. Or was it the back of his mouth. He heaved. He puffed. He could feel his face reddening. Eyes must have been turning to look at him. The teacher looked on quietly, passively, expectantly. It came now, finally flowing out, as though a dam had been broken. Whether the dam was in his epiglottis or pharynx, he could not be sure. Besides, it was to say something of no great importance since it was only school. Outside of class, it never happened.

But for months that year in 8th grade, it always happened. Whether he was called upon or tried to speak out in class, he must have known it would happen. It became as though he expected it to happen, waited for it to happen, this stuttering and stammering. He tensed up. Something in his mouth and throat. It didn't last long, a second or two or three at most, but when it happened, it stretched out like an eternity to him. He just could not get the words out. Only another deep breath or two helped, and then he would expel the words that flowed forth like water over a boulder-strewn mountain stream.

Why did he stutter for some months in 8th grade only? It may have been ordinary growth of the body. Hormones, girls. Fear. Fight or flight syndrome. Anxiety of adolescence. A puberty he did not understand. Maybe a repressed something in his consciousness related to home.

Sketch: The Astrodome

Tickets to sit in the bleachers were all of 50 cents for children 12 and under, $1.50 for adults.

He used to pass for 12 years old for a number of years. If asked by the ticket-seller behind the wire mesh, he'd say "Twelve". Nothing to lose.

These were group outings with neighborhood friends Wassel and Tommy. They would ride bicycles from the apartment complex off Old Spanish Trail, past the old armory, up Fannin, down side streets hosting glass office buildings. They would find a place to lock up the cycles, being careful to lock the frame with the big bike locks they swung around their shoulders. And then start walking, crossing the busy street to walk on the grass path by the fence of the huge parking lots in front of "the Dome."

Bleacher tickets were unassigned and unreserved. The booth opened at 5 PM and the gates at 5:30 PM. The boys would be sure to get there early, line up with a few regulars, enter the huge air-conditioned Astrodome, and take a pick of front row seats. This was always a thrill, claiming one's own spot for the next four to five hours. The players from both teams would already be on the field playing catch and taking batting practice. The crack of the bat called one's attention as did the pop of the glove. The echo of the dome, its dim lights still, the colored seats in the mezzanine and upper sections, the green "astro-turf" along with the crowd slowly filing in and filling up the place all leant an aura of drama to come. One could feel extra special viewing the electronic scoreboard that periodically flashed, "Welcome to the Astrodome, the 8th Wonder of the World."

As practice continued in the two hour wait to 7:35 PM game time, the boys would yell out the names of the players closest to them, sometimes with a croon as in "Jose Cru-u-u-u-u-u-u-u-z-z-zzz"! If a ball came all the way to the wall and a player ran to pick it up, the boys would plead, "Throw it up here, throw it up here!" And if it was a famous player, they would ask for an autograph on the ball too. It wouldn't be long before they would buy the first round of nachos and cheese "with extra jalapeños", as they relished saying to the seller. Crudely, because they were boys, the jalapeños had a higher purpose, which was to draw out one's saliva and see who could shoot the jalapeño juice through one's teeth really—not spit it—the furthest out onto the field. Apart from yelling to the players and anticipating catching a homerun ball, this juicy activity was the other main reason to get there early and get a front row seat. And this had to be followed by the inevitable Coca Cola filled with ice to slurp on and crush between one's teeth maybe even into the third inning.

When the game began, things got more serious. Each of the boys would take a player. Wassel liked Art Howe, the third baseman. Tommy liked Cesar Cedeño in center field and later José Cruz in right field. For the longest time, Sanjay's favorite player was Bob Watson, the first baseman. Later, he followed Terry Puhl, in center field, whose birthday was close to his. Taking a player meant saying to one another, "Art, you're about to come up—what are you going to hit this time?" Single, double, homerun, etc. Take a walk? This continued to when the player was actually on the plate and batting, "You swinging next pitch?" Before the player came, it was math—"You're coming up, what's your average going to be?" This was new every time because the scorer calculated a player's new average (hits per "at bats") and reflected it on the big scoreboard as the game progressed. Sanjay, being good at math, could always figure it out in his head, but deliberately guessed wrong sometimes so that Tommy and Wassel would keep playing along.

If there were a homerun, the crowd would erupt in a happiness of the moment, stand and throw their arms into the air, and grin joyfully, even to strangers several rows away. Eyes would gravitate to the scoreboard, which would light up and "the bull" would appear in a series of flashing lights.

Meanwhile, the boys would feed on nachos and peanuts, eye any open seats in the home plate area or along the baselines, and wait for the "seventh inning stretch" when "the gates would open", meaning the barriers between the bleachers and the rest of the stadium. The boys were ready and knew just where to head and get a closer seat to the action for the last two innings or more if it went extra innings. The ushers no longer asked for tickets and a seat number and the boys would glide down the steps to find good seats, keeping a lookout for any empty cups as well. If they were plastic, which was acquired when you spent the money on a large size drink, they would be tempted to keep them and take them home. If they were paper, they were fair game to be used as "pop cups" just as soon as the game was over. It would be a thrill to hear the "pop" of the cup you stamped on with such force and precision that it echoed across the Astrodome as an attention-getter to all the departing fans.

Thus ended an evening at an Astros' game, with lines of cars and headlights and taillights waiting to exit while the boys would stride by in confidence, in the humidity of a summer evening, on their way to pick up their bicycles and ride home to Parkwood Apartments.

Sketch: Paperboy

"I believe he can do whatever he puts his mind to."

Simple statement, motivating effect. He had never thought of it that way until his father told him what Mr. Williams had said.

Mr. Williams was the man who used to drop off the Houston Chronicle for him to deliver on weekends. In the pitch black of a Saturday or Sunday morning, the boy would meet two other boys in the carport and get to work. It was too early to talk much and there was too much work to do. Some people wanted their papers before dawn even.

So they would get busy snipping or untwisting the wire that bound the stacks of newspaper together. The first thing to do was to "fold the papers," meaning to put the Lifestyle section with its classifieds within the main sections of the paper, usually following the Sports section. It was impossible not to take a quick glance at the Sports section—at least the box score of the Astros or Rockets game the night before—even in the dim light of the carport. Then the boys sat cross-legged on one stack of papers and folded quickly as though it were an assembly line. The fresh ink of the newly printed papers rubbed off little by little on their fingertips.

They were provided with only one piece of equipment and that was a shoulder bag bearing the insignia of the newspaper. After "rolling" some papers with rubber bands, the boys would load up the bag with flat papers on bottom and rolled papers on top. Then they would set out on bicycles, bags around their shoulders but resting on the bicycle's metal frame, each going their own route.

He might start with the houses on the other side of Wyndale on residential streets with English names like Canterbury. It was a thrill to fling the papers on the driveways and sidewalks next to the lawns. Little could go wrong in such open area. Then he would drive further along to another neighborhood entirely, down Braeswood and into a section of apartment complexes. There, he would drop the papers on a doorstep or loft them onto a terrace or balcony. Once he flung a paper onto a balcony and heard the glass break as it hit a window. Rather than flee with such blatant evidence, he waited for the resident to come out so he could apologize. Delivery could coincide with dawn and once he saw an Indian gentleman, barefoot and in white kurta pijama, praying to the sun from his doorstep. It left him with a sense of the sacred and a reminder of different traditions of the country of his father and his origin.

Then, he rode his bicycle back to Parkwood Apartments and dismounted in strategic places to carry out the bulk of delivery on both sides of the street. Each red brick building housed four apartments and there were four boxes at the entrance facing the street. One or all four subscribed to the Chronicle. He had it memorized and inserted the flat papers accordingly. Wanting to be done quickly and knowing his friend was doing the same, he would almost sprint to the next building, fling open the door, drop the shoulder bag on the floor with a smack, remove and insert papers into the slot in one swift motion, and exit.

At the end of the route, the boys re-grouped in the parking lot, revelled in their sweat, and smiled with satisfaction. If the Astros or Rockets had won the night before, it was especially satisfying and they would talk about the game and winning streaks and losing streaks and who was up and who was down. With an extra paper at hand, they could read about it or flip to the section on movies they could dream about seeing sometime. Or they might count what they earned that day and think it deserved getting a Coca Cola and Snickers bar somewhere. The satisfactions of youth!

The money he earned was deposited into his bank account at Texas Commerce Bank. He was 12 years old when he began "throwing papers" and he did not use some of this money until he was 21 years old during a short spell of unemployment.

Sketch: Sweeping the Garage

"Keep bending your back like that—" warned an older and wiser co-worker sweeping the garage. "You might not feel it now, but you will when you get old! Your back don't forget."

It sounded like the voice of wisdom all right. But he couldn't feel anything now really. He kept pushing and dragging the sweeping broom across the parking spaces in the eight-story garage. It was mostly dust and some dirt mixed in with a few pebbles the cars had brought in.

"Hold the broom from up top, don't grab it low like you do," the co-worker remonstrated. "And take a break every now and then. It ain't to nobody's benefit overdoing it."

They swept up so much dust that he noticed his nose blew black mucous. He thought nothing of it. Instead, it was a point of pride, to be able to work long and hard, doing physical labor. It wasn't the pay, it was the pride. His back felt fine.

The garage itself was like other garages that he and friends had ridden their bicycles up and down for fun in the Texas Medical Center complex. Bicycle chains slung across their shoulders and a Burger King soda cup in hand, they would ride around the entry gate and ride up or take the nearest elevator to the top. From the roof, they would gaze down on the people below or look across the skyline to Hermann Park one way and the Astrodome the other way. This was their haunt, their riding grounds, their little fiefdom. There was no better way to show that than conquering the parking garages by riding up and then gliding down slowly, keeping an eye out for the brake lights of any cars backing up to exit and keeping a foot on the brakes to negotiate the curves from one story to the next. Emerging from the garage came with a feeling of triumph, a sort of "who owns the garage—we do" bravado.

They also kept a lookout for medical center security vehicles but they could not do much other than tell them to leave. Signs may have said "no trespassing" and "violators will be prosecuted", but that was all part of the thrill. The violation was too small to be prosecuted and nothing they wouldn't enjoy talking their way out of. The boys' confidence and "bring it on" attitude was bound to be challenged one day but that day was not this day.

Sketch: Lonely Forgotten Hoop

He would play alone. Shooting the basketball on a lonely forgotten hoop hidden on one end of the Texas Medical Center. The bike trail along the bayou was close behind it as was the South Braeswood Avenue bridge before it joined West Holcombe Boulevard. Hospitals, medical education buildings, and parking garages towered close by.

He would shoot mostly on Sundays when neighborhood friends were at church. It didn't matter if there was light rain, sleet, and snow. He just couldn't bounce it as high in the cold. It didn't matter if the hoop didn't even have a net. All that mattered was to play—to imagine the opposing players, fellow teammates, a 24 second clock and game clock, and a cheering crowd. He would get his own rebounds. He could play until his wrist hurt or it was time to go back and watch the NFL football games starting at noon.

He used to ride his bicycle there, carrying the ball in a Houston Chronicle newspaper bag slung over his shoulder. He played alone there since by this time, most friends in the apartment complex had moved away. This place was in the middle of all their old haunts: the bayou and bike trail, the bridge and its birds, Hermann Park and the hill full of rabbits. The hospitals and parking garages he once swept for Republic Parking and often rode bikes down, the first nearby Burger King and Scurlock Tower Garage where he worked as a cashier, the Prudential building where they used to sneak in to swim, and even the old Houston Oilers training camp where they would hang out for autographs. Further down was the Marriott Hotel where they played video games and where for years his mother would take the kids swimming and enjoy a post-swim steak and cheese sandwich.

This lonely old hoop was in the center of it all, of so many of his childhood memories. It was as though someone forgot to remove it as the medical center expanded. Decades later, on a visit as an older adult, the hoop was gone. Nearby, he came across a plaque and a statue outside a building whose ground floor he used to know well. It used to host a self-serve snack bar where he and neighborhood pals had collected many quarters, dimes, and nickels from under the machines. Amazingly, it now bore the name of the graduate school whose extension he had graduated from on the other side of the state. The plaque and statue existed to recognize and honor the owners of the house and undeveloped land that existed before the medical center was built. The statue represented the girl who lived in the house, arms raised in carefree play and delight in the natural world that was once her backyard by the bayou. Looking at that statue, in spite of the stark differences in her life and his, he felt he knew her. It was a love of place and especially one's childhood place, lost amid the churn of development, that accounted for that bond of unity, even if for a brief moment of reflection and being.

Narrative: Stirrings of Religion

Both my mother and father wanted to raise me "free" of any "complexes" or beliefs, any dogma or ideology, especially of the religious variety. My mother was not a great reader or intellectually inclined, though she had travelled widely for her time and nurtured wide friendships, which included maintaining an active correspondence with favorite female family members in India. She, like my father, was an admirer of the philosopher and sage Jiddu Krishnamurti, who was popular in Switzerland and abroad and whose books she kept, books with titles like "The Awakening of Intelligence", "You are the World", and "The Only Revolution." With that Old World awareness of the burden placed on children by religion and ideology, my parents seemed to want to raise me with as much "free thinking" as possible, as opposed to "conventional thinking." It was important to think for oneself and have the courage of conviction. This meant no deliberate exposure even to Krishnamurti. It was up to me to ask. At the same time, my father held a clear sense of right and wrong, i.e. no moral relativism. Better and worse existed, even if I must find that out by trial and error.

Meanwhile, my friends were busy going to church on Sunday morning. I occasionally tagged along, especially if I had a sleepover with them. Going to the Lutheran Church with friends, I found that it was all soberness and silence, even the irrepressible moving, fidgeting, and giggling of a child whose friend accompanied him was looked at askance and severely too. Nevertheless, feeling that we as a family were missing out, I sort of pushed my parents into finding a church for us to go to. They consulted our neighbor across the hall, a young and serious medical student from the Connecticut raising two young children with his wife. He suggested the Unitarian church, which he also attended whenever he had the time. I remember my first "Sunday school" there, sitting on the floor and watching a documentary about Mahatma Gandhi! The message was about non-violence. But the mystery behind church-going was gone for me, and we went no more than perhaps a total of four times. My father and I went back to our pleasurable Sunday morning zoo-going routine followed by kicking a "soccer ball" to one another under the tall pine trees in Hermann Park by "hippie hill" and the amphitheater there.

My mother had long since left off going to church, since her own mother had been excommunicated from the Catholic Church for marrying a Protestant and church-going was never part of her makeup. My father knew the Bible well, better than my mother, thanks to his upbringing in private schools in India where conversion was not the object but scripture was a subject and he always received top marks. Religion in South Asia permeates society, such that "Hinduism" is not just a set of beliefs and rituals but a way of life, affecting dress and eating habits and marriage and holidays and a myriad other social customs and attitudes.

While he never used the term, I learned later to consider my father a "cultural Hindu", as I also consider the most Westernized and educated members of the family and myself. Aware of our history, with respect for our ancestors and countrymen in a majority Hindu society, none of us need make a show of being a Hindu. Such fanaticism is—or once was!—in fact alien to a religion that is organic and natural, in keeping with thousands of years of absorbing local deities and beliefs as equally valid expressions of the divine. "Tolerance" is a word I heard at home, as completely natural to "our" way of looking at the world, and it did not have the sub-optimal or negative connotation it does today compared to "embracing diversity", not just tolerating it. Unfortunately, this "live and let live" outlook of my father and his family has come to be wrongly characterized as excessively weak and meek by the politically motivated Hindus who have exploited an ancient way of being into a matter of suppressed pride and therefore one of great show and form at every opportunity. Every now and then, this view has culminated in violence such as the destruction of the Babri masjid mosque in Ayodhya on 6 December, 1992 by a mob wielding tridents and sledgehammers. My grandmother could not sleep that evening, she told me later. It felt so contrary to everything she felt as a Hindu.

My father found ridiculous the religious claims of the Hindu chauvinists and yet, unlike most of the family in India, he empathized with the prospect of "Hindus" finally running the country "after 1,000 years of foreign rule." As to who had been running the country since 1947 was conveniently overlooked in the long sweep of Indian history with so many grievances to stew on. This sympathy of my father's, while never strong and now and then extinguished by some detestable act of the BJP political party, is a psychological hazard to the overseas Hindu wishing to connect and be faithful to the land of his birth. In my father's case, it was otherwise very much out of character with his own life's choices and ecumenical worldview not to mention the many books on his shelf that took a sceptical if not critical view of religion. In fact, my father went out of his way to acquire the various articles with titles such as "Why I am not a Christian", "Why I am not a Muslim", and "Why I am not a Hindu." He later moderated his views.

My own interest in religion undoubtedly stemmed in part from not going to church like most Americans. Then my questioning, curiosity, and hunger for meaning and things of the spirit began. All this was part of an adolescent search for identity, perhaps more acute for me, given my far-flung and mixed origins, my immigrant parents, my unique upbringing and so on. For years, I had aspired to grow up, saying "wait til I'm 15 years old", imagining it as a marker of sorts, of near entrance into adulthood in some unfathomable way. Little did I know that 15 would stand out as an age in my life for something I could hardly have suspected.

I had completed 9th grade and was about to enter high school. Rather than spending so much of the summer out playing baseball or riding bikes, I spent a large portion of the summer of 1981 reading all the entries in the Children's Brittanica encyclopaedia related to India, A-Z, as a means of further understanding who I was. I had no sooner got past Akbar and Ashoka when I had come to Buddha and Buddhism. I remember the day when I went to my father in the living room, having read of the Buddha's life and the Four Noble Truths and the Eightfold Path, and I re-read a part of it to him and said, "This makes a lot of sense to me." I remember him sitting in his white chair, listening, his legs crossed, probably smoking a cigarette, and saying when I finished, "That's how it has to hit you, all at once, that's when you know something is true. Now you must think it over and decide for yourself."

Ah, free thinking! And he just happened to have a shelf full of books on Buddhism. Four books in particular became my reference books: "Some Sayings of the Buddha", by F.L. Woodard; "The Life of the Buddha", by Mary Rhys Davids; "Buddhism" by Christmas Humphreys; and especially the thin paperback, "Walk On!", also by Christmas Humphreys, which I read a second time before the first day of high school, staying up late at night to mark key passages. The freedom and invitation to think and experiment for oneself appealed instinctively to me.

"Now Kalamas, do not go by hearsay, nor by what is handed down by others, nor by what people say, nor by what is stated on the authority of your traditional teachings. Do not go by reasoning, nor by inferring, nor by argument as to method, nor from reflection on and approval of an opinion, nor out of respect, thinking a recluse must be deferred to. But, Kalamas, when you know yourselves: 'These teachings are not good; they are blameworthy; they are condemned by the wise; these teachings, when followed out and put into practice, lead to loss and suffering'—then reject them. Or, when you know yourselves, these teachings are good; they are not blameable; they are praised by the wise; undertaken and observed, they lead to benefit and happiness,' enter on and abide in them."

Continuing, the Buddha taught: "One thing and one thing only I teach, o bhikkhus, suffering and the way out of suffering… cease to do evil, try to do good, cleanse thine own heart… death is inherent in all component things, work out your salvation with diligence." Such a philosophy suited me immensely and has always been the lens in which I have viewed any teachings or philosophy. Similar to Hindu philosophy, the ways to the Goal are as many as the lives of men. Let experience be the teacher. If it doesn't work out, chalk it up to experience, as fellow Americans would say.

Sketch: Bhikkhu

His room as a teenager was on the first floor of the apartment building. A large tree stood on the ground outside, throwing out its many branches all around. He could always spot a squirrel or two moving about on the limbs outside his window.

His bed was by the window and in front of his bed was a small plastic desk and on the wall above this desk hung several items of symbolic value. One was a length of cloth, folded over itself, blue in color with a pattern and texture that offset the bare standard whiteness of the wall and communicated the connection he felt still to a distant land, that land was India. Above this, on a rectangular-shaped piece of white cloth, he had written with a black marker in Devanagari script the word "dharma." To him, it meant the teaching of the Buddha. It also meant the "path" to him, the Way.

Finally, on the side, on a white posterboard, on which he had pasted various sayings of the Buddha on yellow post-it notes, he had drawn a picture of himself in the future, walking on a path, barefoot, dressed in a yellow robe—a bhikkhu and part of the Sangha, or order of Buddhist monks. He rarely sketched or colored, but the image of the bhikkhu, and what the bhikkhu meant, had moved him so much that he dreamed of becoming a bhikkhu or rather wished he were a bhikkhu in the time of the Buddha some 2,500 years ago. He would think if he could go back to any time in history, that would be it.

Sketch: Christ in the Garage

It was the day after Christmas and he had to work. So he took up his position in the small cashier's box facing the garage's administrative office and the ramp down which cars would come towards him and the exit gate. But it promised to be a slow day, being also a Sunday. School was out for the winter holidays and he had no homework to bring. Instead, in between catching snatches of football games on a tiny miniature black and white TV in the cashier's box, he planned to read the New Testament and learn more about Jesus Christ who was the reason for the holidays.

It was not as if he didn't know, but he didn't know much. Childhood friends had invited him to church more than once. He had been to a Lutheran church, where the friend who invited him kept turning his head in the pew, making a series of funny faces in an attempt to get him to laugh and break the silence of the parishioners sitting so solemnly. There was also "Sunday school," which didn't sound appealing. He attended with his friends once and, for a reason he couldn't understand, it was important to know that Jesus rode into Jerusalem on a donkey and not another animal. Children drew a picture of it.

Since friends in the neighborhood had somewhere to go on Sunday, namely "church," his father had made a different tradition. They would go to the zoo to see the animals and then to the park to kick around a soccer ball. Later, however, he felt he was missing something and urged his parents to go to church as a family. His father consulted the nice neighbor across the hall and he suggested his church, the Unitarian Church. But it was not what he was looking for in going to a church. He did not know what he was looking for anyway, other than a place to go on Sunday like other families in the neighborhood.

This expression of interest in Christianity led his father, who maintained a deep interest in all religions yet practiced none, to acquire a Bible for him. It was a deep red in color, soft and textured and pliable, with golden-yellow pages that were thin like rice paper. His own name was engraved on the bottom right corner of the cover. In the section that was the New Testament, and in the first four books that were known as the Gospels, all the words that Jesus spoke were highlighted in red.

On that Sunday after Christmas in the garage, he began with the gospel of Matthew. So many parts were so very moving and eminently quotable.

"What does it profit a person to gain the world but lose his soul... Lay not up treasures on earth, but rather treasures in heaven, for where your heart is, there will be your treasure also... If a man strike you on

your right cheek, turn the other cheek... If a man take your cloak, give him your coat too... Love your enemies, resist not evil... Reconcile with those who have wronged you before making your offering at the altar... Blessed are the poor, the meek, those who grieve... The kingdom of heaven is within."

While he felt the various miracles ascribed to Jesus must have been symbolic, the teachings were so clear and convincing, and the identity of the teacher so full of peace and love, that he felt quite swept away. Looking out at the empty garage, he then wondered at the paradox. For Christians do not practice this! This did not seem like their Bible at all. Instead, anger and ill speech abounded and peace and love fled every scene, every occasion. Could this be the same Gospel of the Christians? It did not seem so at all. One flipped on talk radio or the news in this Christian country and heard wrath and recrimination, war and retribution. Voices for peace and compassion in the world were as likely to come from non-Christians, and especially a man like Gandhi whose film starring Ben Kingsley was showing then, as from so-called Christians. Indeed, how could one really be called a Christian if he or she did not follow the teachings? Christ himself seemed to call out that very same hypocrisy at every moment.

A few years later, he visited family in India. His grandmother, proudly "convent-educated" and interested in any authentic expression of God and religion, told him about the comfort she derived from a book called "The Imitation of Christ" by a 15th century German priest named Thomas à Kempis. She also knew about Thomas Merton, the influential Trappist monk and author who she said was discovering the religions of Asia when he accidentally electrocuted himself in the bathroom of a hotel in Thailand. His father had a copy of Merton's autobiography, titled "Seven Storey Mountain". The boy read this and it moved him deeply.

Once away from home, and due to the influence of Merton, he began to visit Catholic churches from time to time. These were years of blending in and seeing how much he could integrate into mainstream life. There were also difficult moments he experienced and a verse from any holy book appealed to him. During basic training for the U.S. Army, he sometimes carried the small green Gideon's version of the New Testament that the Army had given all soldiers in the upper left pocket of his uniform. Passing through stretches of "boot camp" that were tough and made him full of self-doubt, he would whisper a phrase or the Lord's Prayer, which he found beautiful and calming. While stationed at Fort Campbell, he occasionally visited the church in nearby Clarksville, Tennessee. These were also years when he was captivated by the personality of Martin Luther King and the struggle for civil rights. He flirted with the idea of conversion.

Later, he would frequent Catholic churches in Charlottesville, Virginia; San Antonio, Texas; and Baltimore, Maryland. Yet always, even from the first visit to the church in Clarksville, he felt strangely that he was absorbing the words, vision, and persona of Christ in a different way compared to the other parishioners. His perception was undoubtedly colored by his previous identification with the Buddha and Indian religious thought in general. He had read Louis Fischer's biography on Mahatma Gandhi and had been impressed how Gandhi could say with great conviction that the Sermon on the Mount "went straight to my heart" and yet he could remain a Hindu. He felt the same way and a similar eclecticism in general when it came to matters of religion. And he was put off by the adherents who insisted Jesus was "the only way" to salvation. An old Indian saying, Hindu in inspiration, that the ways to God are as many as the lives of human beings made more sense. Thus, the thought of conversion passed. It seemed less and less necessary and never entered his mind again.

Yet, the life and sayings of Jesus had provided great comfort in his early adulthood, and Jesus remained a figure of reverence and inspiration to him for the longest time.

Sketch: Burning Bridge

Standing on the bridge over the bayou in the middle of the great city, he looked around for the cars to disappear. It was a Saturday in spring but already there was weeding required in the garden of thought. He had come here, as he had before, to dispense with the distillation of doubt, insecurity, and longing he had put down on paper. The bridge was clear and he took the crumpled paper and a cigarette lighter out of his pocket and quickly lit a corner of the paper. As it caught the flames, he dropped it over the guardrail and it soon disappeared below, leaving only a burning scent.

It was symbolic of course, like a ritual. He might have thought or done something not in line with the lofty ideals to which he aspired. Feeling shame, he would write down words of self-reproach above all. And then, wanting to be free of it, he could not let whatever he had written stay a moment longer in the apartment, not even the trash or the dumpster. He had allowed himself to be caught in a struggle between the flesh and the spirit and being young, the flesh often won out, temporarily but again and again. Longing for an equanimity that was not part of adolescence by design, and with no sibling or close friend with whom to confide his innermost thoughts, which he could barely disclose even to himself, he was left with this ritual of writing them down and then destroying them in fire.

Sketch: Diagnosis

His mother, in her mid-50s, began to feel an unusual weakness. She had confessed as much to her husband, but husband and wife assumed this to be only a passing phase.

Her son was never aware of his mother's increasing fatigue and weakness until the trip to Venezuela. They had been invited by friends from the neighbourhood who had now resettled in their native country. Three adults and two children, they travelled together across that lovely tropical land from the plains up to the mountains and down to the beach.

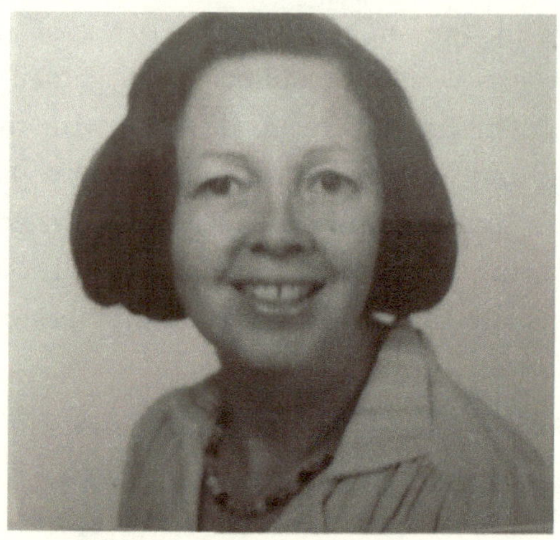

Mama, early 1980s

It was on a boat trip and hike to a cave that his mother suddenly couldn't continue. She was tired, she said, but the day was still young. In his eyes, she was young too. He never thought about her age. He looked at her brown walking shoes, the same ones she used to walk across woods and pastures in Switzerland. Did she just not want to go on? They were at the mouth of the cave. Sure, it required walking down a bit but adventure lay before them. She couldn't be tired when his friend's mother was just fine.

"What do you mean you can't go on, Mama—why?" he exclaimed.

"I just cannot. Maybe it's my knee," she said. And a bit ruefully, with resignation, she added, "I am surprised myself. But you go on—I'll wait here."

She did not know what was wrong at the time. After returning to Houston, she visited multiple doctors until one particular neurologist asked her to walk up a hallway with a gentle incline. She did so, holding on to the banister at one point. The doctor observed her from behind and immediately recognized the gait of a person with Multiple Sclerosis. He confirmed the diagnosis and told her in no uncertain terms. It was a moment she would never forget.

After returning home with her husband, she cried in the morning for days when her son was at school and her husband at work. She hated the neurologist although he was right—because he was right. She hid her tears from her teenage son, who in any case was preoccupied with sports, school, and the quandaries of adolescence, belonging, and identity. She began using a cane and then a walker.

"Mama, why are you creating this dependency? You don't need a cane. You can walk if you want to! Put your mind to it. This is all in your head that you can't walk!" the boy protested.

She took it mostly in silence, while the father reproached the boy gently but sternly. The disease was not so well known. Who got it? How and why? It had no treatment. That much seemed to be clear. She became weaker, dropping things all of a sudden, needing to sit down, slumping to one side as though struggling to balance herself even while sitting. Her sensitive skin became itchy and red.

"Every time you go to the hospital, you come back worse!" the son said accusingly though trying to side with her. "I hate doctors, I really do. And the charges! I will never become a doctor, that's for sure."

He felt a frustration that he did not have the words or demeanour for. He continued to rave.

"You get charged and they do nothing for you, in fact you are the worse off for it. Are they experimenting on you? You should charge them!"

She was confined to the sofa, feet on a stool to prevent swelling, magazines at her side along with the TV remote.

"You always say I should not watch so much TV, now look at you!" he exclaimed.

"I have no choice. Now I cannot turn the pages in a magazine. And I cannot walk or do anything else," she said meekly. Her eyes communicated impotence and he felt shame and kept quiet.

The face which brightened up so many birthdays and dinners at home with friends began to fill with resignation though never dread because she learned to simply ignore her disease. Her husband noticed that most days she still woke up with a smile. She bore her slow debilitation with a courage that seemed to push the disease into remission and that prolonged her life long past the survival of the average MS patient, said to be four to five years only at the time.

Still, the ravages of MS to scarring her nerve tissue and thereby disabling her muscle movement continued. Her vision became less, as did her hearing. She began to wear earphones to listen to the TV. She began to fall asleep in the middle of TV programs. Pillows were brought for her. She could still get up to go to the toilet, but then she began not to make it in time. Incontinence was coming on. This marked the need to get a helper. Bedsheets became wet and occasionally dirty. She began to wear adult diapers.

"Diapers?" he exclaimed. "But that is for babies." By now, he had begun to accept the slow deterioration and wasting away of his mother. He no longer thought it was psychological. But it was not fair. It reminded him of the neighbour whose young wife had died of cancer in spite of living a blameless and fit and healthy life. The surviving husband was in medical school and his parents had to move in to help raise their two little children. Indeed, such examples and stories were there, but one just didn't think it could happen to one's own mother.

With the acquisition of a motorized tri-cart, she retained a level of independence. Later, in their apartment in Chicago, she could even get into the elevator and go down to the first floor to the beauty shop to get her hair done. But one day, during one of his visits home from the military, her son found her on the floor of the bathroom in the apartment. She had just come back from getting her hair done but had not been able to transfer to the toilet and now could not get up. How long she had been lying there, she could not say. It was then that she told him, "I want to die, let me die." She repeated the dreaded phrase with conviction.

"No, Mama, I love you, Daddy loves you. You don't want to die. You say that now, but I will clean you up nicely and put you back on the sofa."

The periods of abatement and remission of the disease were temporary. They were always followed by progression and exacerbation. Having returned to Houston from Chicago, she could no longer take food by mouth since it was too difficult to swallow and she might choke in a spasm of regurgitations. She developed anemia. So there came the day for a stomach tube to be put in. He was surprised that it only required local anaesthetic and could be done at home. Medical science was so sophisticated yet there was still no cure for MS.

Her nutritional status improved and the color returned to her skin and cheeks. She then put on some weight. Lifting her from the sofa was like lifting dead weight. She could no longer use the tri-cart herself but her helpers used it. Then she required a Hoyer lift in order to be lowered down safely on the tri-cart. Then she required the wheelchair to avoid fracturing a hip. Later, she had to be turned from side to side at night to avoid bedsores.

Her son learned to put a catheter in his mother's urethra to drain the urine from her bladder into a plastic container. But even the act of cleaning his mother, or occasionally cleaning her bedsores, would draw a reproach.

"You don't like me, that is why you are hurting me!" she would exclaim.

"No, Mama, it's because I love you that I do it!" he protested.

"That is not true," she said in her weak, broken up voice. "If you loved me, you wouldn't do it. It hurts! You hate me, that is why you do it."

These words hurt him if he took it too seriously, but he knew she was in an altered frame of mind and had been for a long time. Who would not be.

Towards the end, her speech was intelligible only to a caregiver and to her husband and son. Then speaking became too much effort and ended only in slobber. Her eyes communicated resignation to the inability to communicate except through her eyes. Long-term memory had faded. The days went by now mostly in bed. She was perhaps no longer aware of the change in seasons outside her window or even of day and night.

And yet, she was aware of the last big shift to her son's house 1,000 kilometers away, from Corpus Christi to El Paso, Texas. It was now the year 2002 and she was 73 years old. She made the all-day trip stretched out on the back seat, her head resting on a pillow in the lap of Sarah, a caregiver, while her son drove down the West Texas interstate. Her husband followed by plane. And she was aware of her new set-up, her bed, her reclining chair, her toilet, her son and his wife and young son and daughter.

Most of all, she knew her husband was now in good hands. He was the one, the only one, who had really been with her all these years, these 23 years since the diagnosis. He changed her clothes, washed her clothes and towels, took her to the doctor, never left the apartment without a caregiver present, never took a vacation without his son present. He held her hand when he knew it needed to be held, squeezing her hand and communicating love on a daily basis by being so steadfast, present, and devoted. The caregiver never complained yet it had taken a toll on him too.

She could see he was now in good hands with her son and his family. She no longer had to worry about him. She could let go now. And so one December evening, having moved into her new home only one month earlier, she breathed her last. Her body ceased to struggle, her spirit was released, and in her own mind, she became one with Nature. God bless.

Coda: Debt of Gratitude to Parents

There are things one should not take for granted when viewing our particular "inheritance", or what we have received or been given by our parents. It is not a question of material wealth. I have been blessed to know those raised even by the "poor" with no resources who received an engrossing unconditional love and affection from their parents, along with a guiding hand, firm at times, that set them on a path to grow up independently, as individual human beings happy and self-made in their own right. These parents, who could not give the gift of education themselves, nevertheless did everything to assure that their children received it.

To my own parents, I thank my mother for the mother's love I felt, especially on those trips to Switzerland, her home country, when I was her boy, uniquely dependent on her yet feeling her love. Those trips also gave me a love for the mountains and the outdoors and probably triggered an in-born aptitude for languages that my mother certainly had. And I thank her for the independence she gave me and cultivated in me from the start. It was she who undertook a courageous journey to India as a young Swiss girl and single female, meeting my dad aboard the steamer from Genoa to Bombay. Along with the best cooking, from the most wholesome foods, it was the space to grow independently, and the trust and freedom therein, that led me along and gave me confidence. Years later, when she became ill with Multiple Sclerosis, there were times I was less than a good son, once thinking that she could walk and abandon the cane or the walker if only she really wanted to, if only she willed it. I was wrong. Later still, there were times I came too late to attend to her needs, especially those brought on by incontinence, since she became utterly incapable of moving or controlling any muscles at all. I ask for her forgiveness.

I thank my father for the spiritual and intellectual freedom and guidance he gave me, and thereby for that bookshelf, itself a legacy of the uncles and the education he was privileged to receive in India. Though he never inculcated it, I have not only respect for the worldview of his generation and his father's generation in India, but large components of it are my own—the valuation and appreciation of cultures and civilizations while never forgetting one's own or seeking to better one's current understanding in an ever-evolving world, taking care to fulfill one's duties to self and others.

This Daddy did exceptionally well, especially with my mother, whom he tended to over 23 years while she dealt with Multiple Sclerosis. Towards the end, he began to decline rapidly and I became impatient at times, for example when I discovered how behind he was in packing his things to leave Mozambique. With characteristic honesty, he later said it was shameful of him, a "disgrace." No, it was only old age, to which we are all subject, as the Buddha was wont to remind us. But he seldom asked for help. Ultimately, however, and without intending to, Daddy also passed on India to me. He greatly under-estimated me when he said I belonged to India merely by "accident of birth." By birth, blood, and spirit, I felt and feel a certain belonging to India, my father's country and a motherland of religious expression and heritage.

Part III

Young Adult

❖

I shall be telling this with a sigh
Somewhere ages and ages hence:
Two roads diverged in a wood, and I—
I took the one less travelled by,
And that has made all the difference.
– Robert Frost, *The Road Not Taken*

"Don't let schooling interfere with your education."
– Mark Twain

When do we step into adulthood? Or do we? Not simply by our 18th birthday surely, except in the eyes of the state. Not by leaving home—do we automatically become responsible? Not by wisdom certainly. As my father once wrote home to India, "Sanjay has grown in stature; wisdom comes hard!"

I think of a mere 12 year-old girl I knew in a village in Mali who was preparing meals for a household of a dozen people of all ages. A child with the responsibilities of an adult, I thought. Such is life for many children all over the world! And not by choice.

But is taking on adult responsibility equivalent with the "social and emotional maturity" we associate with adulthood and how teachers often evaluate children? No. Others can be quite mature, or look the part, but they remain untested, too young, and are more often just afraid.

In traditional societies, becoming an adult was also related to marriage and entering the householder stage of life. Marriage all over the world was arranged by families and the community. The individual was not so very free to choose or shape his destiny in myriad other ways. Often one left one home and web of relationships only to enter another home and a different web of relationships. One lived for the collective, the group, the family, the community. This was as true for Europe as anywhere else.

I, on the other hand, had been raised deliberately, that too in a new country far from extended family, with "freedom" and the expectation that I would shape my own destiny. William Faulkner once wrote, "People cling to that which robs them", and I've often reflected on the truth of that statement. And yet, while I have always felt keenly responsible to family members and to society at large, I cherish the modern notion of freedom that I have had—to decide what I will do in life, where I will live, whom I will marry. It is what I am most grateful for from my parents—freedom.

How did I use it? Against the wishes of my mother, but with the support of my father, I joined the Army! Which can seem like a prison to many, as they come not to like it yet cannot leave it lest they be given a dishonourable discharge. They must live out their enlistment, be it 2, 3, or 4 years. They must accept the consequences of the decision they made. They must grow up.

In my own estimation, I "stepped into adulthood" when I left home and joined the Army on July 24, 1984. It was no casual decision. I always felt good about it, even proud of it, and still do.

Thus began an adventurous period of 14 years between leaving my birth family and starting a family of my own. While it is the norm for many today, it is the exception in history. What did I do with my freedom? This I ask still.

Essay: Joining the Army

*Written in 1994, at age 28, looking back on 1983 – 84, age 17 – 18.

"I am joining the Army for three reasons: one, a natural feeling of duty and patriotism; two, a welcome amount of money for college; and three, for the experience of military life and company."

Thus read the last entry in a notebook of news items and quotes I kept in high school. The next day, I left for Ft. Benning, Georgia. I often had occasion to remind myself over the next two years of my reasons for joining the Army. But I never once felt so much as an ounce of regret.

A young man, insightful but shy, reflective but restless, idealistic but full of doubt. The only one in a graduating class of 646 to enlist in the Army, the only one in the International Baccalaureate (I.B.) academic program not to go on to college. Such faith in reason, reason in faith, in the power to direct one's own destiny. And so little beset by fear of condemnation, by the protective love of elders.

As much as the child is the father of the man, so am I his shadow today. **Ten years older**, I marvel at his confidence and sincerity, his belief in the ability to match the word to the deed. And I admire even more his belief in himself and his destiny. **For the adult finds it ever harder to understand himself and his fellow human beings and the reasons why people do the things they do.**

For the experience of military life and company. I knew this was the greatest of my reasons for joining the Army and yet it was the one I knew least about. What more could "military life and company" mean to me, a seventeen year-old city boy, than the image of setting up a tent in the woods?

Indeed that was part of the image in my mind, for I begged to learn what I thought were the practical arts of living that my urban upbringing had deprived me of. But what I was really interested in was people. Not the college types I was so self-conscious of and estranged from in high school. But those whom I fancied to be "ordinary people", those who didn't go on to college, whose illusions might be many but whose pretensions at least would be few. The kind of people George Orwell wrote about in *Down and Out in Paris and London*, one of many books I stumbled across on my father's shelves.

Nevertheless, I was ignorant and had few expectations of the life and company I was to encounter in the Army. And I was to join the infantry, which is always a guarantee to bring together the most diverse kinds of people. Diverse in the familiar terms of geographical origin and racial background and social class but even more so in the levels of motivation, expectations, and sincerity each individual brings to the Army. In fact, I don't think any soldier has ever been disappointed by the sheer variety of people with whom he comes into contact in a spell of military service, a variety seldom duplicated in the more customary pursuits of civilian life.

Of the many enlisted soldiers I knew, I remember only two others who had joined with some sense of patriotism. That is, when they wore the uniform, they wore it consciously not just as a set of clothes to put on but the embodiment of a higher cause, however imagined, to which they were bound by honor and allegiance. This was the way most officers also wore the uniform: they believed. The word "duty", in the sense of a contract, freely entered into and obligations freely undertaken, had a meaning to them which did not exist for most enlisted soldiers.

And yet I still hesitate to call most officers soldiers (**I wince when I read some of this in 2025!**). One stands out, a captain, who did not hide behind empty words and hollow commands like the others, but who exerted his soldiers even as he suffered the same hardships as them. I remember how he slipped in the mud after dusk one evening in the field as his troops trudged by, and how he effortlessly pulled himself up and made the kind of self-deprecatory remark which soldiers could both laugh at and respect. And in the most miserable of conditions, when a lieutenant was slow getting up, the steady voice of Captain Hayden could be heard: "Lieutenant, get out there and suck with the soldiers!"

Soldiers, with rifles in the field and brooms in the barracks, were conscious of doing the actual work of an Army. Without the accolades, the pageantry, the dress blues. "Don't call me 'sir', I work for a living" was their proud refrain.

Yet the vast majority never got beyond personal needs to the lofty realm of ideals. They had joined the Army for the more immediate reasons of having few other prospects, of getting away from home, of continuing a tradition of military service or heeding a parent's wishes, of earning a living and being respected, of living the exciting life of adventure and women they always imagined soldiers led. And when the Army inevitably robbed them of such illusions, they resorted to counting the days until their contract ended. Doing the minimum to get by was all that was required. Above and beyond the call of duty had no meaning to them. In fact, to do more than what was required had connotations of either sucking up to the officers or plain stupidity. No pretensions. "Back on the block—192 days and a wakeup!" they liked to say, or whatever number of days of "service" remained.

Without doubt, I was an idealist. But my "patriotism" sprang not from a belief in the rightness of the United States but rather from the abstract claim of duty. More than anything else, I believed in self-reliance. And, according to what I had learned in economics class in high school, I owed Uncle Sam a fee for the cost of my education in the public schools, amounting to about $2,340 per year (**writing today, I can say this line of thinking was somewhat misguided, since public schooling is paid for largely through local taxes and not federal funds**). And in my understanding of a social contract, as I had learned in government class in high school, citizens had a duty to serve their government.

I felt doubly duty bound for two other reasons. One, I was conscious of being a new citizen to the country, reflected in the fact I had signed the contract of my enlistment on 2 December 1983, less than two weeks after receiving my certificate of U.S. citizenship on 23 November 1983. Two, I was aware also that as an idealist, I was a critic, and criticism in some quarters was taken as un-patriotic, my volunteer enlistment could serve to dispel such charges.

Do I see this in hindsight? Were these only subconscious reasons? How much easier to explain I enlisted because I wanted money for college and I would not take money from my parents. Or because of the desire to experience military life and company, as though someone like me could separate my actions from my beliefs. These were undoubtedly reasons, but I cannot deny the abstract claim of duty, which was longer in the making and which saw me through my most trying times in basic training ("boot camp"). *I want to be a soldier, I want to be a soldier,* I would say to myself in those times.

My sense of duty was not so much secular as religious (**true but rather misguided, says the older adult in 2025**). After working through the Buddha and agnosticism to the Gospels and the Gita to Socrates and Gandhi, I absorbed the idea of duty as the sum of our providentially allotted appointments on Earth. Probably I held to duty also as a way of stilling the many questions in my mind. And while I knew that duty could not be performed in the expectation of reward, I did expect it to be the path of wisdom. In fact, the intensity of my early spiritual quest had been so ardent that I was already sure that all I wanted out of life was wisdom and understanding.

I told my father as much, when I said to him, "When I am old and look back on my life, I would like to know that I served in the Army." He said this showed perspective, that I had thought the matter through, and this convinced him I was doing the right thing.

"*The service*", it is called, the armed services. "You got to have been in *the service* to know that", I recalled a supervisor saying to a coworker in the janitorial job I held for a few weeks before joining the Army. But very few people join to serve. Very few people thought anything like me. "*Misguided idealism*", I was to hear it called in a newspaper review of the movie "Platoon" soon afterwards.

And I had thought about war, as well as read Gandhi, who became the occasion of my nickname as a soldier because of the bald, brown, and bespectacled resemblance I bore to him, perhaps in addition to the moral conscience. I judged World War II to be a just war and the use of violence as necessary to overcome the forces of evil in that conflict. But I judged the Vietnam War to be a mistake.

I also joined the Army at a time when U.S. participation in overthrowing the Sandinista regime in Nicaragua was a distinct possibility. But I knew enough about the Sandinistas and the dictator Somoza they had overthrown to know that U.S. support for the "Contras" was a dubious cause at best. If sent to fight a war in Nicaragua, what would I do? When I asked myself, I felt instinctively that I would survive to debunk the myths of the war machine firsthand. Invincible youth. Of all the groups to protest the injustice of the Vietnam War, I judged "G.I.s Against the War" as closest to being morally right. Only they who suffer can bear witness (**my line of thinking at the time, says the older adult, nodding in agreement but shaking his head too**).

Sketch: Glasses for Life

John Caynon, a dentist downtown, wrote his first eyeglasses prescription. The need for corrective lens had only been identified because of an eye test required of him in order to join the Army. His left eye was stronger than his right eye, something he already knew since he would unconsciously cup his right eye when reading, allowing the left eye to do all the work in clearer vision. It started in 11th grade and all that reading of fine print given by the history teacher on those mimeographed copies. Now it was confirmed that he was near-sighted. Distant objects appeared blurry. It took the Army to identify his need for glasses.

But just having glasses was no bar for occupational specialties in the Army of that time. It was the colour vision test, however, that did limit his choice. He had failed to identify numbers in green dots against a red dot background and red numbers against a green background. The examiner had flipped through the chart quickly and he let himself get flustered rather than ask the examiner to slow down. It meant that he could not be the Light Wheel Vehicle Mechanic that he wanted to be, to learn something "practical." That was an enlistment of minimum 3 years.

Instead, he was offered the infantry. The minimum was 2 years. He took it.

* I don't think I'm colour blind at all, but there was no do-over. What was meant to be was meant to be.

Sketch: Standing Inspection

The staff sergeant moved into the private's direct line of vision, having turned crisply to face him from about two feet away. The private continued to stare straight ahead like a cheetah transfixed by some target in the distance.

The sergeant meanwhile began his inspection, top to bottom. The cap, the straightness of the "mosquito wing" insignia on the cap, the indentation of the cap on its top, its crease free of any sweat stains, it being cocked above the ears with visor parallel to the ground. The hair must be short and not touching the ears; the eyebrows must be trimmed and especially there must be no sideburns. Most important was a clean shave. He carefully checked if any spots had been missed, if there was any fuzz around the neck. There should be no moustache and, if there was, it should be neatly trimmed. The position of attention demanded a closed mouth, with no teeth showing, and a level jaw and a chin up but not too high and haughty. Don't let there be even the trace of a hair follicle on the chin itself.

The private was an inch or two shorter than the platoon sergeant. He held his position, arms at his side, fingers curled, a gaze that was impenetrable, fixed, statue-like. The sergeant's eyes lowered to scan his uniform—collar first, the mosquito bar insignia of a private fixed close but not too close to the tip of the collar. The uniform, had the private really ironed it carefully? He examined the area around the buttons and the shirt pockets. He then moved to glance at the proper folding of the uniform's sleeves to a point just above the elbow. The pants, did a crease indicate a set of freshly ironed pants? Were the bottoms tucked neatly into the boots?

With him staring ahead, the sergeant now looked straight down to examine his boots. Did they shine in the right places? Were there scuff marks? Did the soldier use a lacquer on the sides? Were the laces tied properly, preferably left over right?

"When's the last time you put Kiwi on your boots, soldier?" he said softly but clearly, almost like a whisper in the silence that made one forget nearly thirty soldiers were standing nearby in attention.

The soldier said nothing, showing only the slightest movement of his lips around the edges. He knew the sergeant knew he had plenty of polish on his boots.

"A bit more water on your spit shine the next time", the sergeant quipped.

As the sergeant turned to move to the next soldier, the young private adjusted his vision imperceptibly to take a look at the sergeant, black hair touching his ears, brown shaven face, large nose jutting out like his jaw, hailing from the island of Samoa. It was altogether a friendly face, an approachable face, just going through the motions. He knew the sergeant liked him.

The private resumed his distant look, across the parking lot, to the buildings beyond, while the sergeant examined 30 soldiers thusly. Was there nothing better to do?

Sketch: Ft. Campbell in November, 1984

"Pull your poncho out and we'll set up a hooch."

Dusk and a cool breeze whispered in the branches of the trees on the ridge. I loosened the straps of my backpack and groped for the camouflage nylon poncho I thought I'd packed at the bottom. Corporal

Helms rustled about in the bushes not far away. When I no longer heard his heavy boots breaking the backs of the crisp fall leaves, I heard the trickle of urine running on dry leaves. Big Johnnie returned with several short branches in one arm to where I stood waiting with my poncho in hand.

"What's that mess you got there?"

"I had my poncho at the bottom and I had to take everything out to get to it."

"Didn't nobody tell you how to pack your bag yet? You keep your poncho on top 'cause you need it more than all that other shit you got in there."

"Well I had my wet weather gear on top."

"You won't need that unless they tell you that's the uniform. A poncho is good for the rain most times. Now since you got all your stuff out, gimme your E-tool and move them rocks out from where we're gonna set up our hooch."

Helms took out his poncho from a side pocket on his backpack. Kneeling down, he took one end of the E-tool, or entrenching tool that was a folding shovel, and began to cut the branches he had collected and drive them in as stakes. He drove them first through the eyelets down one side of his poncho facing the wind coming off the top of the ridge.

"See, I set up like this so we stay out the wind. Now you can lay one end of your poncho over that end of mine so that the eyelets line up in front. Put a stick through them if you have to and then tie up the hoods."

"What do you mean 'tie up the hoods?'"

"Pull the draw string tight and tie it around the hood so we don't get wet if it rains tonight. You ain't never set up a hooch before?"

I pulled the draw string tight and fumbled around trying to make a good knot. Thoroughly city-bred, I had never even slept outside before the Army. And when we had spent 10 days on bivouac for BRM (Basic

Rifle Marksmanship) in basic training, we had set up A-frame tents using the standard issue shelterhalves, stakes, poles, and rope.

"You not done yet, private?" Helms said as he grabbed the other hood, tied it off, and handed me a straight branch. "Take this and run it through the eyelets in the middle and hold it up. This'll be one tentpole."

I raised up one end of the makeshift tent with a stick while Helms ran a cord from the pole to a stake several feet in front of the tent. Johnnie had spent the first eighteen months of his three-year enlistment in Germany and the last ten months in Ft. Campbell. He bordered on being overweight but carried himself with the dogged persistence of a mule. When we first met, he kidded me about spit-shining my boots and said I wouldn't be doing that after two years. Helms himself never looked the part of a soldier but he got the job done. From somewhere outside of Gainesville, Florida, I heard he went back to driving a truck there after getting out of the Army.

"You bring any 500 cord?" he asked,

"No, but I got my tent rope, poles, and stakes. And my shelterhalf."

"What you want all that for? Ain't you got enough to carry around already?"

"Well, it was on the packing list and Sergeant Denman said to pack everything on the list."

"Listen. These ten days we got in the field, we're never gonna be in one place long enough to set all that up. You don't need it anyway and you just wear yourself out carrying it around. What you need to set up a hooch is 550 cord. You get it from the supply sergeant, and once you get it, hold on to it. You'll always need it."

Helms bent down to fish more 550 cord out of a pocket on his pack. After we set up the other end of the tent, he used the cord to tie the hoods of the ponchos to tree limbs on either side of the tent. Then he pulled the creases out by tightening up the slip knots on the cords running off either end pole.

"If they'da dropped off in the right place, we woundn'na had to set up in the dark. But when do pilots give a damn for grunts? Not then, not now, not ever."

The helicopters had dropped us off far from where we were supposed to be that morning and we had spent nearly all day just regaining our bearings. The day had begun in the barracks long before, around 4 AM, when the word came to move out. At the time, we were sleeping in our uniforms in our quarters, packs and rifles at our bedside. We left the garrison marching in single file down both sides of the street until we came to an open field. Then the whole company crossed the field in a wedge formation, squad leaders in front with their teams spread out in wedges ten metres apart until we reached a long wood line. There we waited among the trees, packs in front of us and rifles in our hands. Watching the sun slowly rise and change the frost in front of us to dew and then to mist, we waited for the "birds" to come.

When the UH-60 Blackhawks finally swooped in, we scrambled aboard and my heart rose with the treetops and the cool breeze and the sun dappling the frosted fields beneath us. We sat facing each other, hunched forward with our packs on our backs, gliding in the line of helicopters and veering with them to the left and to the right. We suddenly dropped into the landing zone, where the crew chief in back unceremoniously pushed us out by our heavy packs. We ran to a distance beyond the blades of the choppers and fell on our bellies, our backs to the rotor wash of the birds and rifles pointed towards the ubiquitous enemy. No sooner were we down than the Blackhawks took off, leaving us to the quiet of the Kentucky backwoods and the vagaries of military intelligence. We soon discovered we were in the wrong place and we spent the rest of the day walking because of it.

"… Spend all day humping 'cause your own people can't read a map straight. And I bet they're laughing, too. With buddies like that, who needs enemies? I'm too short to worry about it anyway."

What Helms meant, big and stocky as he was, was that he had little time left on his three-year enlistment in the Army. He was ready to go home at last.

We had spread out another poncho on the ground under the hooch and were laying out our sleeping rolls when we heard someone groping in the woods and coming our way.

"Johnnie," called the gruff voice I recognized as Sergeant Chapman's. He always talked as if he were hoarse, clearly but raspily, and from his chest, as if cigarettes and whisky had taken too great a toll on his vocal cords.

"What you want, Chap?" said Corporal Helms.

"You all got guard from 2330 to 0100 (zero-one-hundred) and 0400 to 0530," he declared. "And whoever's on last 'uz got to wake us up for stand-to at 0530."

"You can say 11:30 and 5:30 to me, Sergeant. I'm about through with this. 132 days and a wake-up. How long? Not long!" Helms recited that typical short-timer's refrain with relished gusto.

"Yeah, well they're gonna drive us hard this time, Johnnie. It's Captain Alexander's last field exercise. Just make sure you wake us up at 5:30. I don't wanna catch no shit."

"Oh, I'll wake you up all right but don't you fall back to sleep. Mathur here'll take first shift, and tell whoever wakes him up not to wake me up, 'cause I'll be cutting logs, see what I'm sayin?'"

"Cut'em too loud and I'll have Mathur throw a boot over your big head."

"Get the fuck outta here, Chap."

We could hear Sgt. Chapman scampering away through the woods to the next position. I blew up my air mattress while Helms put on his chemical suit.

"We gotta put that on?" I asked.

"No, I wear this to stay warm. I don't tote no longjohns around these woods. Packing things you don't need, private—you'll learn after a while."

"Then what do you pack?"

"Food, man. You can't live on the shit they give you to eat out here. Ramen, peanuts, granola bars—that's what everybody packs. They can keep them MREs."

MREs were "meals-ready-to-eat", the replacement for C-rations at that time in the Army. They came in hard brown plastic bags stenciled with mouth-watering names like "turkey diced with gravy" or "ham and chicken loaf" or "pork patties." Those were the names of the dehydrated main meals to which were added more savory items like crackers and peanut butter or even applesauce if you were lucky. Besides MREs, we might be lucky to get a hot meal every other day or so. As long as the supply truck could keep up with us.

After we rolled out our bedding, Johnnie took out his metal canteen up and poured it half full of water. Then he poked out a small hole in the ground between us and set in a can of flammable Sterno. Laying the bent wires of a coat hanger across the hole, he flicked a match into the Sterno and balanced his canteen cup on the hanger. The faintest hint of light flickered out of the hole and around the edges of the hooch. We sat cross-legged on our sleeping bags.

"Being in the field don't mean you can't be comfortable. Get your cup out and we'll drink us some hot chocolate."

Sketch: Ft. Campbell in November, Part II

"Sergeant Chapman, your team has a special assignment. You are to march down to Range 24 for a live fire. Assaulting an objective on line."

So we took off marching down the range roads, packs on our backs but single file and in close intervals. We stopped only once, for Sgt.

Chapman to read the map and to sip water from our canteens. We marched towards the airfield as if we were marching home, but it was only the fourth day of the field exercise.

It seemed like over a week had gone by already. After the first night, it began to drizzle and we were told to put on our wet weather gear. To my deep shame, I found I carried two wet weather tops in my pack and no bottoms. I thought back to the day when I was not issued but thrown all my gear and I'd had to sign for it and pack it before I'd had time to check it or even identify it. And since I was out of uniform, I'd not been able to continue with the group and I'd had to stay behind with the supply truck. I had all day to think about it because when we did finally move out, it was late afternoon. And I was lying on top of boxes of MREs and other gear in a trailer being pulled by a jeep over the ruts of an old jeep trail. I remember how it grew dark and I could see less and less between the canvas flaps from the roof and the trailer's tail gate.

Anyway, now here we were. We continued walking, passing Ranges 25 and 26 and closing in on Range 24. As we approached, I could see two men in the top of the covered range tower. We walked through the gate and up the gravel road, where a captain in a soft cap and a master sergeant in a steel pot for a helmet waited for us. The sergeant looked at the watch on his wrist and said something to the captain as we walked up. The tall but stout officer with the black rim military glasses greeted us.

"Gentlemen, you're on time. Now listen up. There's a full-bird colonel up in that tower and looking down on us even as we speak. Neither you nor he has come all this way to blow it now. This isn't a difficult range. You got three hundred metres in front of you. There are targets down range but you probably won't see them until you get up close. That doesn't matter. One team has got to lay down a sheet of suppressor fire while the other team advances. You got that?"

"Yes, sir", replied Sgt. Chapman. The captain in his soft cap, .45 calibre pistol slung around his chest, looked so light and lithe next to the Sergeant Major in his heavy steel pot for a helmet and his LBE (Load

Bearing Equipment including ammunition magazine pouches, canteen holder, and first aid pouch).

"Just remember, Sgt. Chapman," said Sgt. Major Cook, "'I'm up, I'm seen, I'm down.' Make sure your guys understand that. Three to five second rushes, you hear?"

"Yes, Sergeant Major", deadpanned Sgt. Chapman. He stood like the rest of us behind him, his left arm resting on the ammo pouch at his side and right hand grasping the sling of his rifle slung over his arm.

"You done good so far," said Captain Bishop again, "but you can't rest yet. Now take your positions and the range sergeant will give you your ammo. Live rounds, you hear, this is the real thing. And remember, you got a colonel looking at you."

"Good luck, men," said the Sgt. Major as they turned around to ascend the tower.

"Cheese-eating motherfuckers", Helms said as we followed Sgt. Chapman up to the range line. "Brown-nosing sons of bitches."

We could see the places carved in the dirt behind trees and logs where previous rifle squads had positioned themselves for the assault. Sgt. Chapman turned to us like an American football quarterback and said in his raspy West Virginia voice:

"Listen, if you're like me, you don't give a damn if it's a five-star general or Joe-fucking private up there watching us. Let's just do the best we can and get this over with. Like Sgt. Major said, three to five-second rushes. 'I'm up, I'm seen, I'm down.' And if you're not moving, you're shooting. Main thing is we gotta stay on line. Team leaders gotta make sure nobody's getting ahead of anybody else. This is live fire so you could hurt yourself. If you don't lock the safety switch on your weapon when you get up, you better be damn sure you don't pull the trigger when you're running. And when you get down, make sure you keep your rifle in front of you at all times. Everybody got that?"

"Sure, Sergeant, we done this before," said Corporal Fahe. He was leader of B team, which was short two people. Helms was A team leader.

Sgt. Chapman continued:

" A team, you're on my left, B team on my right. When I say 'A team, move out', I want you to move out your team, Johnnie. Two at a time. Make sure they can hear you and make sure they stay on line. When I say 'B team, move out', Fahe, you take your team and go. You got a lot of room on that right side so don't go off into the woods. If you don't hear me saying anything, that's when I'll be moving. And don't be scared to fire your weapon. After running through all these vines, you're going to have to clean it anyway. Captain wants to hear us lay down a good line of suppressor fire, so support your buddy. And nobody will fire on rock-n-roll, got that? You're not gonna be able to see what you're firing at anyway. All right, take your positions and grab a drink while you can."

I walked along the range line to the left behind Helms. The range was overgrown with vines and logs and vines growing out of the logs and up the trees for as far as one could see. Not a single target or silhouette could be seen, save for a gentle rise far down range.

"Brooks, I want you here , so I can keep an eye on you."

Helms motioned for Brooks to get down at a spot behind a log. He pointed to where he was going to be and told Laughlin and me to take positions about five to seven metres apart on the left side of the line.

"Five metre intervals all the way to the end. When I say, 'Left side, move out', that means both of you. Get up, move up five metres, and get down. You better not stay up more than three to five seconds. And don't carry your rifle pointed to the side. Keep your weapon pointed down range at all times."

I moved ahead to a position scratched out in the dirt behind a tree. Laughlin got down behind a tree between me and Helms. I lay on my left side and took out my canteen. I could barely make out the top of the range tower through the branches of the trees above me.

Helms was coming back down the line with the magazines of ammunition in his hand.

"Here you go: 4 magazines, 120 rounds, so don't be stingy. Lock and load, but don't fire until you hear Chap say, 'Move out.' Anytime you're not moving, you're firing."

I looked over at Laughlin inserting the 30-round magazine in his rifle and letting the bolt fall forward. I loaded 3 magazines in the ammo pouches on my belt and locked and loaded the fourth one as I had seen Laughlin do. I wondered how fast he would move down this range. He was slim and trim but about the least energetic soldier in the platoon.

"B team, move out!" I heard Sgt. Chapman yell out. Helms initiated fire on our side and Laughlin, Brooks, and I followed suit. I aimed at nothing in particular down range and fired. Live rounds kicked more than blanks. I tried to stagger my fire with Laughlin next to me.

"A team, move out!"

"Left side, move out!" I clicked on the safety switch, got up, and moved forward. I hopped over the vines and brambles as best I could, keeping my rifle pointed in front of me, and came crashing down at a point to the left of an old log.

"Right side, move out!"

I saw Laughlin in position a little further away from me now and laying down suppressor fire as Helms and Brooks were up, seen, and down.

"B team, move out!" Sgt. Chapman called on B team to move up twice as we continued firing down range. It came our turn to move up on line and we pushed forward around the trees, over the depressions, under the lowest branches, and through the vines, sticklers, and brambles. Sometimes I could make out a place to run about five metres in front of me. Other times, I just got up and tried to stay on line with Laughlin to my right. He moved slower and I felt I was up too long. We threw our rifle butt on the ground in front of us, landed on our knees first, and then hit our elbows, clicking our rifles onto "semi" and laying down a line of fire.

After we had got up and down about ten times, I began to feel a light stinging in my right eye. I was a left-handed shot but I was shooting right-handed so I could better face Laughlin and hear Helms. I turned to fire left-handed. We had no time to think. Fire flashed from rifle muzzles, the smell of carbon and probably hydrogen rose in the air, and above it all boomed the voices of Chapman and Helms and Fahe faintly on the other side of the line.

We continued to advance, throwing our bodies forward with disdain, ignoring the scrapes on knees and elbows. My rifle jammed and I took out the magazine to drop the round which wouldn't fire. I reloaded and fired again. The hot shell of the round ejected on my neck and rolled around on my back when I moved to flick it off.

"Left side, move out!" Laughlin and I got up and ran forward. I fired again and another round ejected hot onto my back. I can't remember whether I imagined or saw the brass cartridge on my reddened skin. I shook it off and fired again. The sting in my right eye grew worse. My eyes were protected by my glasses but they must have been very sensitive to the carbon and hydrogen in the air. I made the mistake of rubbing my eye with my right forefinger and probably inflamed it much worse than it had been.

Our advance was beginning to seem interminable when the terrain finally rose slightly. It was clear of vines and bushes at the top and the enemy bunkers could be clearly seen. Sgt. Chapman assaulted past the empty bunker in the middle to fall on line with Fahe, James, and Chappell.

"A team, move out!" As left and right sides, we moved forward again and fell on line with Sgt. Chapman and the B team on top of the objective.

"Cease fire!" Sgt. Chapman yelled. I flicked the switch onto "safe" and looked over at Laughlin. His left trouser leg had come out of his boot and his laces were untied. Helms came over to us and said we were to consolidate the objective and hold the perimeter in a 180 degree angle faced to the front. We told him how many rounds we had left and whether we had lost any equipment. This was standard procedure. My eye felt better already though only then did I feel the scrapes on my knees. It was over. We only waited for the range sergeant to come and lead us off the range. When he came, we all got up and locked the bolts back on our rifles and he collected our ammunition and ran a rod down the barrels of our rifles and we marched back, rifles pointed downrange on our shoulders.

Sketch: Footrace at Ft. Campbell

The hotshot young lieutenant just out of ROTC school threw down a challenge to the platoon on his first day and his first PT run. As part of introducing himself, he boasted about how fast he was and challenged anyone to beat him in the 2-mile run that morning. This was friendly competition yet not taken lightly. One soldier guffawed, another snickered, and a third in back grunted "ooh-ah". The men continued their warm-ups with a touch more purpose now.

The young enlisted soldier with a foreign last name that could be corrupted to hark back to an old TV series thought he would give the lieutenant a run for the money. An officer cannot be allowed to beat all the enlisted soldiers. He squatted and stretched his legs, eyeing the lieutenant between the pairs of legs in front of him. A crisp and brilliant morning it was, a day to upstage the new officer.

Suddenly, they were off and the lieutenant jumped out to a lead faster than a rabbit. He was soon far ahead on the long road that ran straight ahead from the barracks.

Mathur could see the lieutenant and he kept after him. His heart pounded, his ligaments stretched, his diaphragm rose, his chest sucked in more and more air. By the third leg, he was narrowing the gap. Was the smooth-talking new officer from South Carolina slowing down? Was he tired or waiting? At the start of the fourth and final leg and home stretch,

Mathur passed him without a word. The lieutenant was gasping for air and off his compact running form, flailing his arms and legs and looking distraught.

Mathur beat him to the finish line easily and waited for his new boss. After crossing and bending and placing his hands on his knees to catch his breath, the lieutenant looked over at Mathur and remarked, "Soldier, you took me too seriously, congratulations on a first victory."

"Thank you, sir," Mathur replied, with the verbal respect given an officer. With an enlisted soldier's pride in his heart, he added, "I couldn't let you win the first time, sir."

Sketch: Parched Earth in Egypt

Desert training, Egypt, 1985

Parched earth like this he had never seen. Baked and cracked, mud that dried up in geometrical patterns reflective of water that once soaked the area. It was so hot in July now. Suddenly, he saw a farmer below as the helicopter veered in the air, turning and blowing down its rotor wash. The farmer wore a white tunic against his dark skin and he stood bending against the wind of the blades, looking up and waving. His head was wrapped in a white cloth. He continued to look up and wave, not for help of any sort but just to greet the Americans.

The young private had almost missed this trip. The First Sergeant somehow thought he should not join the rest of the platoon headed to Egypt as part of Operation Bright Star. This was a blow to his morale and seemed an odd reward for recently earning Brigade Soldier of the Month honours. He had gone to plead with the First Sergeant, a tall yet approachable African-American with small eyes who looked older than his years. He congratulated the young private and listened to his plea. Then his face changed and with upturned lips and head thrown back, he exclaimed, "So you want to have your cake and eat it too?"

The private remained standing, in the usual form of straight-backed respect, not knowing what to say in the face of an expression he had never heard before. It was not as though earning Brigade Soldier of the Month should reward him with missing out on desert warfare training if that's what the First Sergeant thought. He just didn't want to be left out, alone in the barracks while the platoon and entire brigade travelled to Egypt. Nominally, the deployment was announced as training Egyptian troops but the exercise was more about the American troops building up their own desert warfare skills. Plus, they would have to bear the Sahara's July heat, a survival skill in itself.

The farmer waving up at the American helicopter from the middle of that cracked earth with no one else around for miles and miles seemed to epitomize something else about the deployment. Whose side were the Americans on? Was it his side? It bothered the young private to no end to hear fellow soldiers, starting with the officers who were supposed to set an example for others, use terms like "ragheads" and "camel jockeys." For Arabs and Egyptians, they invariably used the epithet "Abdul" as a general moniker just as they used "Ivan" as the personification of all Russians. There had even been a nighttime exercise in which the fictional enemy for the "war game" was "Abdul"!

It struck the young private, with his own foreign background, as contemptuous and contemptible. He was left to think about it but could share his disgust with no one. As usual, the hypocrisy was apparent, since the very soldiers who kept the dirtiest quarters back in the barracks were the ones who were mostly like to say "dirty Arab" and "we're here to train fuckin' camel jockeys and ragheads." The audacity of it all, the gall, he thought in his own naïve way—running down the people whom you've come to train and that too in their country and supposedly at their invitation, although he couldn't be sure how that worked.

They had received a cultural briefing and a summary pocket book. To the American troops, it seemed strange to hear of men holding hands with men or walking down the street with an arm around the neck of another man. When the First Sergeant heard of the soft handshakes of the Arabs, he took the opportunity to remind the troops, "And when you shake hands, I want you to shake hands like a man—firm and hard—no Tiny Tim handshakes!" It all seemed a wilful and gross misunderstanding driven on by something he could not understand. Not only did it go uncorrected by senior officers and non-commissioned officers (NCOs) who should know better, but it had all the flavour of being condoned and encouraged. Why? He could not understand.

Oddly enough, his roommate in the barracks was quite different. He had ordered cassettes to learn Arabic and he was much looking forward to speaking the language when he got the chance. Of all the soldiers, Lawrence Laughlin was a loner and eccentric. He kept mostly to himself and seemed quite happy to fiddle with gadgets or his beloved jeep which he called endearingly "the beast." He had a slovenly aspect about him and kept the minimum of minimum standards when it came to ironing his uniform and shining his boots or keeping his bed and personal quarters clean and tidy. He almost seemed to take pride in being a proverbial "dirtbag." The other roommate in the barracks was "Brooks", who had a sunny disposition strengthened by a naivete and un-curiosity about anything of significance in life. His pastime away from home early in life was to get drunk every weekend. He regaled with pride at having once filled up the bathtub with beer cans in "party hearty" with fellow troops on a long weekend.

One day in Bright Star, someone came back to the open air tent in which the platoon passed the hottest portion of the days and just happened to mention that there were some Egyptian soldiers nearby on the other side of the dunes. The young private told Laughlin who, like him, was waiting for just such an opportunity. Sensing it was better to be safe in numbers, they invited Brooks along as well.

It was against orders to mingle with any Egyptians, so they had to be stealthy about where they were going. They found a way to disappear discreetly over the dunes and soon came upon the half dozen Egyptians. Their uniforms were unbuttoned and they wore flip flops or rubber sandals instead of boots. Most didn't have military caps, not even to keep the sun or long hair out of their eyes, as opposed to the crew cuts of the Americans.

In a characteristic mumble, Laughlin braved a greeting, "Salaam aleikum." He looked up uncertainly with a faint smile as he said it. A moment passed, then the Egyptians squealed in delight almost in unison, their faces suddenly flashing wide smiles. Only one could speak much English, but the mingling and bonhomie was evident without language. They gathered closely, with less sense of personal space, just as the cultural booklet had indicated. The one who could speak English passed questions to the Americans. At one point, he asked the young private where he was originally from. When he heard it was India, he forgot translating and exclaimed spontaneously and loudly with his head to the sky, "India we love you, Rajiv Gandhi we love you!" It was quite unexpected and the young private had no idea why, but he was delighted. Everyone laughed at the spontaneity of it all.

The Egyptians then initiated a game in which one person blindfolded himself with a bandana and stood with his back to the others, hands behind his back and palms open. He had to guess which of the others slapped him on the palms. The time passed like this with gaiety and laughter as the slap of palms grew louder and louder. The Egyptians did not seem to grow tired of such sport and the silly game among men went on and on as the sun began to set in the desert horizon. If this was breaking barriers and making friends with "allies", then it was mission accomplished in spite of officialdom.

Operation Bright Star, July 1985

Sketch: Bar Hopping

Military days were also the time he even subscribed to Playboy magazine, which arrived under black cover, and to Gentleman's Quarterly (GQ), a men's magazine. The jokes and articles and interviews in Playboy he found as educational as he found the girls adorable. Having to buy his own clothes for the first time in his life, he learned something about style from GQ and became more selective in everything from jackets to shoes. A shirt the color of lavender or light purple seemed to suit him well.

He and a friend in the platoon had a routine for perhaps the monthly night on the town. It started with going to a gym off base in the small town of Clarksville. It was as though building up the muscles and breaking a sweat in a manly environment were required to fit in the designer clothes and reward oneself with a night of high living. Then came the long drive to Nashville in his car, a two door Mustang that was sure to be cleaned inside and out and even waxed for the evening. Coming into town, the first stop was usually Bennigan's for steak, or it could be Red Lobster. He had learned the technique of consuming a lobster from another friend on base—how to break open the shell, remove the claws, crack the joints, and scoop out or suck in the white flesh. People did it and it seemed worth knowing and it tasted all right dipping it into a creamy sauce.

It was early yet and dusk might only be falling and they enjoyed their first drink of the evening, typically a cocktail such as a Long Island Iced Tea. It was syrupy and invigorating. These were all new experiences for an adventurous 19 year old wanting to experience different sides of life for the value of whatever such worldliness could teach him. And he learned from peers in the military, who spent what little income they had on alcohol above all and waited until the end of the month, when their hair might be just long enough to disguise the reality that they were soldiers. Because that would never do, leading any girls who might possibly be interested in them to have second thoughts.

It was on to the first dance club as the sky turned gray and darkness descended. Chevy's was known for its old Chevy on the floor and its 1950s décor and older crowd and older music. It was a well-lit place with a large dance floor surrounded by booths. It was enjoyable to feel the beat and watch the couples on the floor. Here, the ogling of girls began but they were older.

Then it was on to another club with modern dance music and a younger set and fewer couples. It felt like the music was banging off the walls and even ordering a drink at the bar required reading lips. The girls wore more glitter, their heels were higher, their makeup more indulgent, and they were more striking. He and his friend would stay a while, this being the heart of the evening. Every now and then, they would get up the courage to ask a girl to dance. It was not easy getting up the courage and they would ponder and discuss the rejection in their mind and challenge each other to go for it. Another gulp of beer would make them both brave and indifferent to whatever might happen. They were two scared cats and it didn't bother them, since it was never about "getting laid" as the guys would talk about and lie about back on base. They were somehow wanting to be love-struck and were looking for a connection of the heart and yet knew in advance it wouldn't happen. At bottom, they were both deeply afraid of girls and were ok with that. It was safer that way.

On the occasion when a girl or better yet two girls out for the evening said yes, then they would attempt to dance and move their body and wriggle and sway and clap their hands every now and then. The girls could not have been impressed, but the music was loud and hopping, the lights dim and glittering, and it was pleasant just to dance with girls harmlessly, since the boys were indeed harmless. It was difficult to hear one another anyway and smiles and dancing was enough. They would depart the floor when it was a slow song.

The final stop of the night was a piano bar in a Marriott hotel. Here one could talk and be heard and even find a seat. His friend, inevitably inebriated by this point, would invariably buy a rose for a girl who looked alone, but he would never approach her. She could only accept the rose and wonder who her secret admirer was while the boys averted their eyes to keep her guessing.

It was a long drive back to base at night's end. His friend would try to stay awake but would often fall asleep. The night was dark and his ears were ringing and the miles seemed interminable. The highway would loom up going over a bridge and strange thoughts and impulses would come to him. What if he hit the guardrail, either by accident or on purpose, what then and where would the car end up. Was it a death wish? Why? He flinched looking at the guardrails and came back to himself and raced down the midnight highway.

Narrative: Visiting India

My two-year Army enlistment ended in early July 1986. I was someone seen as a good soldier, a potential "lifer" even, because I showed the sort of serious attitude that was wanted and a pattern of continuous improvement rather than slacking off and developing a bad attitude. I was asked several times to re-enlist, even to consider Ranger school. But I declined because I knew my next step was university, which I had saved up money for with the help of the Veteran's Education Assistance Program (VEAP), the successor to the G.I. Bill that had helped so many veterans to obtain an education. I had written admissions essays to the University of Virginia and been accepted into the College of Liberal Arts starting in August. Unbeknownst to me, I was to be the only freshman in the dorms who was not 18 years old, who had been living independently from his parents, and who had other life experience besides school. That kind of traditional school and culture did not bode well for me. Already sceptical of higher education, I was headed for a fall.

Before starting university, however, with a few weeks to spare, my father had arranged a trip to India for me. It was time to meet and get to know "extended family" members, starting with his brother's and sister's families. I was 20 years old and did not know them. I had grown up all these years without extended family at all, with almost no contact even with grandparents, without any brothers and sisters either. Family was, for all practical purposes, only my mother and father. And yet, I had many family members in India, whom my father sketched out on a tree and even provided a few biographical notes for. He also knew of my inclination towards Buddhism and general interest in history and religion. In his enthusiasm about the trip, and he and Mama had just visited in April that year in what was to be my mother's last trip to India, my father correctly adduced that for someone like me, India would prove to be "endlessly fascinating." Still, he maintained that I belonged to the country merely "by accident of birth." So much for a phrase.

I had grown up with a few friends, and friends of friends, whose parents were from India but who were like me—"Americanized", speaking American English, playing American sports, watching American cartoons and TV shows, and—especially—listening to American music. Classic rock was a favourite. Music exerted a powerful role on acculturation. As for the home environment of so-called Indian American friends, it consisted of Indian food, parents speaking in Hindi or another Indian language or accented English, mothers in sarees, statues of Indian deities, Indian music such as bhajans, ghazals, and Bollywood played on cassettes in the stereo system, the Bhagavad Gita on the shelf, and the occasional Hindi film at the cinema (no home video until the 1980s), and wearing Indian clothes on festival days. Watching over it all in Hindu homes was the ubiquitous framed picture of Lord Krishna as charioteer to Arjuna, discoursing in lofty terms how he must rein in the horses of passion, desire, thought, mind.

These friends were not interested in India. If they did visit, they got sick, just like I did. They were anxious to get back home, which was the United States. Who can blame them? America was the place to be. India in those days did not even have cable TV or foreign brands.

So why me, with a Swiss mother and only an Indian father, how to explain my interest? My father did not even speak Hindi at home and he listened only to Western classical music. He did not even acknowledge let alone celebrate important festivals such as Janamashtami, Dussehra, Diwali, or Holi. He had, however, purchased cassettes for me to learn Hindustani and a book to learn Hindi. His shelf was stocked with books on India and he could converse on any topic at all about India, and with authority. He also loved to talk about family history and his own life in India.

He also subscribed to India Abroad, a weekly news journal published in New York City for the ex-pat or immigrant community. What interested me most was reading the letters to the editor, deciphering the matriomonial ads in the back, and articles especially as related to the youth. I remember an article on Indian American youth in California and their fondness for skin whitening creams and so on, which struck me even at the time as just misguided and shameful. Such are the dynamics of an immigrant community. I did not like the term "Indian American", preferring instead "American of Indian origin." As a student of history, I was aware that people, especially "minorities", fought for the right to be Americans, simply Americans, and that should be clear, I thought. It only made sense. And, despite our foreign passports, for immigrant friends from young age like me, the United States was the only country we really knew, the only one that could have formed us, made us who we were, whose mores and values we imbibed almost subconsciously.

Besides that 1976 visit under the wing of my father, I had no real first-hand knowledge of India. Traveling in 1986 also meant my first international plane travel alone, first time getting to know various family members, and first time travelling alone in India. Thousands visit India—

some like it, some dislike it, some fall in love with it. Even for other visitors from Asia, such as the Japanese, India also has a way of making you face yourself, your discomforts, your beliefs, your adaptability. For me, just as on my 1976 trip, every trip I subsequently made to India stimulated yet more interest, as though I were being drawn closer and closer or at least not being let go. For whatever mysterious reasons, this was not true of course for my friends with roots in the subcontinent. I, on the other hand, already began developing the idea that I ought to live and work in India one day, must do something for the country just as my relatives had done. This sense of India, a sub-continent so enormously diverse, stayed with me such that whenever I felt I didn't belong where I was, whenever I felt a sense of alienation, I imagined that perhaps then I belonged in India. An escape? An illusion? It certainly might have been so at the time, but looking back, after these years of living and working in India, which I consider my spiritual home, I don't think I was wrong. That feeling first began to develop in 1986.

Time in India

July 1966 – April 1968 (infancy)

1. December 1975 – January 1976

2. July – August 1986

3. July 1993 – January 1994

4. December 1997 – January 1998

5. December 1998 – January 1999 (after marriage)

6. December 2000 – January 2001 (after 1st child)

7. December 2002 – January 2003 (after 2nd child)

8. November 2006

9. July 2009

10. December 2012 – January 2013 (cousin's wedding)

11. December 2014 – January 2015 (cousin's wedding)

12. December 2017 – January 2018

13. September – October 2018 (father's ashes)

August 2020 – May 2025

Sketch: Living Room with the Brothers

The two young brothers came to visit the cousin-brother. One sat on the living room floor in his kurta-pajama. The other stood, palm against the sofa. The cousin-brother sat relaxed in his chair, one leg swung over the other, wearing his rubber house flip-flops. They were all engaged in an animated conversation.

"You see, RB, people are good!" exclaimed the one on the floor. He seemed to be clasping in his fingers a thin-rolled cigarette known as a beedi along with a lighter. RB was short for Ranjit bhai, brother Ranjit.

They might have been talking about an article in the news, an incident in the family, or a matter at work, whether that was the railway, the publishing business, or the United Nations.

It struck the young American nephew as among the most relaxed, erudite, jovial, and frank conversations he had ever had the privilege to hear. The accents, while sounding to him "English" or British in the main, had those touches of Oxford and Cambridge in them and of course Indian English.

Or was it going back further, to a common boarding school in the hills of Naini Tal? Or to the uncles working in the civil service of the old Raj and the foreign service of newly independent India?

Their language, their diction, their knowledge, their cheerfulness, their comfort with one another, so brotherly, so warm. They were conversant on so many matters, not just India, vast as it was, but also England, America, Europe in general, China, Africa, even Latin America.

His father would have fit right in. Indeed, the four of them had all grown up together, in the hills, all fatherless, as they were wont to say and remind themselves. Their mothers shared a home, at least for a time, and an uncle or two or three looked after the lot of them, regaling all with stories of a family climbing the rungs of government service in the shadow of the Raj and the sun of new beginnings and boundless promise.

Sketch: Culture Shock in Agra

He did not want to leave the hotel. Outside the door was a language he did not understand fully, people he did not trust, poverty of the kind he had never seen before, food and water that might not be safe, dirt, filth, squalor, despair.

The woman he saw when the train had made a stop came to mind. She was elderly, squatting atop a great mound of gravel in the heat of the sun, hand resting on her head, her long gray tresses dishevelled and unkempt, with an absent, distracted, forlorn air about her. Who cared for that woman, he thought, why was she there, what does she do, who is with her. Discarded, abandoned, bereft, he imagined.

Arriving at the station in Agra, all the rickshaw-wallas eyed him as he came out with his backpack. *Aaiiee saheb, Taj dekhne, accha hotal,* restaurant, guide, etc. Come this way! It seemed like dozens called to him at once. He walked past all of them, walking he knew not where but pretending to walk with a fixed destination just to be rid of them. Then he selected one man who was the least assertive, most humble, and spoke passable English. The man pedalled in the fading light past alleys, roads, and markets to a hotel but not without stopping first at an arts and crafts shop and a restaurant he did not ask for and did not want to go into. But it was all part of the game, as he observed the rickshaw-walla knew the people everywhere and seemed to get some sort of pay-off, including from the hotel manager. One shop owner asked him if he could speak Hindi. He said only a little and the man looked askance, leaving him feeling shame.

The trip had started more innocently. Ranjit chacha had sent the cook Mani with him on the crowded bus to New Delhi station. He couldn't help but notice what Indians take for granted: entire families camped at the entrance with all their meagre belongings alongside solitary sadhus with next to nothing. He got the ticket his chacha had reserved for him at the counter and found his seat in a second class coach. Soon after the train embarked, the lady next to him struck up a conversation. Where are you from, what is your name, are you married? Hearing such agreeable answers to those simple questions, the mother smiled widely and said she would really like him to meet her daughter, that too at his earliest convenience!

Although he himself grew up in a humble apartment home, he had a certain sensitivity to poverty, to need, to being without, for the have-nots of the world. And in India, venturing beyond the walls of comfortable middle-class homes and carrying a sensitivity to poverty with you, especially coming from the West, is like going out into the cold without a coat. You will feel the chill.

From the train, he saw the inescapable sights: hovels along the tracks, shacks made of ripped canvas, bent sheets of aluminium, and moulded strips of wood, the black water of stagnant cesspools, people urinating and defecating alongside the tracks. He found it depressing and overwhelming. There was the open countryside, too, brilliant green paddy fields.

It was true, his father had insisted with his relatives that he not be "pampered." And he himself, fresh out of the Army and feeling used to hardship and "reality", did not want any special treatment. He wanted to do things on his own.

Now, after about an hour in his room sitting on the side of the bed and looking at a guidebook, allowing his own sensations, reactions, and thoughts to come to his mind in a quiet and safe space, a resolution formed. He would go out and just get a plate of biryani and a lassi. Nothing more for today. He found it in a restaurant next to the hotel.

It was a moment of "culture shock" that lasted for the better part of an hour and that then he would never experience again. From the next day, with no better knowledge of the language or the strange and unfamiliar aspects of his surroundings, he would go out with a direction and a purpose, insist on being taken where he wanted to go, wear simple clothes even kurtas and not jeans, have basic phrases in Hindi on the tip of his tongue, mind his money and never show it in public, and ignore unwanted attention and walk away. Before stopping anywhere to eat, he always observed the place and made a judgement as to whether or not it was clean enough. He always carried Bisleri mineral water or bought a Limca or Thums Up, never drinking water out of a glass. He still got sick but over time, he became a sharp observer and developed a high degree of comfort in navigating any place such that the more orderly and hygienic ambiences of a city's modern areas began to appear dull, uninteresting, and a waste of money.

Sketch: Spark of Recognition

With the thought that Gautama Buddha must have walked these same footsteps, he felt a tingling sensation in his spine that seemed to last for minutes. He stood gazing at the Dhamekh stupa from under a tree some distance away. A young monk in orange robe sat facing the stupa and meditating in front of him. It was a warm humid July mid-morning.

The Buddha gave his first sermon or talk at Sarnath on the outskirts of Varanasi, called Kashi in those days. The listeners were those five fellow seekers and ascetics who had accused the young Siddhartha of going soft by taking food and now, returning an Awakened One, the Buddha discoursed on the Middle Way, the path of moderation between self-mortification and self-indulgence.

I can feel his presence, the young visitor marveled almost aloud. Yes, the Buddha must have walked nearby. This grove of trees must be offshoots of the grove in Deer Park of that time, nearly 2,500 years ago. It was like a spark of recognition. He felt something almost crackle in his mind, having risen up from his spinal cord, it was a novel involuntary sensation. What did it mean? Aware of it now, he took in again the meditating monk before him. When first he had come across the life of the Buddha in encyclopedias and books on his father's shelf out of curiosity about his Indian heritage, he had felt such closeness and inspiration that he drew a picture of himself as a bhikkhu in the sangha of those days. As if he were there, and now he was here. It was as though time stood still.

When he returned to Delhi, he told his dadiji or grandmother about the sensation he had experienced in Sarnath. She looked at him in seriousness and said, "You have been touched by the Buddha."

What did it mean? He was just a young man on a journey exploring for the first time a country to which his father said he belonged merely "by accident of birth."

Sketch: Tikse

He loathed taking the camera out but he forced himself to do it from time to time. He had spent the night sleeping on a charpoy outside the cell of a lama, as Buddhist monks were known in Ladakh.

With more than a little embarrassment, he trained his Olympus 3 on a boy squatting and kneading dough to make tsampa for the leavened bread that was a staple of Ladakhi cuisine. The boy looked up and down, silently smiling in the awareness that his picture was being taken. He wore the maroon robe of a young lama. His dark eyes sparkled, his skin was the color of copper, his short hair stood up like sprouts on his head. He was the picture of a young lad used to and content with the routines of his station in life. On the wall behind him was painted a faded and peeling mural depicting in mandala form a main figure or deity in the center and several minor figures at the sides and corners of the mural. It was a green pastoral scene alive with peacock, stork, tiger, and deer, each with its own symbolic meaning. It seemed to put humans in the context of a meaning and significance of which we are all too often blithely unaware.

By chance and odd circumstance, he was even here. He had never heard of Ladakh until he picked up a Lonely Planet guidebook in his uncle's house in Delhi. It was titled "Kashmir, Zanskar, and Ladakh" and had been left behind by several female British tourists who had stayed with his uncle and family while he was away. This would be a good opportunity to see Buddhism in practice. It had taken two days to reach Leh, riding by lorry with fellow passengers including an economist and a Buddhist monk. Once over the passes, the land opened out into a part of the Tibetan Plateau. Endlessly, the lorry rolled on amid a desolate and forbidding mountain landscape with the Indus River fervently winding its way among the green trees and barley fields of barley in the valley below.

Tikse lay even beyond Leh though not by much. He carried all he had in a simple backpack fit for a school boy or a day hike. He could look for a guesthouse, but a lama named Lobsang had offered him the charpoy on his veranda. The gompa, like all lamaseries, sat high on a ridge with a commanding view of the valley. Snow-clad peaks could be seen in the distance. It was a mystical night whose spell was broken only by the early morning sounds of the lamas commencing their prayers in a chamber below. The unearthly sounds of deep bass wind instruments seemed to reflect and bring on a slow awakening, perhaps symbolic of the Self or Soul.

He decided to walk back to Leh through the fields that bounded the river. A breeze was in the air, the blue waters of the river crested and rippled, and the walk was in every way idyllic. He loved to see the chortens and to walk around them to the left side. And he loved to say "Jullay" to the Ladakhis, or "hello", as though he lived there. The entire land and way of life felt like something precious and to be cherished.

Yet it too was a disappearing way of life. In the past, every family sent one son to be a monk. No longer. The opening of Leh to tourists like himself also meant that market vendors could command higher prices for simple foods such as apricots and the locals could not pay the cost of inflation. Increased contact with the outside world via the highway, which was still blocked by snow for half the year, brought in merchants who were more aggressive than the Ladakhis and who outsold them. Culture too was changing. It seemed nowhere in the world was really remote any longer. Every place in the world was subject to the same forces of change—social, economic, cultural, political. Even religious or spiritual.

Sketch: Stranded in Ladakh

I begged the airlines to board. I was so desperate I pleaded even to be loaded with the cargo. It was such a small plane anyway. But it was not to be. I did not know I had to call and re-confirm my ticket.

"I have no money to stay, no money at all, and my dadiji is expecting me," I appealed at the counter.

"I'm sorry, there is no seat for you. You must come back tomorrow."

I was devastated, perhaps more than I should have been, but it really was the thought of my dadiji and chacha and chachi expecting my arrival in Delhi and my not being there. At least, they would know I was in Leh, or would they? I must send them a FAX and let them know I am here and missed my flight.

An Indian Airlines worker overheard my plight. She waited and then offered, "You may stay at my home until tomorrow." I gladly accepted. I really had spent all my money, or the very little I even brought with me leaving Delhi. I don't know how I under-budgeted so much. I was feeling short on money already in Srinagar, on the first leg of my trip. I thought I would save money and enjoy some adventure by taking a lorry over the mountain passes from Srinagar to Leh, but I was still short.

Her name was Yang Chan. She led me to her home first via public transport then via a short walk along a stream and amid the ubiquitous chortens of this Tibetan Buddhist land. She wore her mid-length dark hair straight with gentle waves in a modern style in contrast to the long braided hair of Ladakhi women. Her eyes twinkled remotely. She wore a maroon-colored overcoat over a long dress.

She said she lived with her parents, but I never saw them. That night, as I lay down on the mattress on the floor, and she lay down on a mattress some distance away, a strange game ensued.

"I hear something," she said.

"I don't hear anything," I responded.

"Something is moving on the floor," she continued.

"I still don't hear anything," I said naively.

"I'm afraid. Can I come closer?" she asked.

"Sure," I said, still innocent of what was to come.

And she moved her mattress closer to mine.

"I still hear it," she said. "It's coming closer."

I was silent for a while, finally drawing an intimation of what was really going on.

"Can I come in with you?" she asked.

I paused for a moment, rationalizing to myself that I was the guest after all, and said, "Sure."

The moment her body touched mine, she snuggled up close to me, and my arm went around her. Afraid myself of how far this was leading, I was satisfied with the warmth of her body next to mine and one arm awkwardly around her.

One thing led to another and we wrapped ourselves around each other in a multitude of ways, but our clothes never came off and it was never consummated. One thing I remember was her warm breath and the smell of chiles. Another was her softness, her lips, her overwhelming passion.

The next day there was still no sign of her parents, supposedly occupying the upper floor. More concerning, the plane I was to be on could still not land due to clouds. It had turned back to Delhi.

A day went by in the anxiety of wanting to leave and the thought of the last night and the night to come, with this sort of illicit opportunistic passion we were living. I really was the guest, and unsure of how to respond. I had no desire at all to consummate with the real act of lovemaking, which at the time was still foreign to me! Loveplay, on the other hand, had its delights.

Yet another day went by and still the plane was not able to land. Then a message came, asking me to go to the District Chief Magistrate's home that evening. Apparently, they knew I was staying with Yang Chan. Even she went with me. The DCM, who lived in the grander home typical of someone in the Civil Service, introduced himself warmly and looked me over as though wanting to assure himself that I was this certain Sanjay Mathur, U.S. citizen, nephew of Ranjit Mathur, friend to the DCM in Srinagar, his colleague. Yes, it was all true, down to my American accent.

"Tomorrow, an Army helicopter will arrive from Chandigarh. It is for people who are sick and need to leave urgently. You may get on it."

"But I am not sick, sir."

"Doesn't matter, just say that you are sick—pretend!"

"Yes, sir—thank you very much." And the feeling of gratitude arose in me with the certainty of the prospect of an end to this strange unforeseen plight of being stranded in Ladakh. As pleasant as the surroundings were, as sweet as Yang Chan was, I just wanted to get home. I remember that the thought of my grandmother and uncle and aunt waiting on me in Delhi, even though they well knew where I was, was uppermost in my mind. The next day would mark 11 days away from home.

I remember the sight of the Himalayas from the helicopter and the tarmac of the airport in Chandigarh. I then walked across the tarmac to board a small plane to Delhi that already had its passengers. The stewardess offered me a sweet candy.

I wrote a letter to Yang Chan from Chicago. I still remember the address: Yang Chan Shanya Dolmer, c/o Tashi Shakspo, Shopkeeper,

Leh, Ladakh. And I received letters from her, full of passion and longing, of the "you have driven me crazy" type. I felt bad for her. It could not be a good feeling at all. She was suffering. I had been a part of it. I missed her and thought of her but I did not suffer in the same way.

One thing Yang Chan wrote, and that I remembered from time to time over my many years of working abroad in development. She said, "For poor people like us, we do not all want to make money. Health and education are the most important things."

One day, perhaps one year later, a letter arrived to my parent's home in Chicago. It was not from Yang Chan but it was from Leh. Yang Chan was due to get married, it seemed. The organizers needed to know in which room we had slept and in which direction the mattress pointed. Was it east-west or north-south? Evidently, a ceremony was to be done to cleanse the room.

I responded clarifying that we did not have intercourse. Once again, I felt bad for Yang Chan. I did not think she would stay in Leh. She was quite the modern woman for Leh in 1986—in her non-traditional hair length and hair style, her job with the airlines, her knowledge of English and her ability to read and write, her concept of an individual self yes, perhaps that most of all. What had happened?

I never got a response or another letter from Yang Chan after that.

Narrative: Making My Own Path

"Not all who wander are lost."
– J.R.R. Tolkien

In "Seven Storey Mountain", Thomas Merton recounts how over time he came to know what was his calling or "vocation" in life. Such spiritual search led him to the Catholic Church and eventually to become a Trappist monk. Later, he became an author.

When I was a student in high school, three possibilities of what I was most suited for, what my calling was, began to form in my mind: 1) to be a writer; 2) to run a homeless shelter; or 3) to be a teacher. I had already absorbed the idea of service as what gives meaning to life. Well along from my phase of sports heroes, I had it clear that the five persons I most admired, past or present, were: the Buddha, Jesus, Mahatma Gandhi, Martin Luther King, and Mother Teresa. Then I joined the Army out of a sense of duty, money for college, and especially the experience of it.

The older person looking back might say the young man was confused. After the military, he did not know what to do. He joined and then dropped out of university. He thought he might be suited to a trade like carpentry. He re-joined university, studied history, with the idea to teach but didn't stay the extra year to get a teaching certificate and declined a teaching job. True, he joined the Peace Corps and had a life-altering experience but he came back still not knowing what to do. He had an idea to start a dharamshala (pilgrim's rest house) in India where the Buddha died but he gave that up. Then he had an idea to start a factory in Mali making Mangalore roofing tiles in Mali but he gave that up, although after a legitimate feasibility and cost study. He got into a graduate school program to teach English as a Second Language but dropped out. Eventually, at the age of 30, he got a Master's degree in Public Health and his first "real" job in terms of pay and responsibility. Then, he got married and settled down, but not before changing jobs and cities again, and again once more. This is a certain outline of my life from the age of 18 to 33, counting first year of marriage. Does it appear errant and confused?

Yet, on the inside, I was rather more clear. I would do only what I found meaning in. I would feel out my purpose. I would not compromise my principles. I would live with integrity and purpose. Service to others was important, but I would be true to myself. I would make my own path.

To justify such freedom, I took no money from my parents. In fact, my father once gave me a $500 check for college expenses and I kept it for the longest time and never cashed it until disposing of it many years later. Self-reliance and personal responsibility, in a very American way, were values I lived by. For this reason, and because I was interested in work and people, I undertook a host of jobs, believing like Gandhi, whom I admired, in the innate "dignity of labor."

If I didn't like something, I stuck with it long enough not to make a hasty decision but then I moved on. I learned from companions, including the phrase "Chalk it up to experience." I was responsible but carefree. Learning was my mindset. Relaxation was something I found hard to do, always feeling the need to justify my existence. I was a seeker, on some type of quest for a life of meaning. I struggled with loneliness. I struggled with balancing what might be called becoming somebody with just being who I was, just enjoying the moment. I struggled to relax. But people and places were good to me. Eventually, I made my own path.

In terms of career, this is how I used the freedom my parents gave me. It is difficult not to conclude they also gave me such freedom because we lived in the United States. Is it easy everywhere to drop out of university, hold a string of labor jobs, and go back and complete university? I did this throughout my 20s. Others have a similar story.

As for meaning and purpose, I found something close to a calling in what I see as my three careers: 1) Executive Director of a non-profit educational program (AVANCE-El Paso) helping young families break the cycle of poverty; 2) Country Director of a government volunteer program (U.S. Peace Corps) placing volunteers in organizations supporting health, education, and development in Peru and Mozambique; and 3) Teacher of social studies (history, political science, and geography) in high school in India.

Notably, these careers, in my case, also happened to come hand in hand with marriage and children. Family is what kept me balanced, kept work in its place, allowed for other joys. At the same time, balancing family and work and one's own inner life is also a challenge.

Looking back, I was both confused and clear in my 20s. It is hard to regret anything when you are largely true to yourself. Yet I had my struggles.

Sketch: Always Alone

He often found himself alone at the university. It could seem that he was not alone when he walked to the school cafeteria with his roommate and others from the dorm. But even then, he could be quite alone in his thoughts. His mind was always moving, always searching.

Did he think himself superior? In some ways yes, since as far as he knew, he was the only freshman who was 20 years old. Everyone else in the dorm was 18 years old and fresh out of high school. They came mostly from Virginia and other states in the south like Alabama. The school was said to recruit the "cream of the crop" from the South. The overwhelming majority of the students were White. Integration had come late to the university. Perhaps this helped explain the apparent militancy of some Black students who could be seen marching to the cafeteria at right angles and in high steps, eyes straight ahead and swinging their arms like soldiers. One almost had to move out of their way.

He had spent the "extra" two years in the military. The contrast was stark. Soldiers came from far more diverse backgrounds, whether measured racially or by region or by rural versus urban or even by age. Not to mention life experience. Here, however, all freshmen were the same age and with enough wealth and connections to get into UVA, since it was not cheap. He was paying out-of-state tuition in year one, made possible only by the money for college he had earned in a college savings program while in the military. He refused to take money from his parents. He imagined himself to be self-reliant that way. And he was proud of his service in the military, especially having been in the infantry.

These kids were spoilt, he thought. He held up as the example the roommate across the hall whose father was giving him a car for Christmas since he had gotten a "B" average in the first semester. Not even an

"A." And there was a general lackadaisical attitude towards studies that seemed to go in sync with the great enthusiasm for fraternity parties. In his unusually serious bent of mind, he thought this one more sign of "decadence", although it was the norm in every college campus across the country.

It was not just being alone, it was being lonely. He longed to share with someone. There was a girl on one of the upper floors of the same dorm hall who caught his eye but more for reasons of intrigue than beauty. She was petite and appeared always wrapped in coats, such as the knee length dark overcoat she wore when it was even just a little cold outside. It was rare even to see her face, hidden as it was even behind short hair that fell like a curtain along the side of her face. She sometimes carried a book in her hand. He wondered what she was reading, what she was thinking. He was so bad at small talk that all he could think of was talking about books, thoughts, life experience—anything that had actual meaning. She seemed a seeker in her own right. And yet, even when the opportunity arose and she was walking on the pavement in front of the dorm, he could not bring himself to say anything to her.

What might he have said. "Hello, I'm so-and-so. I also live in this dorm. I just wanted to say I've often seen you with a book in hand. I love books myself and enjoy browsing in the bookstore or the library. May I ask you, what are you reading?" Or, to continue, "I have so-and-so for English class. Do you have the same teacher?" Or even, "It would be nice to sit and chat one day, maybe over a coffee or drink at the cafeteria if you like." He simply could not fathom such an encounter. He didn't have the ease for it.

With few friends or social life, and with an interest in work as well as needing to supplement his income, he took work as a dishwasher in Bryant Hall, the cafeteria for athletes. He also volunteered weekly for the Charlottesville Housing Improvement Program (C.H.I.P.), painting and assisting in carpentry for homes that were being built or repaired for low-income families. And he volunteered for the M.S. Society, who placed as a companion for an elderly man with advanced M.S., like his mother suffered from.

He also spent quite a bit of time in the library. Stacks of books, which is why they called it "the stacks." His interests ranged far beyond whatever classes he was taking in school. He knew where the Herman Hesse books were, and he would often find a spot near the window, looking out onto the great trees on the campus, and read Hesse's odes to nature and to trees. He was dreamy that way. It led him to drive up to Skyline Drive on the Blue Ridge Parkway on weekends. He would find a place to park, put on his green REI backpack, and walk down the trail, through the woods, admiring every leaf fall and leaf litter at his feet. It was entrancing, a type of enchantment with the song and sight of the wild.

Yet he did this alone. He ate alone. He walked alone. He thought alone. Altogether too serious, too alone.

Narrative: Dropping out of University

It took me only one semester to decide I wanted to drop out of the University of Virginia. However much I might not have jived with my fellow students or might have quibbled with the "ivory towers" of academia, I did not blame them. I came to want something else at that time of my life.

I wanted to go talk to the Dean of Admissions at the University of Virginia and explain my reasons, even have them challenged. The kind of person I was at the time was represented in my Admissions essay of the previous year. It reflected certain qualities of mine as a young adult, qualities like the "healthy scepticism" that my high school history teacher had fostered, independence of thought, and courage of conviction and to go my own way.

For the essay, prospective students were apprised of the school's "honor code", that required conducting oneself with honor in "matters of ethics, integrity, and character," and were asked to respond what the policy meant to them. I took an approach, influenced no doubt by my favorite social critic and commentator George Orwell, and gave a gutsy response. I chose to analyze the question itself and I posed it as a dilemma. Applicants, I wrote, must choose whether to write authentically and truthfully, based on their limited life experience, or to embellish and exaggerate about "the unbelievable meaning of travelling abroad" or "the invaluable experience of being a member of the band." I was implying that asking students to write about honor when they were competing to gain admission could have the unintended effect of encouraging dishonesty. Pointing out similar competition and dishonesty as part of society, I concluded with the provocative sentence, "Life in these times may require a degree of dishonesty."

The Dean was a thoughtful man who always made time for students. The following is a re-construction of the conversation. It is more imagination than reality but represents why I dropped out of university. I had spoken with him once before, during his office hours, and he remembered me.

. . .

"Good morning, Dean, thank you for granting this appointment. It's a bit unusual, I know. But you granted me admission last year and for that I'm grateful. I've enjoyed various classes here and yet I feel university is not for me. I thought I should tell you the reasons why."

The Dean sat back in his chair, looked at me searchingly, and motioned for me to continue.

"As you know, I was your non-traditional applicant, coming out of the Army, with that life experience under my belt. I found everyone in the dorm is just 18 years old and coming straight from home. Not only that but some are rather spoiled. The boy across the hall got a car from his father for Christmas simply for maintaining a "B" average in the first semester."

"You see we do capture the elite from across the southern states. What you are observing are children from highly privileged backgrounds. But what that does that have to do with your decision? How does it affect your education? History you're interested in, right—teaching history in secondary school?"

"Yes, Dean, as one option. I really don't know for sure. But I've had second thoughts. I'm not sure I'm against a university education at all, I see its value. But I want to work with my hands. I want to build something or fix something. I feel our society undervalues labor and manual work in general."

The Dean raised his eyes and looked both surprised and thoughtful.

"That is very noble of you and I agree with you. Labor is undervalued whether it is pay or status. And it is supremely important. At one time, it was valued more, but society has changed, our economy has changed. Most everyone agrees that a university education is to be aspired to."

"But why exactly?"

"Well, as you know, I'm also the Dean of the College of Liberal Arts. Don't you think there is something to be said for the value of critical thinking, inquiry, and analysis. And for the skills of communication. This leads to careers in law, media, government service, and so on. These qualities are needed in leadership, be it a business, non-profit, or government agency. I could also cite the value of a degree in terms of statistics on earnings, and with earnings comes lifestyle, and even longevity…"

"But can you cite happiness, fulfilment, meaning?"

"Well, I was coming to that… those things, those intangibles let's say, are not a guarantee in any line of work. Not everyone is suited for every line of work. It depends on the individual, don't you think? You have to find your passion, don't you? Then happiness follows."

"It's why I've thought a lot about vocation, about calling. What is my calling in life."

"I see," he said and demurred, before continuing. "It's my perception that most students choose a field of study leading to a career they think they want and then adapt themselves, make compromises along the way, even change their mind. But it is rare to opt against a college education. What makes you think that your vocation, as you say, lies elsewhere?"

"I don't know, but I won't know if I don't try. It might mean that I come back to college but I might not. I'm not sure I like academia even though I'm intellectually inclined. I just don't deal well with things that are too abstract. For example, I attended a lecture on campus, it had to with the peasant in India, as the title of the lecture said, and at one point, I just thought to myself, he is talking about the peasant in terms that the peasant would never be able to understand. The farmer, who knows his life very well, would not be able to make heads or tails out of this presentation. What does the professor know about it anyway?"

"Ah, the question of knowledge, epistemology, how do we know what we know. I would advise you to take a class on this, it is offered in our philosophy department, but you have made up your mind to leave already. Isn't it?"

"Sir, it's that I prioritize experience above all else. How can I know something if I myself have not experienced it?"

"But you will find this a very limiting point of view. There is far more to life, study, and knowledge than you can possibly experience. And is what you want to learn, and presumably teach one day, a matter of personal experience? I think not. I ask you again, how do you know what it is that you want to do?"

"I don't know, but I've got to try, I've got to go figure it out."

"What will you do then?"

"Well, I had wanted to learn auto mechanics when I first thought about joining the Army, but I failed the color vision test. Got nervous. Still, that is something that interests me. Also, I wouldn't mind learning more about carpentry. I might tell you I have volunteered with the Charlottesville Housing Improvement Program, the C.H.I.P. program as you know, and I enjoy what it takes to build a house or make a repair. Virginia is such a beautiful state, and I've admired all the farms, but I've already thought I can't really try and be a farmer, I've read about it and it's too hard these days."

"There are courses for auto mechanics and carpentry, vocational courses. Will you opt for one?"

"Maybe. I will find out."

"Where will you go?"

"Back to Texas. San Antonio, this time. If I decide to go back to university, like the University of Texas, then I can still get in-state tuition if I go back to Texas now. Plus, it's more familiar to me. I also want to use my Spanish."

"Sounds like you have a plan."

And he wished me the best.

...

In fact, I had decided to drop out after only one semester. I did a second semester to satisfy my father. I told my parents over the winter break I spent with them in Chicago. Hearing me talk about the "ivory tower" and my idealistic expectations of professors to have more real world experience and be more involved in work outside the classroom, my mother's comment was, "You expect your professors to be saints."

My father too felt I was being unrealistic and impractical. Later, however, during that second and final semester, he wrote to me in unforgettable terms: "I haven't solved any of the basic problems of living so I would be wrong to impose my solutions on you. However, I feel you do yourself a disservice by forgoing a university education." He listed out a few reasons but then, recognizing the courage of conviction in his son, whom he was always proud to say "marched to the beat of his own drummer", he enclosed information on vocational training for carpentry and related fields in Texas. I found these words and this gesture utterly liberating. It came from a place of wisdom and love. A love that granted space, was not overly protective, and established confidence. It made me love him for it.

Sketch: Circular Saw

Down, down, down the circular saw fell. He watched its perilous descent, unstoppable and as though suspended in time, while standing on a scaffold under the vault of the church under construction. He could make out the metal saw and its blade spinning once or twice as it became smaller and smaller.

He and the master carpenter Red were nearly four stories high. There was not much space to move on the scaffold. It was also dark in that area of the vault below the ceiling. They had used the saw on ground level to cut the 2 by 4 inch boards they needed but brought the saw with them for the inevitable trimming required to fit them and nail them in place within the vault and what approximated to the base of the steeple of the church under construction. How the black electric cord had slipped from the saw, he was not sure, but there was nothing he could do about it now. He was mortified but Red his co-worker had the presence of mind to call out in his Mexican English, "*Orale*, watch out below!"

Fortunately, no one was there. It must have weighed 10 – 15 pounds and it could hurt or even kill someone if it hit them.

It landed on the cement floor with a thud followed by a great smash. Pieces of it scattered in all directions. The sounds of hammers and nail guns suddenly stopped and all was quiet. He could sense everyone looking around.

"Anyone hurt?" someone called.

"No, we're all good", someone responded below.

"*Todo bien*—just a saw that fell", said Red.

He, on the other hand, was petrified. This felt like a seminal event. He was new to construction and carpentry in particular, and this was just his third month working with Red and the crew. What if that saw had hit someone? How careless he had been not to double tie its handle with the electrical cord! Only a rookie like him would not do that. It could have been a fatal mistake. What then!

He apologized to Red and Red said the saw was old and needed to be replaced and these things happen and not to worry about it. He apologized again and said he would pay for it. Red said not to worry and that's why the boss has insurance.

On the drive home, it occurred to him that maybe this wasn't the job for him. It was one thing to learn carpentry and help as an equal member of the team, doing his part. It was another if he were not cut out for the job and could risk someone's else life or safety. This was made plain to him now. He could never forgive himself if he were to injure anyone else, even accidentally. He should not be on the job.

He drove to the jobsite early the next day, apologized to the boss, announced he was resigning, and asked the boss to deduct the cost of a new saw from his final paycheck. The boss paid him right then and there. He was done. He turned around and said bye to Red and all the guys.

This was not a job any of the others could leave so easily. It's not that he was rich. But he had choices, made choices.

Vignette: Mr. Ed Jones

Portrait of a Man, a Time, and a Place

There was a time in San Antonio in 1987 when I was twenty-one years old, in between jobs, and rapidly exhausting money I had saved since being a paperboy at the age of twelve years old. Although I had put in an application to the University of Texas in Austin to give myself options, I had no definite plans. Despite my relative lack of skill in carpentry, I was still interested in working with my hands and learning a trade. So it was at this time that I enlisted in the National Guard as a light wheel vehicle mechanic. I was assigned to a motor pool at an armory on the east side of San Antonio.

For anyone who had been in the "regular Army", the National Guard was something of a joke. I remember how overweight the "guardsmen" and "soldiers" were. Most of these "weekend warriors" walked instead of ran the two miles at the end of the day. Few if any shined their boots or ironed their uniforms. Their hair was long by Army standards. They didn't even salute the officers. These were truly just civilians in uniform. Except for a spell of weekends learning auto mechanics by an instructor from Palo Alto College and the two week summer camp at Fort Hood, most weekends were spent in the motor pool greasing wheel bearings on jeeps, trucks, and trailers. It was easy money.

The Guard was more memorable for the people one met. They were mainly Mexican-Americans with a few blacks and even fewer whites. The full-time platoon sergeant for the motor pool, Sergeant Roeber, was white while his assistant, Specialist Barnes, was black. The rest of the platoon only showed up one weekend every month. There was Dtee Chaipan, born in Thailand to a Thai mother and father but whose mother had long since been remarried to an American sergeant. Later, when I used to commute from Austin, I would stay at his apartment. Like me, he had been in the regular Army and we regarded the National Guard as a joke, a sort of go-through-the-motions of being a soldier and get paid for it. There was Rocky and Sergeant Perez, both of whom worked for VIA, the San Antonio city bus company, and who later skilfully and professionally painted my 1966 Chevy Impala a brilliant sky blue in Sergeant Perez' garage.

Most of all, the Guard was memorable for the happy accident of meeting Ed Jones, an African-American who was to exert great influence in my life and thought at that time. I still recall vividly the first time I met Mr. Jones or "Jones" or "Jonesy" as he was known in typical last-name fashion in the Guard. It was my first day, a Saturday, lunchtime, and we were sitting on chairs and huge tires in front of a jeep and a truck in the airy expanse of the motor pool. Conversation was low as we finished eating a lunch of chili-mac and green beans off paper plates. Jones put his plate down and crossed one leg over the other in the way I had observed my father and other immigrants do, his legs together. It's the way bluesman "Lightning Hopkins" is sketched sitting on one of his album covers, and Jones too could play the guitar and improvise the blues. I noticed he wore no socks in his boots. Jones then exclaimed in that casual setting:

"You know, it seems to me that life is backwards; when you're young, you don't know what to do, but you got to go ahead and do it; and when you're old, you know what to do, but you can't do it no more. So that's why I say life is backwards."

Reaction was long the lines of "there goes Jonesy again, always got something to say" and conversation rippled off. I, on the other hand, thought to myself, "This is somebody I've got to get to know!" There was Shakespearean truth in what he said, and Shakespeare could have made a poetic soliloquy about it. Mr. Jones, I reflected, was much more concise and straightforward but just as profound and plausibly original (though Shakespeare's originality was always questioned).

Ed Jones was born in Schulenberg, Texas not far from Columbus on the highway between San Antonio and Houston. He used to say, "I've got an eighth-grade Jim Crow education", meaning he dropped out of school in eighth grade and even then his schooling in a small town was under the old system of segregated schooling for blacks and whites. After the Civil War up until the turn of the century, so-called Jim Crow laws legalized segregation of the races in the South, where blacks were often a majority of the population. In the North, where blacks were a minority, de facto segregation prevailed. These laws were only repealed in the 1960s. Even after the Supreme Court ruling in 1957 that said segregated schooling was "separate but unequal," it took decades to undo a system based on systematic, pervasive, and crude discrimination based on the dubious concept of race.

Once at the end of the day in summer camp at Fort Hood, Jones, Chaipan, and I had retreated to a spot in the pitch black of the evening where the only lights were the flickering whites of the stars above and the burning orange of Jones' cigarette. Chaipan remarked on how he had seen what looked to him like a dinosaur's footprint earlier in the day. He had just started at San Antonio College and was taking a class on geology. He started to talk about how the world began. Jones interrupted him and said:

"No, no, that's not how the world began, I'll tell you how the world began, see, God created the black man first. But all the black man wanted to do was eat, sleep, and make love to his woman. He didn't want to cut down no trees, build no roads or bridges or buildings. So the devil went to God and said, 'God, I can't get this black man to do shit, all he wants to do is eat, sleep, and make love, he doesn't want to cut down any trees or build any roads, bridges, or buildings, nothing! You need to give me somebody I can play with!' God thought about it and then created the white man out of a rat, a hog, and a dog, to make him slick as a rat, greedy as a hog, and mean as a dog. Now the devil had somebody to play with, he was happy, and this creature, the white man, tore up the forest and made the black man's life a living hell. So the black man went to God and said, 'What have you done? Why have you created this beast? I have no more peace', and God said, 'Well, if you don't like it, kill him!' But the black man hesitated, and the creature got bigger and bigger, too big to kill, so all the black man could do was drive him out, so he drove him north, out of Africa, into Europe. And that's how the world started! And that's why the black man has been cursed ever since, because he didn't kill the white man when he had the chance."

Jones was 47 years old when I got to know him, and his view of the world was hopelessly colored by race. Race was everything, it explained who was up and who was down, why some things were bound to fail and some aspirations were foolish, why the world was the way it was. Jones was very nearly a purist when it came to race. For example, one Saturday in the Guard, they deigned to serve us spaghetti for lunch, and Jones turned to me and said:

"Mathur, let's eat out!"

"What's wrong, you don't like spaghetti?" I said.

"Hell no, ever since I found out Mussolini bombed the Ethiopians with poisonous gas in 1935, I don't eat no god-damned I-talian food!"

And so we went to McDonald's.

"You want to go inside and eat?" I said.

"No, we'll just go through the drive-through."

"Why?"

"I don't like dealing with no white folks if I can help it."

Jones had an anecdote for everything. I asked him if he experienced discrimination today. He told me yes, for example if he took a piece of scrap metal to the junk yard, he got paid for it differently than did a white person. I said, but if they weigh it, and you know what the cost of the metal is, then why do you accept it, why don't you demand the same price if that is the published price? Jones said:

"Well, I'll tell you why not. You heard about the black man and the white man shoveling shit? The white boss man told the two of them, 'I want all that shit out of that hole by the time I come back. Black man, get down in that hole and shovel that shit out to the white man on top.' Then he left. When he came back, the white man was in the hole shoveling shit out to the black man. He said, "White man, what you doing down in that hole? I told you to be on top.' The white man said, 'Well sir, I don't take no shit from a black man!' So that's why I don't fuss if I get paid different for the same piece of metal."

And his eyes got small and he laughed.

It was tough to argue with history, and Jones knew history, or a version of it, and he knew his own life. He had retired, in his words, not as "sanitation worker" but as "garbage man" for the City of San Antonio. Jones used to collect discarded books from "the dump." He said:

"You've heard that saying, 'one man's junk is another man's treasure?' Well, that's how I look at it. I like junk."

As much as a sense of history, he had an interest in things of a philosophical or religious bent. Knowing that my mother had Multiple Sclerosis, a highly degenerative and disabling disease, Jones presented me with a small paperback book whose cover was torn off and the inside page was titled, "Four Minute Essays" and dated "1919".

"Read one of those every night before you go to bed. They're called four-minute essays because it's not supposed to take you more than four minutes to read one of them. Then you think about it."

He then showed me the essay he wanted me to read and give to my mother. It had to do with the theme that humanity was inclined to turn away from the sick and the dying, and that this was wrong, instead the sick had wisdom and much to teach us, and that we should make the room of the sick person a temple and a shrine in the home rather than a place of avoidance and grief.

Mr. Jones retired from the city as soon as he had paid off his house and property at the end of a dead-end street across from a power plant on San Antonio's black-dominated East Side. The neighbors would complain about uncut grass or junk or vehicles such as an old dump truck or school bus that he kept on his property. He paid many fines but never abided by "code compliance." Since he was at the end of a dead-end street, people eventually ignored him. Of his neighbors, he said, "They're slaves, still working for the white man, they're jealous because I work for myself, I'm nobody's slave." To prove his point, he said they were all in debt whereas he was the only one who actually owned his property and he determined when and how much he would work and what days he would take off and none of them could do that. He mocked the concept of order, saying "If I need a nail or screw, I look down on the ground for it and find it."

Mr. Jones didn't live alone, far from it. He had had two wives, both of whom had died in their late 40s from stroke and high blood pressure. They were both heavily overweight, of which Mr. Jones remarked, with the pleasant thought of it, "Keep you warm in the winter, give you shade in the summer." They had had a total of 19 children, of which

Jones remarked again, irreverently, "Well, the Lord said 'be fruitful and multiply', and that's what we done."

Oddly enough, it was on a sort of religious and philosophical level that Jones and I connected. Since he saw everything in terms of race, he saw me as both an Indian and a "mutt", which is what he said all Americans were, including blacks, and that's what made Americans so violent, "like a pit bull, with that mixed blood in him driving him crazy."

I used to say then that I was born a Hindu but a friend of the Buddha. Jones said what he liked most about the Hindus was that the priest was supposed to be a person of knowledge and it impressed him that the person of knowledge was atop the system instead of the warrior or the person of might, and it further impressed him that the priest or person of knowledge lived poor, without any possessions. Once you own something, it owns you, Jones said, and the more you own, the less you know who you are. Jones was a firm and uncompromising individualist, something that to my mind made him typically American.

"You've got to be able to think for yourself. Most people just follow the herd. They don't know why they think what they do. They just do and say the same stupid thing everybody else does all the time. You and me are different. We can think for ourselves, people don't know where we're going to land, that's what scares them. We're free people, we're not slaves."

Jones had an uncharacteristic ability to know my thoughts, and in my college days when I knew him, I had many long and troubled thoughts that I seldom shared. Jones, seeing me and thinking himself, would say, seemingly out of the blue:

"Mathur, you think a man ought to change himself all at once or little by little?"

And that would be just what I was thinking about! Having thought about it, he would then remark on the merits and drawbacks of both and give an example such as when he tried to be a vegetarian, successful for a time but completely isolated in his family and community for doing so.

After we had not seen each other for a time, and I saw him again, he said, not so originally perhaps but not intellectually either, "You know a person is like a river, he might look the same, but the water has moved on, he's not the same, he's always changing."

One time in summer camp, when he saw me down and perceived what he saw as self-doubt in me, he said:

"Mathur, you can't compare yourself to these people here, they might be higher than you now but they done reached the top of their pyramid. They're not going any higher in life. You're still stretching out the base of your pyramid, you're still gathering knowledge, and when you start climbing, you'll go much higher than they ever even thought about."

After I left San Antonio, we saw each other only once a month, for weekend drills. I'd always call from a payphone when I got into town and I had his phone number memorized for a long time. He'd always look forward to our meetings, either at his house or talking in my car, the big blue Chevy Impala I got after I started school at UT-Austin. Jones himself always drove big old-model cars. Smaller vehicles he would call "suicide buggies", remarking of the Japanese, "They've killed more people with their cars than they did in the war!"

Once I told him that I thought my grade in a college class on European imperialism had been affected because I did not agree with the professor. The area of special study was Italian imperialism in Ethiopia, Somalia, and Eritrea. The professor appeared to whitewash it to such a degree that a fellow student had to ask innocently, "Were the imperialists mean?" "Well no…" It bothered me and I told Jones about it. He asked me where the professor was from, and I told him he had Italian heritage. Jones said:

"Well you go back and ask him if he knows what the shortest book in the world is, see what he tells you. You know what it is, don't you?"

"No, what?"

"The book of Italian war heroes!" He laughed and said, "You tell him your friend Mr. Jones told you that!"

Having dropped out of school in the eighth grade, he had his own way of thinking, influenced mainly by his life experience and observations and what he read in the newspaper and in books he picked out of the junkyard. His opinions could be "extreme" and yet hold that grain of truth that made heads both shake "no" and nod "yes." He knew, for example, that the Italians were miserable in both world wars and that even the Ethiopians, without modern weapons, had surrounded and defeated them early in the century, decades before Mussolini's infamous invasion and short-lived conquest in 1935.

Remarking on the people's movements of the late 1980s that were shaking up the communist regimes in eastern Europe, a time of the exhilaration of freedom for many, Jones said:

"The crowd can't be right. That many people in one place, all wanting the same thing, they can't be right. You know when you're right? When you got no followers, that's when you know you're right. If anybody's following you, then you know you're wrong."

"Well, what about the civil rights movement?" I said.

"They were wrong. We didn't need the white man to give us our dignity and respect. Nobody can take that away from you. The people out marching on the street were stupid and mixed up."

That in particular was something I couldn't disagree with more, but he made his point.

Once, during a summer camp in Austin, Jones visited me in the apartment I was staying in and he noticed the framed picture on the wall of Mahatma Gandhi, drawn in pencil by my Ranjit chacha. Jones said:

"When I was your age, I had a picture of Malcolm X on the wall. But as soon as I found out the Muslims were the first slave traders, I said, 'Malcolm's got to go!'"

Mr. Jones said everything with a certain smile and laugh. Humor was how he dealt with bigotry, discrimination, and inequality as a result of just being black. He didn't take the civil rights movement seriously, saying it was led by ministers who had always enriched themselves while the community remained poor. One of his favorite stories related to the Montgomery bus boycott of 1955:

"You know when they started letting black folks ride in the front of the bus? Well, a black man got on the bus and a white man had to sit behind him. They got on down the road and the black man felt the white man take something off his shoulder. He said, 'What did you do?' The white man said, 'I took a chinch (flea) offa ya.' The black man said, 'What?! Goddamit, you put him right back, y'all don't wanna see black people with nuthin!'"

He used to regale people with a seemingly endless stock of tales like these. Many were as stereotypical of blacks as of whites. He regularly referred to blacks as "coons", whites as "peckerwoods", and Mexican-Americans "chili chokers." All tales seemed to relate, inevitably, to racial differences explaining the simplest of differences, such as differences in hair:

"The white man, the Mexican, and the black man were shooting craps (game of dice) when the Lord was passing out the hair. The Lord said, 'White man, come get your hair!' The white man went up and got his hair. They kept playing. The Lord said, 'Mexican, come get your hair!' The Mexican got up and got his hair. They kept playing. The Lord said, 'Black man, come get your hair!' The black man said, 'You got to wait, I'm rolling hot right now. Snake eyes! Seven-elevens!' They kept playing. The Lord said again, 'Black man, come get your hair!'" The black man said, 'Didn't you hear, I'm rolling hot right now, I'm beating these fellas!' They kept playing. Again the Lord said, 'Black man, come get your hair!' The black man stood up and said, 'Goddamitt, just ball it up and throw it over here, why don't you?!'"

When Jones joined the Guard, he was the only black solider in the unit. I found this out later, during the 1988 presidential campaign, when George Bush's running mate was Dan Quayle, the senator from Indiana who had been accused of dodging the draft and the Vietnam War by enrolling in the National Guard. I asked Mr. Jones:

"Were there many people like Dan Quayle in the Guard back then?"

"It was nothing but fifty Quayles and one coon," he replied, referring to himself. "I was the only black person in the unit, the token!"

All his life, Jones was used to dealing with racism, he expected it, and it got so it didn't bother him. I told him about a book my class read in high school titled "Black Like Me," written by a white man who used charcoal to disguise himself as a black person and see what it felt like and how he would be treated in places like New Orleans. Jones said:

"The white man shouldn't feel guilty. You heard about the snake and the fox? Well see, the snake was in the river and he was drowning and he saw the fox on the riverbank and he said, 'Help me, Mr. Fox, help me, I can't swim, I'm drowning!' The fox said, 'I can't help you, you'll bite me.' The snake said, 'No, I won't, Mr. Fox, no, I won't, promise! You've got to help me, I can't swim, I'm drowning!' But the fox didn't want to help him, he knew he'd get bit, but the snake kept asking him. Finally, the fox said, 'All right, I'll help you, if you promise you won't bite me.' The snake said, 'I promise, Mr. Fox, I promise I won't bite you.' So the fox got in the water and let the snake get on his back. They started swimming back to shore. Then the snake bit the fox. And the fox turned around and said, 'You said you wasn't gonna bite me!' The snake said, 'I know that's what I said, but I can't help it, it's my goddamn nature!' So the white man shouldn't feel guilty, that's how he is, he can't help it!'"

You could laugh but you could also get discouraged by hearing too much of this, too much. Humor was how Jones and many others adapted to dealing with the pain and hurt of discrimination over centuries. It wasn't that Mr. Jones never said anything good about whites. He respected their technical prowess, their ability to fix things. He also recognized what in his experience he saw as differences. For example, he said the English settlers in Texas were different than the German settlers—one owned slaves (the English in East Texas) and the other farmed their own land (the Germans in Central Texas). But everything came back to race and a view of the world in which race explained everything. I asked Jones directly once:

"Jones, do you hate the white man?"

"Yes, I guess you could call it that. But it's an elevated hatred. I don't mean him no harm and I don't let it get me down. It's a raised hatred."

I used to worry about his children, what it must be like in school for them. Jones used to remark about "teachers who always want to tell you what to do with your kids when they got no kids of their own." It was hard to make out what Jones said at times because of his dialect and use of words. I noticed some of his children spoke the same way and I knew the teachers must have a hard time understanding them. Many years later, I found out that my fears about the children of his that I knew were borne out. Not only had they not graduated school but Mr. Jones told me that he had told them not to finish school. I respected Mr. Jones and had learned a great deal from him but this I found sad and upsetting.

It's not that he didn't respect education, it was more along the lines of Mark Twain's dictum, "Don't let schooling interfere with your education." For his part, Mr. Jones was self-educated and proudly so. He was also proud not to drink or do drugs and he pitied those that did and lamented the rampant substance abuse he saw, particularly in the black community. He felt crack and the drug trade in general was a plot to get rid of blacks. He maintained a deep scepticism of progress and any superficial assessment of things in general. Of people offering to give you something for free, he would remark, "It's like the crack dealer, the first rock is always free. I always say, the only free cheese is in the trap!"

Sketch: The Woman Who Passed

He knelt beside her on the floor in the back of the ambulance, his right forefinger on her left wrist. He would remember this, that her pulse was quite faint and deep. It was a cold night and the metallic box which was the back of the ambulance only seemed to make it colder. He had to take his glove off and hers too, and roll up her sleeves. She was an elderly woman, eyes closed, wrapped up in a dark coat and fluffy cold weather hat that the nurse at the hospital would have put on. Her lips were pursed gently, her Latina skin a faded bronze.

He looked at her chest. Was it rising? He could not be sure, bundled up as she was. He put the back of his hand above her mouth and below her nose. Could even the hairs on his hand feel any breath, any warmth, in this cold? He did not think so. His mind quickly registered: "Low pulse, faint breath—elderly, diabetes, released from hospital." He knew to begin CPR, which entailed opening her mouth with his thumb and placing the standard air bag over her mouth to pump air into her lungs and prepare to do chest compressions.

"I think she's fading," he alerted the paramedic driver who looked at him in the rear view mirror that glimmered in front of the darkness of the windshield and the late night city streets. "I'm gonna bag her."

"Do it, just let me know", he heard the nonchalant response.

He straddled her gently without letting his weight fall on her. Placing one hand under the other and clasping the fingers, with his arms extended and straight, he began to press down lightly on her sternum and release. One-two-three-four-five. Then pinching her nostrils tight, he squeezed the mechanical bag that pushed air through her mouth and into her lungs. He watched her chest rise gently. He did it again, then five more chest compressions, then two breaths, five and then two, five and then two.

He could feel her breathing on her own again. He felt her pulse. It was more evident now. She breathed more deeply now. But still, she did not wake up at all, appearing only to sleep, grateful perhaps for the most minimum disturbance.

"How is she now?" the driver asked. Had she not responded, he knew the driver would have been ready to turn the sirens on and go back to the hospital.

"Her respirations and pulse are back," he replied. You always hesitated to say "ok" in this job, since you could never really know. A patient could "crash on you", as they said.

Soon the driver backed into the driveway outside the adult foster home. It was a poor side of town and after ten in the evening. He put her glove back on, pulled her sleeve down, and unstrapped the arm restraints. She lay motionless, arms at her side, looking quite peaceful. He was ready to lower her and release her to the caretaker.

After a knock on the door, a gentleman in a white uniform came out to the ambulance with a stretcher. He lowered her down on the ambulance's stretcher and they transferred her smoothly. "I've got her now", he said.

The next morning, she was dead. She had passed away sometime in the night.

He was informed. It made him sad. He reviewed everything in his mind. He recalled her face, its peacefulness perhaps not of this world entirely. He recalled the faint pulse and the effort of bringing back her respirations. She had seemed ok, yet something told him she might not be long for this world. She was already on that edge, he could sense it. She had never been awake the whole trip from hospital to adult home. She was in her late 60s only. Had they done enough?

The very peacefulness of her face and the depth of her slumber said it all. That is what he most remembered and was most reluctant to interpret. But there was dignity in that face, neither pain nor struggle. She had been ready. God bless.

Narrative and Letters to a Young Friend

I did go back to the University, this time 45 miles up Interstate-35 to the University of Texas at Austin. I joined in January 1988 and graduated with a Bachelor's degree in History (concentration in 20th century history) and a minor in English in May 1990. President George Bush came to our graduation and many of us, including myself, wore broccoli on our graduation caps, as a joke, since the President had said he did not like broccoli. Presidents could take a joke back then.

I had few friends until my last year, when I was a "Normandy Scholar", part of a 30 student pilot program that studied all about World War II including for 2 months in Caen, France at a new Museum of Peace. In that program, my good friends included my roommate, a girl who liked me, and two guys from Costa Rica. Other than that, my other close friends in my university years were two Mexican-American buddies who worked at the Sears garage, where our job was "tires, batteries, and oil changes." I worked 24 hours weekly while maintaining a full course load, 36 hours in the summer. The garage, and the rhythm of physical work and the camaraderie with all the guys in the garage, balanced out my serious side. And I commuted to San Antonio one weekend per month for the National Guard, sharing everything about life with friend and eccentric mentor Mr. Jones. I visited my parents twice a year in Houston, where my mother's health continued to slide and my father was nearing retirement age.

I really don't see so much aloneness as good for the psyche, and I do feel college years in particular should be more balanced, more carefree. Looking back, to myself in particular, I would have written:

I often think that you are too much alone, are too serious, are too preoccupied. If I could lift the burden of your thoughts from you, I would. I would love to see you feel light and carefree, if only for the moment. You were not meant to brood and ruminate so much. A touch of melancholy is ok but do not let it descend into the condition of being morose. Learn to let thoughts, emotions, and moods come and go rather than to chase them, hold them, stew in them. They can exert a power and control over you if you are not watchful. Do not see only the suffering of the world without also seeing the joy of living. There is so much to be shared in good company, in wisdom, in Nature. It all awaits your discovery, my young friend, if only you will allow it.

And to someone like me today, or to anyone starting college, I would write:

Your college years should be years of discovery. Follow your interests, develop your abilities, ask good questions. Make friends along the way. Be social, be free, learn to make mistakes and be ok with it. Chalk it up for learning, for experience, as they say. Love the outdoors, nature, the life of the senses. Learn to use your discretion and judgment when it comes to people and peers. It is not the number of friends you have but the ones you can count on for a sense of fellowship and support. It is natural to have far more acquaintances with whom you are simply on good terms or perhaps no terms. Respect your teachers and professors, even when you suspect they may be wrong or when you disagree with them. They too are on a journey. Try not to be too judgmental of others. We are all on a journey. The important thing is to be open in general, to learning, to discovery, to new ways of thinking, to seeing others in a new light, to new relationships. This is living.

Content yourself more with observation than a need to change the world around you. Understand yourself first. Cherish relationships more than fixing problems. Learn to be a listener. Learn how to reflect what others feel and say and to express compassion, but be content to give advice only in the quantities the other person takes it, and no more. Understand that problems come in the way, both naturally as part of life and because of our own thinking and approach. Do not bear the pain and suffering of the world on your shoulders. First learn to handle your own issues. Develop your own awareness, and not just of external matters in people and society and nature. I refer to internal matters such as the senses, the body, the mind, the attention you give and that you direct. This is what it means to live an examined life, to be aware of oneself, to feel the unknown before it makes itself known, to be privy to all the murmurings of the self and its interaction with the world. Find moments where you are as aware internally of what is happening within you as you are aware externally of what is happening around you. You will find such occasional living in the present with full awareness to be strengthening like medicine.

This is sort of perennial advice for the older adult I am now as well as the younger adult I was then.

Narrative: Joining the Peace Corps

Coming out of University of Texas at Austin, I had an offer to teach English as a Second Language in 8th grade at a school in Los Angeles. This would be with Teach for America in their inaugural pilot program in 1990. I was to attend a Summer Institute that basically would be a crash course on how to teach.

However, one day in the spring of 1990, I stopped by the Career Services office at UT-Austin. Flipping through various binders, I came across information on joining the Peace Corps. I had read about the Peace Corps when I was in high school. It was just a two to three page article in a big book on the 1960s. Peace Corps had been established by President John F. Kennedy in 1961 "to help developing countries meet their needs for trained manpower" and to "promote a better understanding of the American people on the part of host countries" and of "the people of host countries on the part of Americans." Its overall mission was stated simply as global peace and friendship. Its recruitment slogan was "the toughest job you'll ever love." It was unique in the sense that it was separate from foreign policy, managed by an "independent agency" of the U.S. government, and served as a citizen-to-citizen program. Volunteers would live and work side-by-side with host communities, speak the same language, eat the same food, and live in the same kind of homes. The entire emphasis was on community integration, cross-cultural learning, and working on "grassroots development" projects with local counterparts. There would be no salary, only a subsistence allowance and a readjustment allowance at the end of two years of service following three months of in-country training.

I didn't think I qualified. I thought they took only specialists, people with hard skills, like engineers, nurses, and so on. I was surprised to find they took "generalists" like me, with a liberal arts degree, if we had relevant work experience, volunteerism, and foreign languages. I had construction experience framing houses and putting up ceilings plus volunteer work with Habitat for Humanity and the CHIP Program back in Charlottesville. Other volunteer work was with homeless shelters and the MS Society. Foreign language was a strong point with me, being fluent in Spanish and with intermediate German and basic Hindi. I had to get eight references, and my various employers plus professors helped me, even my Latin teacher from high school. I also had to drive to Dallas for an interview.

One day in September, I got a call from someone from Peace Corps in Washington D.C., telling me I had been selected as a Water and Sanitation Volunteer for the country of Mali. If this was acceptable to me, then I should call back and let them know. Final acceptance was contingent on medical clearance and a background check. I thought vaguely of a country in east-central Africa—Malawi. I then looked up Mali in an atlas, found it was in West Africa, and saw Tombouctou was located there. Timbuktu is Tombouctou in French and Mali was "French-speaking", at least at official levels. So much for my Spanish. I knew I couldn't be too choosy in getting into Peace Corps and I figured it could be my one chance in a lifetime to get to know a place in Africa firsthand. Yes—Mali—report to a 3-day pre-training in-service in Philadelphia, January 1991.

Little did I know, I was about to begin the greatest adventure of my life, the best two years of my life, a life-changing transformative period on par with marriage and children. I had also hit the goldmine in getting Mali, a more generous, kind, and hospitable country and people is hard to imagine.

. . .

Inclined as always to advance preparation and to knowing the past in order to understand the present, the first thing I did was to go to Houston's downtown public library to find out more about Mali. In 1990, few people had personal computers and even fewer used the Internet which itself had few websites and information resources at the time. There was hardly anything on Mali in the library but I did come away with two books, one on the Tuareg in the north and one an eye-opening and ground-level work of historical fiction titled *Segou* by Maryse Conde.

I also went to the library at Rice University. I was looking for a government publication on Mali in the library's basement. I couldn't find it myself and asked for help from someone putting material back on the shelves. I gave him the slip of paper on which I'd written the card numbers identifying the publication. He pulled out the government document and saw the word Mali in the title and said, "I'm from Mali." What a coincidence! He told me that he was doing post-graduate work in archaeology at Rice University. He also knew about Peace Corps in Mali, having been taught English by a Peace Corps Volunteer at the Ecole Nationale Superieur ("ENSUP") in the capital Bamako! I later met Don, an elderly Volunteer who spent many years in Mali. That is how everything was in Mali—small enough to be personal.

Looking back, it is curious how my entrée to Mali started and ended with just such a coincidence. When I came back to Houston in 1993, I took my updated resume over to the local 7-Eleven store to get it copied. The clerk saw my resume and said, "I'm from Mali." We later went out for dinner and saw a Houston Rockets basketball game together.

There were 48 of us at the Peace Corps Mali pre-training in-service in Philadelphia in January 1991. Mainly white, young, single—inexperienced, fresh out of college, idealistic. Mainly female. Mostly, but not uniformly, liberal in political views. I considered myself a moderate along with a number others. There was only one self-proclaimed conservative in the group. The reasons for joining Peace Corps were more similar than different—learn another language and culture while helping others, travel and adventure, work experience, the feeling of being useful and helpful, the ideals of brotherhood and community. *Never before had I been reunited at the same time with so many people like myself in inclination!*

Later, I always recalled how one of the trainers was a black American, who had been a Volunteer in the Philippines, and he seemed to be speaking to a few of us Volunteers who were "minorities." He recounted how prior to Peace Corps, his attitude towards white Americans was one of mistrust, how during Peace Corps he made many friendships and realized how much in common all Americans have with each other regardless of differences at home, and how after Peace Corps he maintained the friendships that he made in Peace Corps up to the present day. Likewise, *I was to make lifelong friends in Peace Corps.*

The fellow-feeling that existed being around so many kindred spirits, combined with the useful and practical training I received as a water and sanitation volunteer, the discovery of my own talent for languages, and the warm and jovial reception given to us by Peace Corps Mali staff and the training village of Katibougou gave me the feeling that *finally I was doing what I was meant to do.* This gave me a sure-footedness, confidence, and purpose that was new to me and with that came a tremendous physical and mental vitality and energy. *I never felt so alive as I did in Peace Corps and Mali!*

Here I was, going from a period of loneliness, emptiness, and alienation from peers, ever since I'd left the military at age 20, to a sudden feeling of belonging, purpose, and community. I had also prepared myself, not only by reading and viewing whatever I could find on Mali, but also by studying French in advance. It was easier for me since I knew Spanish. So I felt pleased with myself when on the 6 hour flight from New York City to Dakar, Senegal, I found I could read and understand as much of the magazine *Jeune Afrique* ("Young Africa") as another Volunteer who had actually majored in French in university. More remarkably, unlike other Volunteers, I found that learning Bambara came so easily to me that I almost didn't have to study. I would hear it, remember it, repeat it. I conversed with all of the teachers, training center staff, and Katibougou villagers without fear of making any mistake. To their credit, Malians tend not to judge and not to over-correct—only to laugh, joke, and encourage. In addition, one could learn through songs on cassettes that people listened to in the village, singers at that time like world famous Salif Keita and even Alpha Blondie. This was the training village that was used to Americans. It would be different in the provinces, and after three months, every Volunteer would be on their own, with no one to speak English to and no phones.

Bambara	**one of a dozen languages in Mali**
Good morning	*I ni sogoma* ("you and the morning")
Good job	*I ni baara* ("you and the work")
Tree	*yiri*
Branch	*yiribolo* ("tree arm")
Fruit	*yiriden* ("tree child")
Bicycle	*negeso* ("iron horse")
Airplane	*sannakurun* ("sky canoe")
Rain	*sanji* ("sky water")
Leaf or medicine	*fura*
Pill	*furakise* ("medicine seed")
Sickness	*bana*
Germ	*banakise* ("sickness seed")
Green	*binkeneman* ("like fresh grass")
South	*worodugufe* ("towards the village of kola nuts")

Bambara	**one of a dozen languages in Mali**
Goodbye	*k'an ben* ("may we meet again")
Someone who keeps his promises	*kantigi* ("the owner of his voice")

Katibougou was about 20 miles from Bamako and a short cycle ride from the training centre, which was called Ntubani So, "home of the doves", after the emblem of Peace Corps. We were divided up into twos and assigned host families. My roommate and I stayed with a host family headed by brothers Kanda and Lasina Diarra, whose names, in Peace Corps Mali tradition, became our Bambara names for the duration of our time in Mali. I became Lasina Diarra. The real Lasina was young, unmarried, extremely jovial, always smiling, pleased, and delighted. He was proud of his name, of an American like me bearing his name, of teaching us basic words and phrases in both Bambara and French, and of teaching us basic cultural etiquette. It was the dry season, so there wasn't much farming to do. Lasina spent his days chopping and selling firewood for 500 CFA, or $2 per day, an inflated price since we were close to the capital. Sometimes, he would arrive home after dark, obviously tired after a long day of labor, but ready as always to engage his guests, to laugh, and to take us out to visit his friends in the village.

Like most of the Volunteers, I could only marvel at how hard people worked and yet how fundamentally content they appeared to be. I remember writing home something to this effect, "These are the happiest people I've ever known!" It was over-stated, and yet the happiness I could see in the village consisted quite simply of having one's basic needs met, playing cards in the evening, drinking tea, listening to music, making conversation, telling jokes, and having the honor of hosting and initiating Americans in the Malian way of life. Then there was family, meaning extended family, everyone seemed to be related in some way or another. In the Army, cynically speaking, I'd been told "expect the worst and you'll never be disappointed." In Mali, it wasn't about expecting the worst, but it seemed, at first glance, to be about expecting nothing and therefore being content with what you had.

Towards the end of my 2 years and 4 months in Mali, I reflected that the "fatalism" ascribed to traditional societies like village Mali is not really fatalism in the sense of resignation to a pre-determined fate. On the contrary, traditional living, with its feeling that humans are a part of and not above Nature and that humans are dependent on both God and Nature, has much to do with confidence in life. Else how to express the smiles, the laughter, the amusement, the jokes, the merriment, the joviality, the refusal to call it a night, the desire to stay up until dawn, the gratitude at receiving small things—combined with the near absence of qualities like sarcasm—how to account for this zest in living when life is subsistence-level hard and all the possessions a person owned, save for cooking ware and livestock, could be put into one small trunk. Not by chance perhaps, the word "God", or "Allah", was constantly on people's lips, in the form of blessings and greetings throughout the day as well as in conversation. The feeling that God will provide ("anw be Ala bolow", or "we're in God's hands") reflected *an underlying confidence in life, not fatalism!*

It is worth noting that my adaptation to Mali was not true for everyone. By my count, 48 of us arrived in Philadelphia for pre-departure orientation and shots, etc.; 46 of us went on to Mali; 43 of us completed the training and swore in on 26 April 1991, committing to doing two years of service; by April 1993, 28 of us had completed the two years. I spent one extra month to complete work. Two as I recall stayed on for an extra year or more.

Mali in 1991, in spite of the warmth and hospitality, was not an easy country to serve in. Malaria was endemic, paved roads few, and phone and communications almost non-existent. Everything was by word of mouth, face to face, and messages one person to another, plus "common sense", patience and endurance, and confidence in others—no reminders.

The country had a population of 9 million people with another 3 million Malians abroad, especially in the much wealthier Côte d'Ivoire (Ivory Coast) to the south. It was one of the 10 "poorest" nations in the world, going by income, and 2 of every 5 children died before the age of 5 years old, usually of diarrheal disease and malnutrition but also cerebral malaria. During our training, a military coup took place and Mali soon became a fledgling democracy.

Home to three influential empires in West African history—the Ghana, Mali, and Songhai empires—Mali had most recently been colonized by France and had won its independence in 1960. But the resourcefulness and resilience and spirit of the people was unparalleled and consistently impressed and amazed the American Volunteers.

Sketch: Waiting for the Rain

We were all assigned to our sites in rural Mali for the next two years. The cycle of life changed from structured to unstructured, from determined by human beings to determined by the seasons, from living independently to living in community. From electric lighting to kerosene lamps. From sleeping late and waking late to sleeping early and waking early. Any barrier with Nature was about to be broken.

I was assigned to Sirakoro ("under the baobab") as my base for water work (wells for drinking water, hand pumps, repair of small dams). There, in southern Mali, the rains came in May and the farming season commenced, lasting even after the rains ended in September up to the end of the millet harvest in November. Then the cold dry season began followed by the hot dry season. People worked hard, often on empty stomachs. There was the "hunger season", August in particular, when the previous year's harvest was sparse and the new harvest was still in the field, ripening.

The rain often came at night, when one literally battened down the hatches, being the wooden window hatches, and the drops struck like bullets on the tin roof. Outside, the dark night flickered with lightning such that sometimes it was impossible to count to "two" or even "one" without a flicker and a flash. The air was electric and one waited it out inside and watched the puddles form outside. The uppermost walls of one's house might become dark brown with moisture or the rain might enter where nails held the tin roofing sheets to the beams on the ceiling.

One witnessed the absolute power of nature in awe and occasionally fear. Living in village, especially in dry season when people were not absolutely exhausted from a day's work, one felt everything slow down and simultaneously one's own senses sharpen, one's power of observation grow more subtle, and the hyperactivity of the urban mind take a back seat. Conversation could be flowing or in bits and snatches. There was no pressure or compulsion to fill the silence.

The sketch below was my norm at dusk for two years whenever I was in Sirakoro and not off working in another village. It is an evening of the dry season on the bench with my *jatigi*, loosely translated as "guardian" or *responsable* in French, since I was attached to his family for the two-room house I lived in, meals as I chose, clothes washing except for undergarments, and general advice. The rains are coming nearer and nearer from Côte d'Ivoire (Ivory Coast) in the south…

. . .

I sat on a small wooden stool in front of the metal bucket in the shower side of the open air *nyegen* (latrine), hesitating to pour the cold water over myself. Breathing in, I closed my eyes and emptied the cup over my head. I opened my eyes and breathed out forcefully, as if exhaling the shiver down my spine. Quickly chasing the streams of water running through my hair with more cups of water, I rubbed the bar of hard soap in my hands and spread the lather over me. When I had finished rinsing off, I threw out what little water remained in the bucket and turned it upside down next to the drainage hole at the bottom of the cement coated mud walls.

Standing up to dry myself, I saw my *jatigi*'s daughter Fanta drying herself in her nyegen not twenty-five meters away. She blushed when she saw me, breaking into a broad smile before tossing the towel over her head. The sun was setting on Sirakoro and painting the mud walls of houses in brilliant shades of pink and rose and violet. Birds criss-crossed the blue sky fading to black as the stars in the east shone ever brighter.

I pulled the towel around my waist and walked into my house. It felt stuffy and warm under the tin roof. I pulled a pair of pants and a shirt from the line on which I hung my clothes and quickly put them on. Pouring myself a cup of water from the canary behind the door, I could already feel the beads of sweat collecting on my hairline. I slipped into my flip-flops, grabbed the keys, stepped outside, and locked the screen door.

I walked up the short path to my *jatigi*'s concession. Nearly all the mangos in the tree between us had been knocked, pulled, shaken, or blown down. I caught a glimpse of the white head, black wings, and long beak of the solitary *baninko* perched in the treetop and beholding the village like a deity. Its arrival at the end of the dry season was much anticipated, for like the swallows flying in mad circles above in the fleeting light of dusk, it heralded rain.

"*I ni wula, Balakisa, heré tilenna?*" I said to the daughter-in-law of the house. Literally: *you and the evening, Balakisa, did the day pass in peace.*

"*Heré doron. Heré tilenna, Lasina?*" *In peace only.*

"*Heré doron. I ni baara.*" Literally: *you and work*, a familiar acknowledgement.

I had turned the corner into *jatigi* Saidou's concession. Balakisa stood atop the cement slab over the well, drawing water into two buckets beside her. Saidou sat in his hammock and Fanta and her younger sister Basila sat on the bench across from him. They were shelling peanuts, dropping the shells and the nuts into a large basin between them.

"*Aw ni wula*", I said.

"*M-ba. Heré be, Lasina?*"

"*Heré doron.*"

"*I ka kene wa?*" I asked. *How are you.*

"*Tooro si te. So ko yan?*" *No problem at all. People are fine in your place?*

"*Heré b'u la.*" *Peace is on them.*

"*You're shelling peanuts.*" Typical Mali-style acknowledgement of work.

"*Yes, the rains aren't far off.*"

I sat on the bench and leaned over to grab a handful of peanuts. Greetings, however banal, served as a basic affirmation of another's existence and of community as well as an acknowledgement of time of day and work. The questions were standard but much was also conveyed in tone of voice and the extent of exchanges.

"*Tige jeman?*" *White peanuts.*

"*Yes, I sow these first. They'll be ready in three months, God willing.*"

Saidou was always the first one to sow peanuts in the village. He gambled on the rains. When he judged that the rainy season had begun, he and his sons would spend three days sowing peanuts after the first heavy rain. However, if the rains were late, his peanuts would wilt and die under the hot sun. If he were lucky, the first rain would soon be followed by another, and another, and the rainy season would begin in earnest.

After harvesting and drying his peanuts in July, he would load them onto a taxi and travel to Bamako, where the rains usually began later and where he could sell them at a higher price. Depending on the cost of transportation and on the price peanuts would fetch on the market, Saidou's gamble might or might not pay off handsomely for him. While in Bamako, he could buy cheap parts to keep up the motor scooter he had bought back in 1959 and which he relied on to sell bread in neighboring village markets. Saidou worked hard but everything depended on the rains.

When we had shelled the last peanut, Fanta lifted the enamel basin on her head and Basila followed her out of the concession, carrying two baskets to winnow the peanuts and to separate the shells from the nuts to be sown as seeds. Saidou stretched out on his hammock and I leaned back on the flat boards of the bench. Swallows still flew in mad circles above.

"Do you think the rains will come early this year, Saidou?"

"Ah… Ne m'a da la. I doubt it. This matter of rain gets more difficult every year."

"The rains must be close. I saw the baninko. And the tamarind tree by the pump is just beginning to bud."

Like everyone else, Saidou refused to speculate on just when the rains would arrive. He listened to the weather report every evening on a short-wave radio but placed no faith in it. The rains were becoming more erratic every year. A nearby village might get a torrential downpour but the same storm, almost always coming out of the southeast, would pass to one side of us. Or a storm in Bougoula, only three kilometers to the west, might leave Sirakoro completely dry, in which case those fields bordering Bougoula might get some rain but the fields on the other side of Sirakoro would not get so much as a drop.

"It doesn't rain like it used to, Lasina."

Fanta and Basila returned and emptied the basin full of peanuts into a brown cotton bag that Saidou held open. He tied up the bag and stored it in the room where he mixed the dough to make his bread. He had learned to make bread from the American missionaries who used to live on one end of the village. The best wheat for bread was imported from Russia. For a long time, he had sold French-style baguettes when few villagers had the taste for bread, earning him the nickname "Buuru Nango." Buuru meant bread and Nango, a name given to male children whose mother had died upon giving birth to them, was his real name.

Night had finally fallen, concealing us from one another and enveloping us in its silence. We faced south towards Ivory Coast, witnessing the occasional flashes of light across the sky in the distance. The face of Saidou's first wife, Konza, was lit up by the embers she poked in the three rock fire in front of her. At the far end of the concession, I could see Balakisa carrying a kerosene lamp and moving back and forth between her cooking hut and the house she shared with Mousa, her husband and Saidou's oldest son.

Mousa sat on a metal folding chair with his back against the wall of his house. He had just come back from the market in Masigi, some sixty kilometers to the north. For some weeks now, he and a group of other young men had been buying peanuts in the Sunday market in Kebila twenty kilometers to the south. They shelled them in the evenings in Sirakoro, then transported the fify kilo bags on bicycle up to Masigi, and sold them for a few more cents per kilo in the Wednesday market there.

I sat up when I saw Balakisa approach with the lantern and the bowls of rice and sauce. She set Saidou's food down on the ground in front of his hammock and my portion on the bench I sat on. She then fetched a cup of water from the canary under the mango sapling in the middle of the concession and placed it on the bench next to me.

"Dumuni file." Your food.

"I ni ce, Bala." Thank you.

I leaned over to rinse my right hand, letting the water trickle down my fingers onto the ground. I passed the tin cup to Saidou. With my right foot on the ground and my left knee drawn up on the bench, I poured some of the peanut butter sauce onto a corner of the rice in the bowl before me. The rice was hot to the touch but I felt my mouth watering in anticipation. Scooping up a portion of rice and rolling it into a ball in my hand, I lifted and deposited it into my mouth, fingers and all, in one full motion.

Bakary, Adama, and Seku were eating out of a common bowl with Mousa on the other end of the concession. Konza, Balakisa, and Fanta were eating across from us. Basila and her little sister Miyatu were eating with their mother Halima, who was Saidou's second wife, in the concession behind us.

"*A barika, Saidou,*" I said. *Thank you* (after food).

"*A barika Ala ye. Are you full?*" *Thanks be to God.*

"*Tewu tewu*, to the top", I said. As usual, Saidou insisted on giving me more, but I declined. I leaned down and poured some water over my right hand, rinsing it as best I could by moving my fingers over my palm. I returned to sit on the bench with my arms around my knees, clasping my left wrist with my right hand.

When Saidou finished, he called Fanta over to take away the empty bowls and fetch us some charcoal. She drew the coals out of the oven Saidou was heating up to bake bread later that night and brought them to us on the head of a shovel, dropping them before us into a round wire stand which served as a stove. She poured some water into a pot which Saidou balanced on the glowing coals. He gave me two small plastic cups with handles to set on the bench while he emptied two packets of Nescafe and a quantity of sugar into the water.

"*Sanji te na ikomi folofolo. It doesn't rain like it used to, Lasina. We used to have moisture and humidity here, but no more. It was my father who planted those tall mango trees by the stream bed. A lot of rain used to come in those days, and it used to last.*"

At that moment, the crier at the nearby mosque across the open field outside Saidou's concession broke out into his "*Alahu akbars.*" I could hear Fanta in the dark, coyly imitating Ba Siriki's souful call to prayer. Saidou sat fanning air across the glowing coals with a withered straw fan before finally leaning back in his hammock.

"*Were there many banana trees in the village then?*"

"*Where my mango orchard is today used to be all banana trees. There were even pineapples. And there were no stick fences like today, because very few people owned cattle or goats.*"

"There must have been many more animals in the forest."

"You would have thought they would never end! People did not travel between the villages at night like young people today. Wild animals were on the path, waraba, lions even. People were too scared even to walk around the village at night."

Saidou sat up in his hammock to pour the coffee into the plastic cups. I held a flashlight while he cooled the coffee, raising and pouring it at a high angle from one cup to another. He held out a cup to me, which I promptly drank, tasting more syrup than coffee.

"There must have been very few people in Sirakoro when you were a boy, Saidou."

"O mogo tun man ca de! Very few people, Lasina. I don't believe there could have been more than two hundred people in Sirakoro when I was a boy. And noone walked around at night."

"The fields were closer, too?"

"You could not plant too far away or the red monkeys and wart hogs would destroy your crops. But they were scared of people, so we planted everything next to the village."

Konza had retired into the round hut across from us, her outline lit by the karité oil lamp burning next to the wall. Mousa had left on his cycle. Balakisa was sitting on a mat with her legs in front of her, hummin while spinning cotton onto a spool she twirled in the twilight of the lantern beside her.

"And did you grow any cotton, Saidou?"

"We only grew enough to clothe ourselves. No more. At that time, the ground was too moist even for peanuts and mangos. And we had no ploughs or tubabu (foreigner or white man's) fertilizer. We grew many yams and sweet potatoes. Today, you know, I am the only one growing yams, and they no longer produce. All because the rain doesn't come."

"Why do you think that is, Saidou?"

"Mogo", he said instantly, people. *"People are bad and the rain doesn't come. Mogo manyi de. People are bad."*

Saidou seemed to have sunk deeper into his hammock. I wasn't surprised by his response. Everything came down to people. And the rain. At that moment, the loud croak of a frog echoed throughout the concession.

"Ntori. A be sanji wele ka na," said Saidou. *The frog is calling the rain to come.*

I stood up to look for the three stars of Orion in the western sky. Saidou called them *che saba*, or the three men. When they dropped below the horizon, Saidou said, the rainy season would be here. The first star to fall would become wind, the second rain, and the third wind again. They marked the winds that began the rainy season, the rains themselves, and the winds that closed the season. When the rain retreated south in October, *che saba* would again rise in the eastern sky.

"U jiginna kaban, Lasina," he said, *they've gone down already.* "You won't see them."

A faint breeze could be heard in the tall mango trees by the mosque. It seemed to come through the door of Saidou's concession and blow gently by us. I looked at the clear sky above us and Saidou stirred in his hammock. A second breeze shook the leaves in the top of the trees but seemed to dissipate indefinitely somewhere above us. We could see erratic flashes of light in the southern sky. Then all was quiet.

Sketch: Cut by a Sickle

One day, I was in a field with others harvesting a type of millet with a sickle. We had to bend down, grasp the millet in one hand, and take the sickle and deftly cut the ripened stalks we held. At some point, I noticed bright red drops of blood on the green grass. The blade of the sickle was so sharp that I didn't realize I had cut myself and that it was my own blood. I showed my finger to my companion next to me.

He said, *na yan*, come here, and led me to a particular type of grass that he cut with a machete. He had me hold out my finger and squeezed the juice out of the grass onto my wound. The bleeding stopped.

Again, *na yan*, he said, come here. He took me to a particular tree and cut sideways into it with the machete. White sap oozed out. He had me hold out my finger for the sap to spread on it. The swelling went down.

He then cut a strip of cloth from his shirt and tied it onto the wound and said, *an ka baarake*, let's get back to work. And we did.

So little said, so much done, so much knowledge. In fact, the word "fura" in Bambara meant leaf but it also meant medicine.

I was 24 – 26 years old. A university education. Military experience. Odd jobs that taught me a few things, even a stint on a medical ambulance.

But at no time in life did I learn more than I did from the humble villagers of southern Mali who had only the bare minimum of formal education, if any at all.

Generosity, hospitality, knowledge, wisdom, resilience, forbearance, patience, love, caring, growth, togetherness.

Sketch: A History Lesson from my Malian Mother

The afternoon sun loomed high overhead and beat down hard upon the tin and straw roofs of Sirakoro. Dust rose with the *harmattan*, that high and dry wind which blew across the Sahel, thickening the air and marking the true beginning of the hot season. Cattle roamed the fields in search of water, sheep and goats loitered about wells, donkeys blinked in the dust, and chickens strutted about aimlessly from concession to concession. Dogs sat in the shade with their tongues hanging out and their sides quivering while lizards creeped in the corners of every house. Leaves shook in the branches and people sought refuge under the lofty trees or on log benches or under straw hangars. Active minds sought out neighbors to converse with and active hands occupied themselves in weaving rope or spinning cotton.

On this particular day, with no work scheduled, I lounged about in a hammock under the straw hangar outside my house, immersed in a book detailing the adventures and escapades of the first Europeans to stumble across these lands in search of the course of the Niger River. Tales of gentleman dabblers and intrepid travelers, of science and geography, curiosity and speculation, ignorance and accidents, valor and chance, setbacks and successes, betrayal and friendship, illness, murder, death and the fever to renew a quest which became a conquest for a while but ultimately a retreat and a withdrawal. So engrossed was I in the reading of these exploits that my mind only vaguely registered the sound of little feet scamper around the mud brick wall behind me. When I felt eyes upon me, I turned to look where the wall ended and caught the face of young Fanta smiling with glee. She burst out in giggles and stepped up to me with her hand on the hammock.

"Lasina, Awa ko, ko i ka na," she said in pauses, *"Awa is calling you to come."*

This was not Fanta, my *jatigi*'s daughter, but Fanta the younger daughter of Awa, my adopted mother in the village. Awa would save rice and beans for me from the market, bring me back fritters and hibiscus juice from the market, call me over to begin and end Ramadan fasts, keep me abreast of gossip and advise me on village issues in general. If I chanced to spend the night in another village and a hunter had come home with a wild boar, she would cook and salt the meat and save it for me in a plastic container. In turn, as time allowed, I accompanied her to the fields—sowing, weeding, harvesting, and beating rice—and I gave her a ride to Sirakoro from the Zantiebougou market on my motorcycle. I bought rice for her on the Ramadan fête *selidon* and did things like shell peanuts and shuck corn with her and other women in her concession in the shade of a hot day or by the fire of a cold night.

"N kono doóni, n be na sisan," I said to Fanta. *Wait a bit, I'm coming.*

I set my feet on the ground and rose from my repose as Fanta flung into the hammock with a smile and a laugh. I put the book on the counter inside my house and reached into the canary behind my door to scoop out a cup of water.

"Ayiwa, an ka taa." Ok, *let's go.*

She bounced out of the hammock and led me under the mango tree behind my house, down the path by the pump, and into the group of concessions off to the left. Denkura and her youngest daughter Sali sat inside a round hut finishing off the remains of tô and sauce in bowls in front of them. Tô was the staple dish, usually made of millet or corn flour, boiled in large iron cauldrons, and served like patties with a sauce made of baobab leaves or peanut butter.

"Aw ni wula," I said. *Good afternoon.*

"N se. Na dumunike, Lasso," Denkura said. *Come eat.*

"N fara." *I'm full.*

"Baasi te", she said. *No problem. "Are you going to see your mother?"*

Yes, I said, as Denkura smiled approvingly. She and Awa walked the ten kilometers to Zantiebougou together every Thursday, rainy season or dry, and they lived almost next door to each other. Perhaps because she was a widow, she was more independent-spirited than other women in the village. She also danced a lighter and more elegant and graceful step than any of the other musokorobas, or old women, that I knew.

Fanta and I wound our way down the familiar pathway between the concessions, walking into a round hut with open entrances on either end. The daughters and daughters-in-law of the different concessions were making *shi tulu*, or karité oil, in three large mortars. They took turns mixing the thick brown oil in a lateral motion with their forearms. Karité oil was used primarily for sauces and cooking oil but also for healing wounds. IT was an important source of income for women who sold it in the markets.

"Lasina, I nana sin min wa?" *Have you come to breastfeed.*

Everyone stopped for a moment on hearing this, arms dripping with brown oil and laughing at the joke Kura made on the occasion of my coming to visit my adopted mother Awa. She and Asetu were wives of Soma, the youngest brother of Awa's husband Baba. Kura in particular always had something clever to say to express the essential surprise of a *tubabu*, or foreigner, coming to pass the time in their concession.

Fanta led me across the concession to Awa's house. She and her daughters had recently crêped the outside walls of the hut in gray, black, and white mud dyes. The walls were gray and bordered with black on the bottom and the door was outlined with black crosses on white squares. Three pairs of plastic flip-flops rested on the two steps in front of the door.

"*Aw ni wula,*" I said. *Good afternoon.*

"*N se. Heré tilenna, Lasina?*" *Did you spend the day in peace.*

"*Heré doron.*" *Peace only.*

"*So kono la ko ye, Lasina?*" *How are things in your house.*

"*Heré doron. And your family?*"

"*Heré b'u la. I t'i sigi? Kuruni filé.*" *Why won't you sit, here's a little stool.*

I sat on a wooden stool on one side of the room. Opposite me was a wooden bed on which I could make out the cotton-filled, cotton-sack mattress behind the line of clothes partitioning the large room. Awa sat on a red and black plastic mat against the wall with her legs in front of her, carding cotton with a hand-held *karanda*. Her neighbor Aminata sat next to her, spinning the carded cotton onto a spool that she twirled on the hard clay floor beside her. Aminata's daughter Geneba sat on a mat made of dried millet stalks and strips of bark. She was also spinning cotton, though the yarn she twirled onto the spool looked less fine than what her mother spun.

"*Lasso,*" Aminata addressed me, "*the next time you go to Bamako, can't you bring your mother a new karanda?*"

"A soro ko de ka gwelen sisan, Aminata," Awa said for me. *They are very hard to find these days.*

"Where can you buy them in Bamako", I asked.

"Suguba kono, in the main market," Awa said, *"but you won't find new ones."*

A *karanda*, a carder, consisted of two wooden handle with hundreds of tiny metal bristle between which sheaves of cotton were rubbed to remove the seeds and fluff out the cotton for the next step of spinning. Sirakoro was known in the area for the number of *musokorobas* who still carded and spun cotton like this.

"The karanda I have now my grandmother gave me."

"But how did you card cotton before you had karandas?" I asked.

"An bolo fe. We did everything by hand."

The thread which the women were used to making was coarse enough to be yarn or string. The *gesedalas*, or the men who could weave in the village, would then take these spools and stretch the string out on their wooden looms to make long, thin lengths of cloth. Kouake and Kotigi were the only weavers left in the village, though I occasionally saw Kotigi teaching his son how to work the loom.

"What did women wear for clothes?" I asked.

"The indigo waist cloth you see young girls wear today for excision ceremonies, that's what I wore as a young girl."

* It must be mentioned that excision, or female circumcision, means the cutting away or excision of the clitoris, a ritual and rite of passage that was done when girls were 6 or 7 years old (in older days only at the age of 15) out of complicated ancient beliefs but basically serving to control female sexuality by removing sexual pleasure. This practice carried on since no one would want to marry a girl who did not get excised but this entire outdated, cruel, and unnecessary practice, once common in West Africa, is being curtailed thanks to innovative

indigenous non-government organizations (NGOs) like Tostan. They began by convincing thirteen villages in Senegal to give up the practice simultaneously so that they could marry amongst themselves without any taboo. Their story, which includes the involvement of a former Peace Corps Volunteer, is chronicled in the book *However Long the Night*.

Back to cotton and women's clothing…

In the old days, the strips of cloth the weaver made would be tailored into short draw-string pants and long sleeveless shirts for men or wrap-around garments and head cloths for women. Clothes for men would be either white or dyed with the mustard-colored dye of a certain plant or the brown and black hues of certain kinds of mud (*bogolan* or "mud cloth"). Cloth for women would be dyed in indigo.

"When did you start wearing pagnes?" Pagnes in French (*tafe* in Bambara, *capulanas* in Mozambique) are the colorfully designed, factory-made cotton prints that women across sub-Saharan Africa wrap around their waists, carry things in, and use for any number of purposes.

"The people who went to farm peanuts in Senegal were the first people to come back with tubabu (white people or foreigner) clothes. Even before the clothes, I remember when people came back with sandals made of rubber from tires. How we looked at them—everybody wanted a pair! You remember Mabilen, Bobar's mother, who died last year? She and her husband were the first to go to Senegal."

"Did they have to go there?"

"They had to pay the tax…"

After the slave trade and the spate of wars and thee drain of population it fostered, the succeeding European impact on West Africa was felt in the form of cash crops, forced labor, and taxes. The French introduced the cultivation of peanuts—a crop brought by Europeans from the Americas—into their colony of Senegal, which proved fertile ground for the export of peanuts as well as for the import of such things as pagnes and eventually the machinery to make pagnes.

"And they went all the way to Senegal for 150 francs CFA," she continued.

"Only 150 F. CFA. How is that—was there a road here?" I asked.

"Forcé baara de fe. They built a road through forced labor. Famas (rulers)—tubabus and jamanatigis—were carried in hammocks by four people each. Some people travelled by horse. Mabilen and her husband paid to go by horsecart."

As French West Africa expanded to include Mali, or what was then the French Sudan, the colonizers demanded forced labor for public works projects such as railroads, dams, and roads as well as tithes of millet to feed the Army and taxes to make the colonies pay for development. Forced labor, millet, taxes. Many people slowly began to leave even the remotest of villages to heed the demands of the jamanatigis, the local rulers through whom French colonizers exerted their influence and greased their rule in southern Mali.

"Do you remember the first white man you saw?"

"Ah oui. We used to go to the market in Zantiebougou on Thursday just like we do today. A white man used to sit there in the middle of the market to buy the rice and millet we brought. He even spoke Bambara—perfectly!"

Zantiebougou used to be the home of a jamanatigi and so used to be run as an administrative center by the French. Villagers paid their taxes through their labor as well as the food they could sell in the market.

"What kind of things did you buy in the market?"

"We bought iron cauldrons to cook in. Before, we used to cook out of clay pots and get up long before daylight to light a fire. But iron pots heat up water much faster and use less firewood."

The system of taxes and cash crops, especially of cotton after the introduction of the plough, became self-sustaining because of the things money could buy. Labor-saving devices and items of convenience such as iron cauldrons and metal pots to cook in, light clothes and sandals to wear, bicycles to transport good, radios to listen to, metal buckets to carry water, enamel bowls to hold food, kerosene lamps to see by, sheets of tin for roofing, and plastic containers for multiple purposes became objects of desire and found a ready market among the masses.

"Even a little money was worth a lot. At that time, you could buy a cow for 25 F. CFA."

"What—how is that?! Cows today cost 60,000 F. CFA."

"Ah yes, but money was worth more then. A cow cost 25 F. CFA and a bride could be had for eight cows!"

Once consumer objects began to penetrate society, their possession became a measure of status. The price of marriage had always been a matter of bargaining, but with so many more objects to bargain for, the bride's family could hold out for more and more items such as pagnes and towels and sandals for various members of the family before concluding the marriage arrangement. And when a wife said her bridal price (not dowry) had been eight cows, she said it with more than a little bit of pride. At present, however, families could afford to give away no more than a single cow or two to compensate a family for the loss of a daughter in marriage. Since the tse-tse fly responsible for disease in cattle had been eradicated and cows were now used not just for beef or a bridal price or a sacrifice upon the death of an elder but also as the means to pull ploughs across fields of cotton above all, the value of cattle was considerably higher than it used to be.

"Eh Lasina, I nyesinnen don kosebe an ka ko korow la de," neighbor Aminata interjected. *You're really curious about our past.*

"Yes, because I've read a lot about it in books, but books don't always tell the truth," I said.

"Eh, seben se ngalon tige wa?" Can what is written tell a lie.

"It happens all the time. A book is only as honest as the person who writes it."

I could see Aminata had trouble believing this, but Awa nodded her assent since she trusted me. The written word was endowed with both power and righteousness since the advent of Islam and the subsequent French colonizers and their lackeys. People were instructed that the written word told the truth and they did not doubt that the scribe, for reasons of his tribe, might be less than inspired to write the truth.

"*Lasina,*" Awa said, looking up at me. "*I te na don weré, an b'a seben?*" *Won't you return another day and we'll write it down.*

"*Ayiwa, baasi te.*" *Sure, no problem.*

I made no great mental resolution to do it. I didn't like the idea of sitting before somebody with pen and paper and the undue attention it might cause. I had a good short-term memory anyway and could write down all the notes of a conversation as soon as I got home. From those notes, which made up no more than seven lines on a page, and my long-term memory, I have written this anecdote today, about two years from the date of the conversation (April 1995).

Sketch: Frog in the Village

It was a dark moonless evening in the dry season. Only the orange-yellow light of kerosene lamps lit up the empty ground in the middle of Sirakoro, a village of 800 souls in southern Mali. The elderly sat on benches, women on stools they had brought, young men on a wooden log bench to themselves, and kids on the ground. I earned a spot on a bench, unseen by the French evangelists standing in front, who were the center of attention. It was rare, after all, to see a white person in the village, and the villagers had gotten used to me, a different sort of *tubabu* or foreigner.

To a villager in southern Mali, the slightest blanchment in skin color could warrant the appendance *je* (white) or *fin* (black) to a name, such that a woman named Maje, only as dark as cocoa, was distinguished from Mafin, undeniably charcoal in color. I had somehow blended in not on the basis of skin color—and mine was bronze, a deep tan under the Sahel sun—but as a Peace Corps Volunteer, someone living on site, there to help with water resources and community projects, and having learned the language and customs of the community. There is in fact no better spy than a Peace Corps Volunteer, but we spy on the smallest details of village life and share our stories with everyone!

And here were these four French evangelists, two women and two men, so obviously foreign—in city slacks and dresses, in pointy-toed shoes and pumps, looking whiter than the muslin sheets used to pray during Ramadan or to wrap dead bodies for burial. The village was Muslim on the surface, but as usual this varied in observance, and people tended to "wear religion lightly." After all, there could be more basic needs, as captured in the Bambara proverb, "*gwa ka koro misiri ye*" translating as "the kitchen is older than the mosque." There was still the old Christian pastor who lived on the edge of town in the grand house of an American missionary and his family who left many years ago. But when the chekorobaw, or old men, in a village in southern Mali spread the word about a meeting, almost all of the village will show up, at least out of respect, as was the case this evening.

After introductions, translated by a Malian interpreter from French into Bambara, the highlight seemed to be the story of one of the women. I forget now what exactly it had to with, but I remember thinking to myself how existential her pain must have seemed to the villagers. There had been trouble in her marriage or with her parents and she had found herself all alone. She was in the depths of despair and by some or miracle or other, after a long fruitless search, she had found God through the person of Jesus Christ the Savior. She looked positively bereft still, abandoned, longing for the God she spoke of, in the throes of this existential angst and emptiness in her life. From time to time, her long blonde hair fell in tresses across her face.

The audience paid polite rapt attention but not with the emotional empathy one might expect. It wasn't the translation, I thought. Partly, it was the novelty of the occasion and hosting a group of foreigners, especially white foreigners and French people, being the former colonial power. People everywhere are fascinated by physical differences. In outlying villages far from the main road, I had experienced children touch the hair on my arms or head and adults of course comment on my hair and eyes.

This evening, however, more than being dazzled by these honored guests' skin color and foreign clothes, physical characteristics, and gestures, I could tell by the look in people's faces, as the translation continued, that they simply could not relate to the poor lady's pain and suffering. *What was it like to feel alone anyway?* Even when they were sick, Malians were not alone, since others must sit by the sick person until they got better. Only a hunter who could go off for days in the forest was really alone, and that was physical aloneness, not "lonely in the crowd" mental aloneness.

While obviously emotional, her pain seemed to a more modern anguish people could not as easily relate to. Pain and suffering to the villagers meant the untimely death of children from malaria or an adult from snakebite; or women who knew the disappointment in a young girl's marriage to an old man or more often the beating a wife might endure at the hands of an immature but dominant husband; or what the community endured at times of hunger and drought or some other natural calamity. God was in the natural world, from the moon to the animals in the forest, each with their own power, and across the sky and maybe even the heavens above. And, it was said, God was in the mosque.

Then, something odd happened. A frog suddenly jumped out from under a bench, and with the startled reaction of the people sitting on the bench, the frog then leaped towards the middle of the clearing, with any children in its way clearing a path for it with all due haste! Malians are inexplicably afraid of frogs. They live close to death in a way, subject to debilitating illnesses like Guinea worm and to lack of medicines that most of us simply take for granted. Yet, something as essentially harmless as a frog will literally send chills up the spine of almost any Malian and cause them to become immobile and gasp in unison.

Just now, their eyes shifted from the anguished French guests exclaiming about heavenly realms to the frog, its every move, its next move, wherever that might be. The French evangelists could not understand this shift of attention and, caught up in their anguish, went on about the drama and relief of salvation. Meanwhile, with the frog's every hop, more people jumped up, gasped, and moved out of the way, taking their kerosene lamps with them as the open area lost its glow.

I thought we would surely recover from the intercession of a lone frog, but when we did, it was impossible to get everyone's attention again and half the crowd had dispersed. We were left in a half-lit clearing with a smattering of women, children, and village elders. One could hear people shuffling to their homes down the dirt paths. And one could imagine the frog somewhere nearby still but likely sitting silently in the grass.

When I think of the great variety of cultural encounters and misunderstandings that exist, I sometimes recall this incident with warmth and laughter. One group of people, with their own suffering along with their own beliefs and respect for an invisible supreme being, found it hard to relate to the very learned, refined, unique anguish of someone from an entirely different society and way of living. *And along came a frog to send everyone home!*

Sketch: Point G Hospital

It didn't require any special courage of him. He was oblivious to the danger anyway.

"Are you Lasina? Mousa is sick. He cannot walk. He needs your help. Can you come?"

Looking up and seeing the young visitor and the outline of the tall tree and a fading orange sky behind it, he would remember the moment. It was the end of the day and the sun was setting fast. Mousa was in the village down the road. He took nothing with him except for an empty backpack. He closed his house, strapped on the yellow helmet, and powered on the Yamaha 125 motorcycle. Lasina expected only to bring his guardian's eldest son Mousa back home to Sirakoro.

The young man led him to an obscure round hut in the next village. It was dark and he could make out only a hunched shadowy figure inside and then the odd eerily hoarse voice of Mousa.

"Lasina, j'ai quelque chose très grand ici", Mousa said, hobbling and pointing to his groin. *Lasina, I have something very big here.* He was almost too weak to stand. The young American with the Malian name of Lasina didn't know it at the time, but it was an inguinal hernia. The bulge of an intestine into his groin. The size of a pineapple. Excruciating pain and extreme discomfort. He was losing blood internally.

"On va a Bougouni au hospital," Mousa said under his breath but with determination. He hunched over and friends helped him to Lasina's motorcycle. He struggled to get on and friends had to sit him up and curl a leg onto the other side and tie Mousa to Lasina with a piece of black rubber called *mana*. There was no time to waste. Bougouni was over 40 kilometers away. The road was bumpy and Mousa seemed to grow weaker with every bump to the point of losing consciousness. His arms, tied also with *mana*, hung over Lasina's neck and shoulders.

It was pitch black arriving in Bougouni and Lasina drove straight to the hospital. The blackout was general and not even the generator was working at the hospital. A doctor came out and said to take Mousa to the capital Bamako immediately. Lasina drove to the taxi stand, arranged for the next taxi to Bamako, dropped off his motorcycle at the Peace Corps house, and ran back through the dark streets to the taxi stand. Everything happened in pulsating speed, driven on by Mousa's weakening condition. The pain was leaving him to shift in and out of consciousness. Lasina paid the rest of the seats for the taxi and they left immediately.

It was a long three to four hour drive to Bamako. Mousa was spread out awkwardly on the back seat, wrapped in a blanket and leaning against Lasina. The night was clear, the sky full of stars, a crescent moon hanging high overhead like the handle of a sword. The taxi driver seemed uncharacteristically silent, engrossed in driving down a dark road with no lights or vehicles but with the ever-present possibility of brushing up against bicycles alongside the road or running into livestock crossing the road. Lasina tried to speak to Mousa to keep him awake or let him know he was there, but there was no response. He had fallen asleep from exhaustion or worse, his breathing labored but with the strength of a young man in the prime of his life.

Hours later, they arrived at the first hospital in Bamako. Lasina got out to explain but they would not take Mousa. They told him to go up the hill to the Point G hospital. The taxi driver obliged and they pulled out in a hurry. At the Point G hospital, a nurse came out to help bring in Mousa and a white doctor in a white coat waited inside the entrance. They hustled Mousa away quickly.

It was almost dawn. Lasina spent the night slumped on a bench in the same clothes he had worn all of the previous day. Then the white doctor came out.

"He will be fine," he said in French-accented English, "but had you waited even one more moment, he might have lost too much blood. That is how weak, how close to death he was."

The doctor explained to Lasina that Mousa had an inguinal hernia and had lost a tremendous amount of blood but the surgery had been successful. In a daze and with bloodshot eyes, Lasina heard what the doctor had to say and looked at him in admiration. He had seen no other white person working here.

"Where is his family? Do you know them?" the doctor asked. Lasina explained his circumstances, and the doctor now looked at him with a certain awe and fascination. These Americans living en brousse! In the bush! Lasina would stay like other family members at the hospital, who were expected to clean the bedpans and bring food and water to the patients. The doctor expected Mousa would be awake by mid-morning. It gave Lasina enough time to go out and get food and water for the both of them.

With relief and amazement at the chain of events, he stepped out of the Point G hospital. The early morning sun was rising gently over the city of Bamako below. Modern medicine had saved Mousa. Yet if Lasina had not been there, with his Yamaha 125, Mousa might not have made it either. How fragile life was, he thought, especially in this corner of the country of Mali he so loved and called home.

Sketch: Death in the Afternoon

We made the day's last bricks in silence. The sobering pall of death fell like a veil over us. The wind seemed suddenly to disappear and the sun to fade away gently into the soft white clouds. The slap of cement in the brick mold echoed long and unanswered.

We had only just seen the sick child. Fever, heavy breathing, clammy skin. He lay unconscious in his mother's lap. Fusini, whom I had trained to fix wells and brought to this village, had advised the women in the hut to bathe the boy in the leaves of a certain tree. I had promised to take the child to Garalo that night if he did not soon regain consciousness. Then no sooner had we started work in the afternoon than his little life had passed away. A mother's love and burden, nine months inside and twice as long on her back, all over in the briefest instant.

The child who passed was the grandson of Fasera, the head of family whose well Fusini and I had come to repair. The child's father had been helping us mix cement and lay bricks under the mango tree next to the well. We quickly washed the mold and the shovels. We walked past the hut where we had seen the boy, and in which we could now hear the women weeping, and into the courtyard, where we sat on one edge of a mat with the *chekoroba*, the big old man, the grandfather. I had met Fasera twice before and had come to look and expect the playful flash in his round eyes and the irrepressible energy in his movements. It was unusual to see him so suddenly sad and dejected. A grandchild was gone.

"We drank coffee this morning and ate porridge together. He went to his grandmother's hut after lunch. Then we heard a scream inside and found that the sickness had seized him."

We sat on one end of a courtyard bounded by three concessions. Fasera spoke like a disembodied voice, empty and far away, like a ghost. He wore a sleeveless cotton shirt and thick homespun cotton trousers which came down to his knees. Quiet and still, he sat with his legs drawn up and his arms over another grandson. The blankness of his gaze, eyes perhaps too old and too weary to cry, was offset only by the moist and intense eyes of the child between his knees who was crying softly.

Men on bicycles had spread news of the death through the village and the young men had left to dig the grave. Children walked about aimlessly and expectantly, sniffling their noses and holding back confused sobs. Groups of old women arrived and filed into the concession behind us to wash the corpse and console the grieving mother. One by one, the elders of the village entered the concession and sat down on the mats and offered their benedictions.

"May God have mercy on the corpse. May the resting place be cool. May God take these blessings."

There was little else to say. Some greeted Fusini and me, and others whispered in hushed voices. The sun continued its slow descent into the horizon and the light faded and grew dull. Word came that the grave was ready. Immediately a young Islamic preacher, the mori, came out of the concession behind us leading a group of men carrying the corpse, which was wrapped in a white shroud and rolled in a straw mat. Women crowded behind them, most stopping at the concession walls, over which they hung their arms and looked on mournfully. We rose as one, walked forward, removed our footwear, lined up, and faced east as the mori led us in prayer over the corpse.

"Alaaa-hu akbar."

We looked up at the dim blue sky in unison and looked quickly back down. The covered child lay before us like a sacrifice, an offering, a petition. I felt like the heavens would open up at any moment and scoop up our little bundle.

Suddenly it was over. Grief was driven back that much, the boy was given up, we were more in acceptance. Two young men swept up the body in the mat like so many dead leaves and a procession of youth marched swiftly to the gravesite. The first steps in dealing with grief and loss as a community had been taken and this knowledge seemed to spread over those of us left in the courtyard. The old men sat with their lags drawn and relayed a speech among themselves as was customary when taking care of more routine affairs.

The burial procession soon returned and washed their hands and hoes in a bucket in front of us and dutifully filed into the concession behind us. The elders were preparing to depart but the young mori stood up now and addressed us. He spoke quickly, as if repeating a well-rehearsed prayer and with apparently as little regard for the content of the speech and its effect on one particularly anguished old man.

"I have something to say before we leave. I would say this only to the family concerned, but the old man has refused to acknowledge the Word of Allah for too long now and I will say it to all of you assembled here… This family's name is tarnished. The younger brother is a Muslim but the old one has still not accepted the word of the true God and His Prophet. And he does not raise his children as Muslims… Sharia demands that I, a marabout, trained in the Koran and entrusted to carry out the teachings of Prophet Mohammed, that I not pray over the corpse of a kafiri, an infidel. But because the younger brother pleaded with me and because had not yet reached seven years of age, I have made an exception, in accordance with the law. Had the child been more than seven years of age——"

"Enough!"

Fasera had risen like a shot and his round eyes locked on the mori like a vise. Anger coursed through Fasera like pain through a wild boar shot in the forest. The gaze, vacant and numb only moments earlier, was now livid with emotion. Short but stout, his arms looked more like branches and his legs like tree trunks. The veins in his thick neck bulged with anger as the pent-up energy of his compact frame burst all restraints, like a raging river rushing into a dry stream bed.

"Bastard! Kafiri!" he poured forth like a torrent, overwhelming the stunned young mori.

"Shameless, ungrateful bastard!" he repeated, rapidly giving vent to his anger.

The crowd rose and I with them. Fusini moved to help restrain Fasera and others quickly escorted the mori out of the courtyard but not out of sight. Women peered over the concession walls and children looked on in confusion.

"I fed your father when he couldn't feed himself. I paid your taxes when no one else could. Kafiri, you say—talk! Your own mother drinks wine with us. Kafiri!"

The elders endeavoured to calm Fasera down but to little avail. A group of young men had gathered around the mori outside the concession. I could see Fusini, a pious believer himself, remonstrating with the young mori who looked surprisingly limp and shaken. They led him into the neighboring group of huts and houses.

When he could no longer fix his eyes on the mori, Fasera's fury began to abate slowly. Yet the crystal point of his anger, the ardent focus of his frustration, could not subside so easily, mingling instead with the other griefs and torments it had awakened. He suddenly turned about and marched into his concession. It was dark now.

Notes:

1. The boy died of cerebral malaria, as I was to learn later. The load of malarial parasites had infected the brain and not only the liver and kidney. Children especially died of cerebral malaria. Of the four main strains of malaria to infect humans, *plasmodium falciparum* is the most lethal and, like many lethalities, is predominant in sub-Saharan Africa more than anywhere else. For example, in India, it is *vivax* malaria, not *falciparum* malaria.

2.   Fasera, while an individual and personality himself, also represented an older Mali, one before Islam, which came to Mali first through trade across the Sahara and then through different tribes in the savannah like the Fulfulde converting to Islam. Other peoples, especially in the more forested areas, remained "animist." If I asked, what did you believe in before Islam, the response would be, *"Bamana cogo"*, or "the Bambara way." The world was inhabited by spirits of many types, good and bad. Rituals using fetishes, which could be masks draped with a special animal skin, were used to appease the spirits. People believed in the power of the fetish. For example, if the rain was delayed in arrival, it might require a special ceremony.

    Alternatively, in the old days, if someone had stolen something, the people would "go to the fetish" in "the sacred forest", perform a ceremony, and come back and announce, "If the thief does not return what was stolen in 8 days time, then something terrible will happen to him or her." If everyone believes in the fetish, one can imagine the psychology of the thief and the feeling of fear and the inner compulsion to return whatever is stolen. As a result, one person remarked to me, "When Islam came, theft increased!" The explanation? Islam said put away the fetishes.

3.   The mori represented a new crusading version of Islam that was spreading in southern Mali in the 1990s. Oddly, "Bambara" is the term used by the French and outsiders for the people and their language whereas the Bambara call themselves *Bamana*. Literally, *bamana* meant "those who have refused their master", and some believe the name was given by Muslims who traded salt for gold from the animist people in the forests south of the savannah. Islam in southern Mali was still relatively new, as in decades only. The new version of Islam was being spread by cassettes and itinerant preachers like the mori. What made it new was a certain strictness and exclusivity, such as saying not to smoke or drink, and that failure to do so meant you were not a true Muslim. For

example, old men like Fasera might go to the mosque and fast time to time or even for the whole month of Ramadan fast but it didn't stop them from believing in the fetish, eating wild boar from the forest, and drinking.

4. Alcohol in southern Mali was available only at certain times of year, depending on the seasons and what could be harvested, since it was palm wine, honey wine, and millet beer. Further, consuming alcohol was ritualistic not merely recreational. It was said of alcohol, "a be hakili dayele", it opens the mind. The old men in particular would gather, drink palm wine, and philosophize. Instead of shirking work, they were proud to work. I once heard Fasera and the old men give a mock evangelism. They called it blominnaw wajuli, or wine drinker's evangelism, in mock imitation of the itinerant Islamic evangelisms. It went like this:

"N fa y'e blo min—ne fana b'a min!" My father drank wine—so do I!

"N ba y'e blo min—ne fana b'a min!" My mother drank—so do I!

"Blo min ka fisa." Drinking is better.

"Kossebe, kossebe." Very much, very much—amen.

"Blo minnaw, olu la banaw man cha." Drinkers, their sicknesses are few.

"Blo minnaw, u be si jan soro." Drinkers, they live a long time.

"Tigi, tigi, tigi." You said it.

"Blo minnaw, u be baarake fo ka temen." Drinkers, they work harder than anyone else.

*"Cheu—friends, "*Fasera said dramatically, a plastic cup in one hand, a horse-tail fly whisk in another, and a triangular cotton hat cocked elfishly on his head.

"N fa y'e blo min, ne fana b'a min!" My father drank wine—and so do I!"

Narrative: Fighting for a Matrône

As anyone who has worked in development will know, at some point there are politics involved—vested interests, which can be quite obscure until touched, rankled, upset. One such incident in Mali is worth recounting for the multiple issues it threw up.

A Volunteer several years before me had helped build a maternity, so that women from Sirakoro and surrounding villages could give birth in safer conditions attended to by a trained midwife or *matrône*. That maternity, a small building with two rooms, had been closed ever since the matrône got married to someone in the village. When I asked why, I was told because the *médecin chef* in Bougouni, the *cercle* town or administrative center, had said that only an unmarried female could be the*matrône*. But why is that? So he could sleep with her when on tour, the old men told me. Is that so? The *chekorobaws*, or old men, wanted to get the maternity reopened and asked me to go with them to Bougouni and make an appeal to the *médecin chef*.

We went one day as a small delegation, a group of five or six. The *médecin chef* said the village is free to find a *matrône* but the following conditions would apply: one, she must be a qualified midwife; two, the village will have to give her a house and food and will have to pay her salary for one year; three, she must attend training in Bougouni for three months; and four, she must be unmarried and must agree never to marry. The villagers could perhaps understand that she be unmarried but how could she agree never to marry? Every woman beyond a certain age, without exception, was married. Living unmarried, villagers thought, would create problems, would not even be safe. This is why they thought he only wanted to sleep with her. When the villagers questioned the last criterion, the médecin chef became suddenly and visibly upset. He spoke down to the *chekorobas*, the revered village elders, in a hostile, derogatory, and contemptuous way I had never seen Malians use. Was it his education, his position, his authority, the fact that he came from another tribe and a different part of Mali, the dialect and humble homespun cotton dress of the old men, the questioning of his conditions, a feeling of guilt perhaps or knowing in his right mind that he had no right to impose a condition based on marital status, or what?

In any case, we had heard the conditions. When we reached back home, the chekorobas told me there was an influential son of the village, named "Falaba Isa" Traore, living in Bamako and maybe he could help. They asked me to meet with him the next time I visited the capital. In fact, he was a well-known filmmaker. With only the vaguest description of where to find him—no phone number, no address, no office—I wound up locating "Falaba Isa" at his home in Bamako. He had not forgotten his roots, which were in Falaba, the village next to Sirakoro and thus the "stage name" he went by.

Falaba Isa wanted time to find someone and asked that I meet him on a return trip to Bamako. When I did, again as a walk-in with no appointment, he was excited because he had found a candidate. He sent for Fanta so I could meet her. I felt I was in the presence of two modern and sophisticated people speaking the same language. There was only one problem: Fanta was officially still married, although a divorce was in process. Isa questioned why all this attention on her marriage status, shouldn't it be on her qualifications and her willingness to work? How many people with education and training would be willing to work in a village? Why does it even matter what her marital status is? It's her commitment that should matter. He was right, of course, and echoing my values. He suggested I take Fanta to Bougouni and present her to the médecin chef. Fanta said she needed just a day or two and she would be ready. She was as decisive and decided in her mind as Falaba Isa. She also had a one-year old daughter.

We met the *médecin chef* in Bougouni. He looked at her and her daughter and repeated the condition that she be single. She was still married. It didn't matter that she was separated and her divorce was in progress, he said. He also seemed to say that she should not have a child. And he said she should agree in writing not to marry! He seemed upset that, contrary to all expectations, the village had actually found a qualified *matrône*.

These extra conditions were too much and nonsensical to both Fanta and to me. Having come all this way, we then went to Sirakoro. The village was thrilled to have her but perplexed at the blockage being put up in Bougouni. A health center worker in the district town of Zantiebougou also told me that is was not only the *médecin chef* whose responsibility it was to fill the position but also the *chef d'arrondisement* or district administrator in Zantiebougou. In fact, I had tried to meet with him, but he had refused to meet with me. I found out through the grapevine that, in a phrase I didn't forget, *"il est alergique au blancs"*, meaning "he is allergic to whites" and that he refused to do anything because *"un blanc est intervenu dans le processus"*, meaning a white person is involved in the process. Well how about that! It so happened that he too was from another region and tribe of Mali. It was general government policy post-Independence to place people of other regions and tribes in positions of local authority based on the idea that, without family members in the area they were responsible for, they would be less susceptible to bribery and favoritism. However, it also seemed they cared nothing at all for the people!

When it came to my further attention, that the *chef d'arrondissement* in Zantiebougou had threatened me, saying if I did not withdraw from the process his hand would strike me, then I decided to let my superiors in Bamako know. I wrote a four-page letter in French with timeline, outlining everything the village and I had done. I asked my supervisor to let the Minister of Health know what's going on. I asked another Volunteer who was going to Bamako to deliver it to my supervisor personally.

Some weeks later, on a Friday which was market day in Sirakoro, I was in a relaxed mood sitting in a chair outside my house when a girl came running from the market and said:

"Lasina, Lasina, they are calling you from the market. They want you to come."

"Who is 'they?'"

"I don't know."

"Well, tell me about them."

"They came in big cars, two big cars. They are wearing nice clothes. One I think is from the health center in Zantiebougou."

"Really?"

"Ah oui!"

I was in simple clothes, my pair of pagne pants and a shirt. I walked up to the market. A big crowd had assembled and were sitting under the trees as though waiting for an announcement. The *chekorobas* and the *musokorobas* (women elders) were present. It seemed like I was the last one to show up. And there were several visitors, including the health centre director from Zantiebougou, his assistant, and the *médecin chef* from Bougouni. I walked up to them and, according to custom, welcomed the *médecin chef* to Sirakoro. He said they had come to announce the reopening of the maternity. That is very good news, I said. What are you waiting for, tell it to the people. At that point, one of the old men of Sirakoro used a proverb I'll never forget.

"Lasina! Fali te den wolo jama nye la." A donkey does not give birth in front of a crowd.

"Meaning?" I said. They all laughed. Everyone was surprisingly relaxed.

"Come here, let's talk first."

We went behind a building and talked. The *médecin chef* said: one, I will direct the health team in Zantiebougou to reopen the maternity immediately, they will bring the supplies in two days time; two, I have accepted Fanta as the matrône for Sirakoro; three, as the chekorobas already stated when they came to my office, they have just said again that the village will take care of Fanta's house, food, and salary for one year.

"What about that condition you put that she be single or at least divorced?"

"Didn't I just say I've accepted Fanta? *Il faut pas preocuper!*" Not to worry!

"And what about the *chef d'arrondisement* in Zantiebougou?" I asked, looking at the Zantiebougou health centre staff. "Is he in agreement?"

"Yes, he is. I've talked to him. Don't worry about him. He is fine."

The *médecin chef* was smiling broadly. This was quite unbelievable. There was nothing to disagree about. Evidently, going to the top—belling the cat, rattling the cage, blowing the whistle—had worked! I thought of my supervisor in Bamako and had to smile. With no phones, she had no means of telling me what she had done, but I had guessed correctly.

A Peace Corps Volunteer is supposed to work only with and through local counterparts. Avoid all outside money, outside contacts. Rely on local resources, local wisdom. Learn how to help, then transfer skills. This is a tall order, and limited in its way. What if the authorities whose job is health or education or some other aspect of development are neglectful or corrupt? The Peace Corps Volunteer is to be a connector, can connect the village to other resources and occasionally advocate for the village, while endeavouring at all times to do this with village leaders or a village committee.

Overcoming that bureaucratic hurdle, now the work began. But it was good to re-start a full maternal child health program in the village, including "baby weighing" or child growth monitoring, following up on underweight babies and ensuring they got adequate nutrition, ensuring safe births in the assigned area of six villages that included working with and not against traditional birth attendants or dais, and organizing health talks of all kinds.

Fali te den wolo jama nyela! I had never thought about how donkeys gave birth, but it must be true, everyone told me, donkeys never give birth in front of a crowd.

Sketch: Blind Chief

He should stop and greet the chief. It was late in the dry season and he was on his way back from work in another village. He drove the Yamaha 125 motorcycle along the familiar winding paths of Falaba village, stopping to enquire where the chief was and coasting up slowly to a round hut. It was the type of round hut—compact, mud brick, straw off, two open entrances, perched on a rise—favored by old men as a sort of resting place.

"I ni tile, dugutigi." Good afternoon, chief.

"M bah, i ni tile. I ka kene wa? Yen mogow?" Good afternoon, how are you, how are the people over there?

The chief wore rough homespun cotton trousers and a sleeveless top. He lay resting on his side but promptly leaned up upon being greeted. He looked with his eyes but could not see. Many long years ago, he had contracted river blindness on a public works project in the north. It was actually a project of forced labor during the epoch of French colonization and that the French stopped only in 1946.

The visitor and the chief went through the greetings at some length. Then the chief asked sharply:

"I togo be di?" What's your name.

"Lasina, Lasina Diara."

"Eh Lasina, tubabu Lasina? You really trick people!"

He said he did not know he was speaking to a foreigner, that Lasina spoke Bambara like a native.

"Lasina, i be bamanankan men de!" Lasina, you really speak Bambara!

It was the highest compliment Lasina could be paid, and that too by a chief and a blind man.

"I togo be fo i ko, Lasina—I ye baara nyuman ke, I ye baara chaman ke de." Your name will be spoken after you are gone. You have done great work, you have done a lot of work.

His wooden staff lay propped up against the wall of the hut next to one of those old plastic containers once used for motor oil and now used for drinking water. He sat on a plastic mat meant as a prayer mat.

As Lasina drove away, he thought again of how much he loved these people, this community, this country and how much he would miss it all when he had to leave a few weeks hence. Truly, it wasn't really fair. His life was about mobility, their life was about stability, rootedness, place. But who was the poorer? What would happen to him now? Moving about had its moments of beauty like these, but it was only because he had stayed for two years, not as a tourist but as a guest and worker. It was the people of Mali who were the source of all the beauty of the place and it was only because he had gotten to know the people, while performing labors of purpose, that he felt the attachment that he did to the people of Mali, a country that could not have been more different than his own.

Sketch: Leaving the Village

He held it in. He had to. He could not break down and cry in front of so many people. It was time to go and they had come to see him off.

The morning would bring an end to many moons of village life. Two years prior, he had arrived insecure, uncertain, with trepidation. He was reluctant even to leave the house sometimes or go very far in a culture that valued wandering around, visiting, and greeting—*yaala yaala*, they called it. It had taken him weeks to overcome the inclination to close up his windows and pretend he wasn't home so that he could read a *Newsweek* magazine brought from the regional capital.

Now they were all his friends, young and old, children and elderly, men and women. He loved being able to visit a neighbor at any time as well as to hold his door open and greet anyone who came into his compound. He had attained a certain comfort and integration in Malian village life that might hardly be conceivable for someone coming from such a different land and culture, that of the fast-paced, consumerist, modern lifestyle.

The build-up to his departure had lasted months, it seemed. Even in the first year, people would ask when he was leaving. "But two years is such a short time", they would say. "When our people go abroad, they stay for 10 or 15 years." Time and relationships were viewed differently in the village. Time was more elastic, relationships closer. Sentiments counted for something.

And yet, unto almost this last day, he would wonder about the sentiments. He could still feel that people always wanted something from him. It was usually something small, such as a photograph taken on market day. Or it could be something else, such as his bicycle, now that he was leaving.

His closest friends in the village weren't like that. They always had much to converse with him about and seldom wanted anything. His adopted mother, Awa, never asked for anything nor did his closest friend Jamaseri. Instead, they shared sentiments, openly saying, *"I be na nyenafinba bila yan, nyenafin belebeleba"—you will leave a big memory here, a very big memory. "I togo be fo i d'a la"*, people would say, *your name will be spoken after you.*

In the end, he had to go. Once tempted to stay and do a third year, he had begun to feel that if he stayed a third year, he might never leave. He was becoming more like a Bambara with every passing day and week. The girls of marriageable age, especially in the villages where he worked, appeared that much more attractive to him, and he entertained the thought of what it would be like to marry and settle down and live here, using his unique connections to the outer world to foster community development projects at a level beyond what he had been involved in to that point.

"*N ye here soro yan,*" he would say. *I have found happiness here.*

"*If you have found happiness here, won't you stay?*" they would respond.

He might explain why he had to leave, that his contract was over. But you can stay on, they would say. But I don't have the money. But you can start a business. He would then explain that his mother was ill, and that is why he must leave. Only this they would understand and not question.

"*N'i ma here soro yen, i be segin ka na*"—*if you don't find happiness there, come back.*

It was time now, and he turned to go. A circle of friends, young and old, gathered round. Eyes and faces were uncharacteristically subdued, downcast, and resigned. A metal trunk and backpack was strapped to the rack of his Yamaha 125 motorcycle. He put on his yellow helmet and threw a leg over the bike and mounted it ever so reluctantly. He then engaged the kick-starter and gave it a little gas. All that was left was to put it in gear.

His eyes welled up. The flood was coming. He looked out from under his glasses and the yellow helmet at the people around him. He then did the inevitable and put the motorcycle in gear. He drove away for the last time, slowly between the tall dry grasses, beneath the tall trees.

The involuntary tears came now, streaming out of his eyes and down his face. He felt the salt and the warmth and later the coolness of their wake, salt clouding his vision. When was the last time he cried like this? When would he cry again? Why was he crying now?

Like this, he guided his motorcycle for the final time onto the dirt and muddy path along the side of the rutted and watery paved road.

The village had meant the world to him, in more ways than he could fathom or express. Everything he had learned from people who were outwardly poor and humble but inwardly so very human and giving of themselves. Everything about what it meant to live close to nature, sensitive to every change in the air, to every drop of moisture. Everything he had learned about himself, a journey from fear and wariness to faith and confidence.

If he must leave, he would carry the village in his heart, carry the country of Mali in his heart.

Reflection: "Peace Corps Made Me Who I Was"

From those lean and raw years, ages 20 – 25, when I was "alone in a crowd", I had now both "found my tribe" among Peace Corps Volunteers and my purpose in being of practical use to people.

About 20 years later, I went back to the Peace Corps as Country Director, first for the program in Peru and then in Mozambique. I wrote the following in Peru in the year 2014, reflecting on my motivations to be a Country Director. I was keenly aware of what Peace Corps and Mali had done for me. The opportunity to be the leader of a Peace Corps post was partly to re-live my service through the Volunteers I was to support.

. . .

I was a Volunteer over 20 years ago, in 1991 – 93, before the cellphone and the Internet, which seems now like a different era altogether. News in English came on shortwave radio via the BBC in the mornings and news in Bambara, the primary language of Mali, came on Mali's lone radio station at dusk in the evenings. I picked up mail in the regional capital of Bougouni once every two weeks at most. Although there were four telephone lines available at the post office in Bougouni, I never called home even once, partly because I didn't want to have to shout into the phone and partly because I wrote regularly to my parents, 48 times in just over two years. ***I had also put the United States behind me for two years, in the sense that I had fully embraced living in Africa on Africa's terms in African style.*** In an important way, that is what the Peace Corps—the brainchild over 50 years ago of President Kennedy,

Sargent Shriver, and others interested in grassroots development and the international youth service movement—is all about.

I still marvel that Peace Corps could take someone like me, 24 years old with a B.A. degree in history, and train me to contribute to village development in a setting so foreign and so unlike anything I had ever known. I became an accepted and valued member of the community, probably my greatest satisfaction of Peace Corps Volunteer service. I could speak the language, eat the food, and live and work like a Malian. People knew that my main job was to build deep and lasting wells for clean drinking water, using a simple and effective technique that I could teach local masons. They also knew that I was available to help on various other community projects such as adult literacy, acquiring a matrône and starting a maternal child health education program, and acquiring a diesel mill to grind grain. And when I wasn't "working", I worked alongside villagers in the fields, went to ceremonies marking births, marriages, and deaths, and drank tea and socialized in the evenings.

Fixing the stilling basin of a small dam, Mali, 1991

In the process of living this way, I assimilated many of the values of the village. Most of all, I came to value ***time spent with others*** and any conversation from the banal to the stimulating to simple acknowledgements and shared silences. It is well said that Africans in general are a social people. I put my Western notions of privacy and space to the side, though not without difficulty and gently easing my way into the full flow of village life.

I also came to value ***time spent outdoors and living close to nature***. Such was outdoor living, and such even were the windows in my two-room house, that the wind never blew in my village without my being aware of it. Many nights were spent looking at the stars or watching the lightning light up the sky in the distance or listening to the sounds of the frogs before a rain and the insects after a rain. Many days were spent observing even the slightest changes in the temperature, in the color of the grass, in the soft and hard ground, in the growth of the corn, cotton, and millet in the fields, in the birds that flew overhead or perched in the trees, in the mangos and tamarind fruits that ripened with the seasons, and in the health of the chickens, cattle, goats, sheep, donkeys, and other animals that we lived with. I was a witness to tremendous rainstorms, sometimes filled with thunder and lightning.

I also learned ***what it meant to live in a traditional society***, the lot of humankind for most of its history, where everyone had a defined role. These roles were determined most of all by age and gender. The old men were the key protagonists and arbiters of decision-making. The old women also held sway. Men who were householders or young unmarried men came together for specific tasks, often physical labor or communal work of one form or another. Men married by age 25 and girls by age 16, although both were often betrothed up to 4 years earlier. Boys were circumcised by 5 years of age and girls by 7 years of age.

Nature gave life its rhythms and men and women gave it routines, proverbs, and meaning. For every season, there was an activity and for every situation, there was a behavior. For example, what one did and said at times of eating, at times of greeting or calling it a night, at times of a birth, marriage, or death was all remarkably consistent—surely the sign of a cohesive culture—varying only according to the occasion.

I admired the social organization, communal spirit, and also the sense of humor. I lamented the illnesses and untimely deaths, especially of children. I lamented times of over-work, especially when people were dead beat and food supplies were running low, right before the first corn was harvested. I lamented a certain stifling of human development, where I could see different talents of people and yet everyone had to be a farmer. I admired people's knowledge of the environment, including for medicinal purposes, but feared the ease at which certain beliefs, gossip, and untruth could take advantage of ignorance, to the detriment of health and even harmonious relations with others.

I could never accept three things: that it was acceptable for husbands to beat wives; forced marriage, not merely arranged marriage, especially between an old man and a young girl; and female circumcision, which was designed to control women. I came to these conclusions separately and later realized that they all had to do with the treatment of women. And yet, I knew women and the society well enough that I would never think of the village women I knew as "oppressed" somehow. After all, they could speak to men, joke with men, did not have to lower their eyes, and they walked around the fields and sometimes the village without their tops on. Women were respected and, like anyone else in the village, including the un-pretty, the crippled, and the mentally unwell, everyone seemed to have their basic dignity. They could look you in the eye and speak to you freely.

Just as I carried the U.S. and my values to Mali, I carried Mali and what I had learned back to the U.S. with me. True to the saying, I felt I had gotten much more out of Peace Corps than I had given. I was the recipient of so many kindnesses and so much learning from Malians that it was not going to be possible to re-pay it. And I had changed: ***more self-confident; more observant; and more patient***. Having absorbed the sociability of Malians, in a society where no one is made fun of, mocked, or ridiculed for what they say, I had also become ***less introverted.***

Peace Corps also helped me realize that I had an ***uncommon talent for languages***. Whereas others had to pore over their lessons in French and then in Bambara, I was able to recall the words and grammar and reproduce both languages without having to spend much time studying or doing homework. It was as if Bambara came naturally to me.

I had also made many fine friends as a Volunteer, since Peace Corps is a magnet for attracting people with certain ideals and a sense of service plus a sense of adventure. I had never had closer friendships, not in my two years in the military nor even in my childhood, which is saying something.

It was the first time in my life that I felt so richly alive, so obviously in the right place with the right people doing the right things.

So, one can imagine, I wanted to re-capture some of that experience. I never quite could, but I did meet Returned Peace Corps Volunteers (RPCVs) in the U.S. and a few Malians here and there. The Peace Corps continued to be a path for me in ways, since it led me to the Shriver Peaceworker Program at UMBC in Baltimore in which I spent a summer and fall semester. Then, my RPCV status led me to a Peace Corps Fellows Program at UT-Health Science Center School of Public Health in El Paso. As part of my graduate school education in public health, I was fixed up with an internship at the local health department thanks to the Peace Corps Fellows Program. In my second year of graduate school, I was able to use this relationship with the health department to obtain a competitive fellowship paid for by the CDC.

In important ways, as a person and in my schooling and career, Peace Corps had made me who I was.

Lima, Peru 2014

Sketch: The Caregiver

He came home late one afternoon, by taxi, directly from the airport, international arrivals, multiple bags. The apartment door was unlocked. His mother was sitting on the couch, propped up by pillows, her socked feet on a stool, her knees together separated by a thin orange cushion. She was asleep though her earphones were on.

He promptly put down his bags and strode to the kitchen where he could hear the water running. His father was washing a towel of his mother's in the sink. It was a Saturday afternoon and his father wore a white shirt and dark pants and brown sandals. His skin was the color of mahogany.

The image of his father—who had cared for his mother by himself the whole time he had been away—quickened his heart while he felt himself catching a deep breath. A tear loosened uncontrollably.

His father, looking up from his glasses, brightened and said, "So you've come! That's good, that's good." He continued washing and quickly finished up.

"Yes, Daddy", he could only mumble in a watery way through the constrictions of his throat, choked up as he was.

"How was the trip? Come, let's sit down."

They sat at the dining table, which was also his father's work table. There was a floor lamp in the corner, a beige and black and red tapestry on the wall, a yellow ashtray next to where his father sat. His mother sat on the couch in front of them. The TV was still on, the earphones on. She was still dozing away.

It had been 2 years and 5 months and he hadn't been home. He had been away in Africa—in Mali, West Africa, in a little village—in an assignment that brought him great joy and satisfaction. The people there naturally asked him, "If you are happy here, then why must you leave?" Living as they did, taking care of large families, he learned to say in their language, "My mother is ill, that is why I must go home." This they immediately understood.

And yet it was his father who devoted himself to the herculean task of taking care of a spouse with Multiple Sclerosis (MS) while continuing to work. Retirement was near but caregiving was constant. Besides a paid nurse visit in the morning and the arrival of a helper on weekdays, his father tended to the rest and to all the needs on weekends. From morning, he cleaned her, bathed her, changed her clothes, lifted and transported her on the Hoyer lift, made her comfortable on the couch, and fed her through the stomach tube. He washed innumerable towels, often due to the unavoidable slobbering of someone unable even to swallow her own saliva. He applied lotion to her dry skin and tended to her hair and hairbands, fingernails and toenails, nose, ears, and the tiny yellow cakes that arose in the corner of her eyes. From time to time, there was a doctor's visit too, and the ordeal of a wheelchair and ambulance ride.

Besides going to the office, his father had not left her truly alone for years. He was always there.

She would respond by opening her eyes, moving her pupils ever so slightly, attempting to speak though too often it ended in a dry cough. Every now and then, her legs below the knees would twitch involuntarily or her throat would make spasms. She had not been able to really speak for years. Undoubtedly, she could listen and understand, but her capacity was much diminished. She spent an increasing number of hours in a state of drowsiness, such that she was essentially asleep most of the day, drifting in and out of consciousness, unaware really of time or the seasons, sensitive only to the comings and goings of her caregivers.

This is what it meant to live with the ravages of multiple sclerosis.

Narrative: India Immersion

For someone like me, it would prove to be much harder to re-adjust to the United States than it had been to adjust to Mali. Peace Corps provided its outgoing Volunteers with a "readjustment allowance", which amounted to $4,800 at that time. I spent my money on travel.

Leaving Mali, I first spent two weeks in Paris and Switzerland. Then I met up with friends from Peace Corps in Boston and we drove to Washington D.C. Then, I reached Houston and met my parents again after two years and five months, as depicted in the sketch "Caregiver."

Soon afterwards, my father left for India and I was left to take care of my mother while he was away. I faced the reality that I was back where I began. I would relax by sitting on the narrow enclosed porch of my parents' apartment home in the humid heat of June in Houston. All around me, I felt the absence of community that was my solace in Mali. I felt the faster pace of life, impersonal and competitive, that came with a big city. I had illusions and no clear direction.

In the way I responded to Mali, might I not respond to India? What would I do there?

When my father returned, I then left for India, reaching on 2 August 1993, which date I remembered because I came down with malaria on 16 August, exactly two weeks later, which is the incubation period for vivax malaria. I had avoided malaria all that time in Mali.

As for what to do, before leaving I conceived the idea of a dharamshaala (pilgrim's hostel) in Kushinagar, where the Buddha passed away. In addition, I also thought I could do something in the way of agriculture in Kushinagar, a place I'd never been and knew nothing about! But my bhua's husband, Kamaljit uncle, had commercial agriculture experience and he managed a successful farm outside Bangalore, growing calla lilies for sale to hotels and other outlets in the city. So after visiting relatives in Delhi, I would go to Bangalore and see about the farm and what I could learn. It didn't take me long to realize that something like that was not for me, but the farm manager Wajid advised me what would make money in Kushinagar: coconut palms interspersed with papaya trees and mulberry trees in another plot, to cultivate silk for the silk industry in Varanasi.

Eventually, I would make it to Kushinagar. Before getting there, however, a different entrepreneurial vision overtook me. Feeling nostalgic for Mali and seeing that the poor in south India could afford clay roofing tiles known as Mangalore roofing tiles, I conceived the idea of starting a Mangalore tile factory in Mali. I wound up doing a detailed feasibility study that included attaching myself to a tile factory outside Mangalore for two weeks. Starting the project, including shipping the tile press from India to Mali, was going to cost me $10,000, which I didn't have and would need to take a loan for.

Then, in December, I calculated just how much wood was involved in the roofing structure to hang tiles, and knowing how expensive and more dear wood was in Mali, I realized it was a break-even gamble with marginal profit. Tiles also needed to compete against tin roofing sheets. Even though tiles would be cooler in summer and warmer in winter, their cost counting the wood needed to hang tiles would be about the same. A day or two after looking and re-looking at the figures, I could feel my mind talk to my heart and tell me, no, this isn't going to work, at least not like you think, it's just not worth it, don't do it.

Before coming to that decision, I was at ease travelling around India and getting to know the country. I travelled simply, with my small green REI backpack, a Lonely Planet guide, and no reservations anywhere. I would show up and, if I didn't like the place, then find somewhere else in the vicinity. I immersed myself in many books, fiction and non-fiction, about India. I always tried to take a city tour or monument tour and I became a great fan of the Archaeological Survey of India.

A friend who grew up with me in Parkwood Apartments in Houston, Ursula from Peru, travelled around Europe and France, in particular, and it opened a whole world to her of art, intellectual interest, and the good life. For me, this trip to India was similar, except that instead of art, it was architecture and intellectually, it was history mainly, and spiritually, it was religion—which includes both archaeology and history in India. It was also society, understanding Indian society, customs, attitudes, and politics as well. Unlike my two previous trips, this was total immersion in all things Indian, and getting to know family members at a much deeper level.

"Discovery of India" Itinerary – August 1993 to January 1994

1. Delhi

2. Bangalore

3. Mysore, Srirangapatnam

4. *Bangalore

5. Madikeri (Coorg), Belur, Halebid

6. *Bangalore

7. Madras (now Chennai)

8. Mahabalipuram

9. Pondicherry (and Auroville for a day)

10. Tiruchirappalili (Trichy)

11. Madurai

12. Trivandrum via Nagercoil

13. Kovalam beach

14. Changanacherry to Allepey (backwater trip)

15. Cochin

16. Ernakulam

17. Coimbatore (arrived over Western Ghats by bus)

18. Ootacamund ("Ooty")

19. Mangalore (arrived over Western Ghats by bus - and Udipi for a day)

20. Panjim, Goa (arrived over Western ghats by train)

21. Margao

22. Bombay (by plane)

23. Aurangabad (arrived over Western ghats by bus - and Ajanta and Ellora for a day)

24. Bhopal
25. Sanchi
26. Agra – Fatehpur Sikri
27. *Delhi
28. Hardwar
29. Rishikesh
30. *Delhi
31. McCluskeyganj, Bihar
32. Bodh Gaya via Hazaribagh
33. Rajgir
34. Varanasi via Patna (and Sarnath for a day)
35. Kushinagar via Deoria
36. Lumbini, Nepal (via Sonauli)
37. Lucknow
38. *Delhi
39. Ranikhet
40. Dhikhala (Corbett N.P. - Ramnagar bus and Garzia mandir enroute)
41. *Delhi
42. *Mangalore (and Calicut aka Kozikhode for a day)
43. Hassan
44. Belur – Halebid
45. Shravanabelagola
46. Hampi (Vijayanagar)
47. Bombay via Hubli, Belgaum, and Kolhapur
48. *Delhi

49. Jamshedpur via Calcutta
50. Calcutta
51. *Varanasi
52. *Delhi

Sketch: The Balls of his Feet

It was still morning when I arrived in Kushinagar. I got off the bus behind an elderly man in a yellow robe. His name, he said, was Buddhamitra or "friend of the Buddha." He ran the traveler's hostel in this out of the way town where Gautama Buddha, one-time prince of the Sakyas, died a mortal death and passed into Nirvana some twenty-five centuries ago.

He led me to a room full of books behind his office where I lay my bag down. A busload of Sri Lankan pilgrims was occupying all the rooms at present, but after lunch they would be leaving for Lumbini, site of the Buddha's birth just across the border in Nepal. I changed my clothes, put on my chappals, and walked outside.

Having just come from Varanasi, it was a relief not to be in a busy place. The air was fresh and crisp and the vegetation still green and rich with the flush of the departed rains. I walked up to the tea stall on the edge of the road, sat down on a bench, and asked for a cup of tea. The young vendor said he had seen me get off the bus with his father. He inquired where I was from. A man selling fruit and peanuts a few paces away joined us. I told them I too was a "friend of the Buddha" and had come to pay homage.

I walked across the street and up a path which ran into the Tibetan monastery, where a monk on the terrace waved me back onto the path. A long field bordered by enormous banyan trees stretched out before me. I could make out a market and a school in the distance.

At the age of eighty and having spent more than half his life elucidating the Four Noble Truths and the end to suffering, the Awakened One had come to what was this daub-and-wattle village of Kushinagar in the kingdom of the Mallas. His body wracked with illness and old age, his disciples and companions had carried him across the rain-swollen river on the edge of the village and had placed him between two great sal trees. Villagers gathered round him and seekers still sought him out. When night fell, the people were full of fear, but he reassured them in his way: "Death is inherent in all component things, work out your salvation with diligence." Then, lying on his right side, the Dew Drop slipped into the Shining Sea.

The path turned and led to a temple. I could hear the methodical tapping of a drum. I slipped off my chappals on the steps, folded my palms together under my chin, and went in. It was dark inside but my eyes soon adjusted. There before me lay the Buddha as he had died—on his right side, one arm gently astride his body and the other folded under his head, looking ever so slightly upward, in a gaze of perfect peace and equanimity. I calmly surveyed the length of his body, every gentle fold of his garment, down to the balls of his feet.

The Sri Lankan pilgrims were doing puja and a saffron-robed monk who looked Japanese sat cross-legged on the floor. He methodically lifted and let fall a leather hammer on a small drum next to the Buddha's ear. The Sri Lankans had laid a bright blue sari over the Buddha's midriff, on which they had lit three white candles on a brass plate. Orange and white jasmine flowers were strewn about the Buddha and offerings of bananas and coconuts had been placed beside him. Pungent fumes of incense filled the enclosed space of the little temple.

The hammer fell for the last time and the celebrants rose. Clutching handfuls of rice, *prasad,* and flowers, they leisurely circumambulated Lord Buddha in a clockwise fashion. I followed behind, palms folded under my chin. We passed in front of the Buddha, around his head, and behind him. The pilgrims laid their offerings beside him, putting their hands on the recumbent Lord and touching their foreheads and hearts.

Overcome with devotion, I felt myself suddenly filled with the urge to place my forehead on the balls of his feet, as I had seen the others do.

We shuffled along until my turn came. I lowered my forehead: *Gracious Lord, I know who you are.* I knew not what else to think or say. I moved on and lingered in the corner awhile as the Sri Lankans chanted a prayer in Sinhalese. Then, taking one last look at the stone figure, I walked into the sunlight and across the long field shaded by the protective arms of the enormous banyan trees.

Sketch: Lot of Love

Jhula Devi mandir is a small temple atop a hill on a long ridge in the Kumaon. Facing away from snow peaks like Trishul, it looks back down on the valley and the plains. The small stone structure, with the usual elaborate assortment of deities, is preceded by a flower garden and a winding path.

His aunt rang the bell at the gateway and proceeded ahead, pausing to admire the carnations and roses. She wore a gray shawl dotted with little red designs in diamond shapes. Always sprightly, one was hardly aware of her age. Realizing her nephew wasn't following, she called back.

"Are you not coming, dear?"

"No, not coming, this is as far as I go, chachi," replied the thin man with the large shock of gray hair. His voice still retained the irrepressible chirpiness of youth.

"My dear, you have no faith, no faith," lamented chachi while looking intently at a white carnation flower.

"No faith, chachi, no faith, but *a lot of love, a lot of love*," responded the nephew almost on cue.

He said it with such verve and flourish. Then he rang the bell on the gateway with enough gusto to make the hills resound with glee.

I stood nearby. While my great-aunt attended to the gods, my chachaji and I passed time at the tea stall outside the perimeter, chatting amiably with the chaiwallah.

*Of all the fond memories I have of my Ravi uncle, this memory outside Jhula Devi stands out. He loved India, he loved the hills, he loved wildlife and people, he loved fiction and non-fiction, justice and equality, and he loved his family. I will always remember him for the person he was, someone who was able to live life on his own terms, with integrity and love.

Sketch: Train from Mangalore

The sun began to rise on Mangalore.

I made a rapid descent down the steps and onto the platform to catch the early morning train to Hassan. I stepped down to cross the tracks and board an open carriage in front as an elderly woman followed behind me.

I slid my backpack under the bench, supported my elbow against the iron bars of the window sill, and looked outside. I felt the urge for coffee, the sweet milky coffee sold on trains and that tasted so good in the south. Two other people boarded the carriage and moved to sit somewhere in front of me. I felt a jolt in front and knew the locomotive must have been hooking up.

Mangalore was on the coast, by the Indian Ocean, and the point from which trains running east and south began. The train I was on would be traveling east to Hassan, where it was not due to arrive until the early afternoon. We would have to cross the Western Ghats, that stretch of mountains lining India's western coast, a footstool really in comparison to the lofty Himalayas.

The train slowly began to move down the tracks and out of the station. Hovels of red laterite slabs and baked clay roofing tiles bordered the tracks. Children were waving in courtyards, women cleaning their teeth in doorways, and men squatting to relieve themselves next to the tracks. Trees of papayas and bananas grew in and around the open concessions and living quarters of families. Yet humanity was still not as densely packed here as elsewhere in India.

In minutes, we had rolled out of the city and into the countryside. The sun was rising, drying the morning dew and throwing long shadows over yellow fields and green trees. The rhythmic clack of the carriage wheels moving over the tracks sounded steadily beneath us. I sat still, absorbing the scenery and sensing the meter-gauge train begin its slow rise.

It must have been close to mid-morning when we pulled into a long and low, spacious and shaded station. The air was cool and I could see many people milling about on the platform. My eyes ranged until I spotted a man boiling water on a gas stove with two tables of disposable clay cups next to him. I put my bag on my seat to save my place, hopped down onto the platform, sidestepped the vendors and hawkers, and bought a cup of coffee. Tasting the richness of the caffeine in the milky brew, I remembered we were not far from Koorg, south India's prime coffee growing center. I bought a second cup of coffee as well as a bottle of mineral water and a few measures of *channa dal* sprinkled with *masala* to savor on the journey.

When I re-boarded the train, I found several other people had moved into the compartment I was in. I sat by the window while the others lounged in the aisle and stood in the doorway, bidding farewell to family and friends on the platform. I was startled when the train began to move backward, unnerved when it continued doing so for what seemed like several kilometers. When we did move forward again, it was further to the north though I searched in vain for the tracks on which we had been. In the dim distance, I could see the hills rising up. They grew taller with our approach as I gazed on in rapt expectation.

The other passengers were still moving back and forth in the aisle on the train's left side. When I got up to see what all the activity was about, my eyes beheld a stunning verdant valley, untouched by so much as a road or a house, and stretching out in front of us and up to the craggy mountain peaks in the distance. People were sitting and standing in the open doorways and looking through the windows along the open aisle, absorbed in the luscious beauty of this ancient land.

I moved to a doorway in which two young men sat and two others stood looking over their shoulders. As our train traversed the escarpment, we gazed down at the vines climbing up to the tracks and at the woods covering the hillsides as thick as a fur coat. Our train ran into a cliff and through a narrow tunnel. Emerging from the darkness into the brilliance of the sunshine, we marvelled at the many streams of water cascading down the hillside, merging somewhere on the floor of this luxuriant valley. The mountain on the train's right suddenly gave way and we crossed a tall and narrow bridge which split the valley. We glimpsed the river rushing against the rocks below us and gasped in awe, delight, and adoration.

Our hearts were lifted up. We pointed out features of the landscape to one another. We inquired where each of us was going. We traded places, now standing, now sitting. When the train stopped at a tea and coffee house midway on the journey, we all clambered down, drank coffee together, and stood on the valley rim, marveling at the enchanted scenery as one. Our hearts were full but ever so light.

Afterwards, the train never really seemed to descend but rather to run down onto a plain. But we had left the mountains behind us. And by the time we pulled into the station at Hassan, most of us had already disembarked, going our separate ways just as before.

Sketch: Train from Hampi

I awoke with a start in Hampi. I turned on the light and reached for my watch on the dresser. It was almost three o'clock in the morning. My train was to leave at half past three and the station was a twenty-minute walk away. There would be no scooters or rickshaws at this early hour. Hadn't I told the *chaukidar*, or nightwatchman, to wake me up at quarter to three?

Fortunately, I had paid the bill in advance, so I had only to pack my bag and go. I rushed to fold my clothes and retrieve my toothbrush from the bathroom. The taste of idli sambar and coconut chutney in my mouth brought the picture of the restaurant where I had eaten dinner to mind. But the dream I was immersed in only moments earlier was already forgotten.

I turned off the lights in the room, closed the door, and fairly leaped down the stairs to the lobby. I wasn't surprised to see the entire hotel crew asleep on mats behind the front desk, but when I saw the chain gates pulled tight across the front entrance, I found I was locked in. I felt the crisp morning air but I could not get out. I tried in vain to wake up the man I recognized as the *chaukidar*. Others were sleeping deeply under sheets drawn over their heads. I began to fret. Then I noticed a ring of keys on the floor next to my feet. I scooped them up, ran to the door, and unlocked the gates. I closed the chain gates behind me and flung the keys across the floor back their way.

Carrying the pack on my back and alternately walking and running, I hustled down the narrow paved road to the station at Hospet. The road was deserted except for the lurking hulks of cattle here and there. The memory of the previous day in Vijayanagar came back to me now: the scattered red granite outcrops, the meandering blue Tungabhadra river, the shady green banana and palm groves, the weathered stone ruins of a lost empire. I remembered walking down a path into a clearing and coming across a local woman and a couple in front of a large rock painting of the goddess Durga. The fiery goddess, blood dripping from the fangs of her gaping mouth, contrasted sharply with the tranquility of the shaded grove. And I recalled now the lingering question of faith. Faith as confidence in life, or faith in the way of the Great Ones and the worthiness of the path they had trod, or faith in something else... The question had not burned in my mind but seemed only to nestle there comfortably, like a bird returning to its nest. I had gone to sleep like that, almost feeling an answer.

I reached the station at 3:25 and bought a one-way ticket to Kolhapur. I would have to change trains at Hubli. I walked through the lobby, past the covered apparitions sleeping on the floor, and onto the platform. I looked back down the track to the red light on the track in the east. I was on time.

Minutes later, the train pulled in. I was almost alone on the platform to meet it at this early hour. I boarded an unreserved second class coach and sat down on the end of a bench in the second compartment. A family of five was sprawled out on the bench in front of me.

The train inched forward ever so slowly. I looked outside at the passing figures of people squatting and huddling around bonfires next to the tracks. The clacking sound of the carriage moving down the track grew faster and faster, synced, and then disappeared in the background as we sped through the countryside. I felt a faint breeze down the aisle of the carriage as the train swayed gently from side to side.

I looked at the family in front of me. The father sat almost across from me with his arms around a young boy in his lap. Another boy leaned against his side. Under the window lay the head of a woman with her feet up and an infant on her chest. The man had been struggling to keep his eyes open but appeared to have finally succumbed to sleep like the rest of his family.

The train swayed and I looked out the window into the early morning darkness. Time seemed to stand still. I felt a warm sensation just behind my chest and above my heart. Suddenly I felt keenly alert and intensely aware of everything around me—the train, the family, the countryside, the darkness, the cool air. I sat still and thoughtless, empty and observant, quiet and awake. I felt an overwhelming peace and calm. For a moment, I saw a lake inside me, a lake in the midst of mountains. Its still waters disclosed scarcely a ripple, appearing only to glisten and smile in splendour. All this was beheld by an observer from a vantage point behind drooping boughs and golden leaves.

Slowly, I came back to myself and I made the conscious effort to remember. I had not anticipated in the least what had just transpired. I recalled my wondering about faith and how the question seemed to have vanished. In my mind, I recreated the early morning darkness, the swaying of the train, the family asleep in front of me. I recalled the warm sensation above my heart, the alertness of my senses, the absence of the "me" in the experience. How indeed could one speak of "my" soul, when in what I had just been a part of there was no "I"? Of that, I was sure. In fact, it was just when I had become aware of the "I" that the experience had ended. Not I, but God in me, so that saints had said.

Sketch: Train from Bombay

It must have been almost eleven at night at Kolhapur when I got down from the train. I had been through this station once before on an earlier trip from Goa to Bombay. In fact, I had taken the same overnight train to Bombay that I would be taking this evening. At that time, however, I had a second class sleeper reservation, while tonight I was only able to purchase the brown cardboard stub entitling me to travel on an unreserved sleeper.

Intent on securing a good seat, I marched up the stairs and over to the platform from where the train to Bombay would be departing. I walked past the numerous first and second class sleepers until I found two unreserved bogeys hooked up behind the locomotive.

I was too late. A few men in dusted white dhotis were already standing in the doorways. I brushed past them but one glance down the aisle was enough to see that not a seat remained. People were doubling up on the single seats facing each other down the left side of the aisle. And the compartment on my right already held four people on either bench. The racks overhead were full of luggage.

So I sat down in the aisle on my backpack. People continued to trickle in and shuffle down the aisle where I could see them sitting on their bags in the train's dim yellow light. A young man sitting cross-legged in the compartment next to me put his legs down and a frail old man squeezed into place in the middle of the bench. I kept sinking lower into my pack and repositioning myself to sit on the frame.

I felt a tap on my shoulder.

"Baitho, baitho". Sit, sit, a young man said to me from under bushy eyebrows, motioning to a place on the wooden bench beside him no larger than what his open hand could command.

I stood up with some difficulty, lifted my bag over the intervening legs, and slipped into the middle of the bench. I looked at the people across from me. Two youths in slacks and striped shirts, the frail old man in his white dhoti, a stout middle-aged man in a tan outfit and his homely wife in a blue and yellow print sari next to the window. And they looked at me, searching my eyes, scanning my clothes, surmising my bag.

The train lurched forward and stopped, as if trying to shake out a few passengers. But stragglers continued to file into our crowded carriage despite the protestations of those already on board. They shouted at those standing by the doorway to close and lock the doors to prevent any more passengers from coming in.

I too thought, yes, it would be absurd to take in any more on an all night trip such as what was ahead of us. And someone in the doorway finally closed and locked the doors to our great relief.

People continued to come up to our carriage. Finding the door locked, they asked us to open the door. There were three of four of them. The train started to move. They ran down the platform with us, leaping onto the doorstep and clinging like prisoners to the iron bars of the door's square window.

"Darwaza khulo, darwaza khulo!" Open the door, open the door.

They pleaded with us and their voices rose as the train picked up speed and the glare of the station's lights grew dimmer and dimmer. We had almost reached the end of the platform when a person near the door finally relented and let the young daredevils in. They shared with us more than a few words of undisguised disgust before squatting on their haunches along the wall in the rear.

We rode silently into the night. A cool and gentle breeze blew through the open windows, dispersing the worst of the accumulated smells of compacted humanity. Along with others on my bench, I pulled my bag out from under the seat and in front of my legs so a man could stretch out on the floor beneath our bench. A wiry young man climbed onto the rack above the single seats on the other side of the aisle, rearranging the anonymous pieces of luggage to sit in what looked like enviable space and comfort. I tried not to press against the toes of the unpleasant foot sticking out from under the leg of the person next to me.

We hadn't travelled far when we pulled into another station. A few people on the platform had spotted the two unreserved bogeys in front and moved to follow us. Finding our door locked, they ran to the next coach, only to return and beg us to open the door. We sat in silence like before.

The train started to move again. The would-be passengers hopped onto the doorstep and shouted through the window.

"Darwaza khulo, darwaza khulo!" Open the door, open the door.

We pretended not to hear, to sleep, to dream. We averted our eyes, deaf to their pleas, insensible as stone but ever so anxious for this uncomfortable moment to pass, to end, to be gone. One man jumped off in the fading light near the end of the platform but the other two held on in the dark.

Bodies shifted, eyes darted, consciences perhaps pricked. Maybe the rest really were asleep. Finally, a man with his back to the door—one of those who had previously pleaded with us to open the door—turned to unlock the door. Involuntary eyes dared to glance at the young men who had just scrambled in and were catching their breath in the rear of the bogey. The few words of frustration and reprimand they directed to no one in particular, however, met with only the same impenetrable, irrefutable, irreproachable silence.

Reflection: A Word on Prejudice and Stereotypes

Bias: *a strong feeling in favour of or against one group of people, or one side in an argument, often not based on fair judgement*

Prejudice: *an unreasonable dislike of, or preference for, a person, group, custom, etc., especially when it is based on their race, religion, sex, etc.*

Stereotype: *a fixed idea or image that many people have of a particular type of person or thing, but which is often not true in reality and may cause hurt and offence.*

I remember watching a PBS travel documentary on the Silk Road when I was young. The engaging narrator and guide looked at the camera and said, "It has been said that there are no foreign lands. It is only the traveler who is foreign." That made me think. He went on to say that *"travel is fatal to prejudice."* I would like to think so! But I am not sure. It does allow you to see the human being and one does learn not to generalize, or to generalize with great caution. Still, I am reminded how in U.S. history, southern Whites would exclaim to Whites in the north, "You don't know colored people like we do!" Perhaps they should have known better but they didn't. Awash in bias, prejudice, and stereotypes, not to mention structural racism, how can you see your neighbor as a human being?

I am not free of bias. We all have biases that we have picked up, and if we are honest, we find ourselves proven wrong and yet we still don't drop our biases, why not? Conditioning is strong, and we need to be aware of it.

In general, however, I experience anything from distaste to disgust when I hear prejudice based on skin color, race, ethnicity, gender, religion, nationality, and so on. Stereotypes irritate me. The study of history is replete with examples of the danger and harmfulness of stereotypes. What we say in fact tells more about us than what we are talking about. One of my favorite maxims is: *We do not see things as they are; we see things as we are.*

Some sensitivity towards the lives and circumstances of others helps. But it is not a mere lesson in history or sociology. Only if we begin to be aware of our own conditioning that forms our views and responses, only then can we check a tendency in our human nature, built up over millennia, towards bias, prejudice, and stereotypes. Who are we to judge, who am I to judge?

Towards the end of 1993 and my 6 months in India, I wrote a letter to my parents in which I expressed my irritation at stereotypes of Americans. Extracts of the letter are italicized below:

Dear Mama and Daddy,

...I thought I would write this to jot down the crude stereotypes many Indians of both low and high education have of America and Americans. The stereotypes do not come to mind in any order but I'll begin with the so-called "substance" (nothing but illusion and misinformation, really) of a conversation with a Brahmin and a Rajput of low earnings on a train from Varanasi to Deoria. I am asked if it is true that Americans drink from the cradle on and when I say that you must be 18, and in some states 21, they refuse to believe it. In India, no drink is allowed, they say, and when I say otherwise, they only reiterate what they say. I am asked if it is true that everyone gets a divorce in the U.S. and when I say that yes, 50% do divorce nowadays, they say that will never happen here. Good, I'm glad. They say the U.S. does not respect the territorial integrity of India, and I say that Robin Raphael's statement questioning Kashmir and the Instrument of Accession was unfortunate. Of course, I don't obliterate their smugness and conceit by talking of the rights of women or of Kashmiris. That would be too great a mental leap, as I could tell from their refusal to believe that Americans aren't drunk from the day they can swallow.

It is the curse of being a superpower that everyone's view of you is colored by politics. Who is the U.S. to talk of human rights, they say, when they have discriminated against blacks for years? True, but do not forget that India has everything including racism. It's hardly a coincidence that the upper classes are mostly fair. And what of the government's subversion and persecution of tribals. Or take the questions posed to me by some upper caste women at a dinner party here. Is it true that U.S. students cannot find India on a map? Well, yes, they are rather delinquent in geography. Is it true that if you wear something different in a U.S. high school that you will be ostracized? Quite the contrary, madam, everyone is competing to wear something different, to be different, to act different. One woman tells me the Peace Corps was thrown out of India because they wanted to convert people to Christianity and because they divided people, one village against another, one caste against another, one religion against another. America and Americans are seen as childish, immoral ("do brother and sister have sex?"), racist, decadent in every way and anti-India, India which is moral, spiritual, traditional, a poor country fighting for respect and all that other ... that people grow up believing. To the dismay of his colleagues, an Indian said at the International Yoga Conference in Munger, Bihar, "India was a spiritual country up to the 10th century, the India that Fa Hsien and Hsuien Tsang visited, but now India is just as spiritually bankrupt as any other country." And India hardly needs the U.S. to pit caste against caste, religion against religion. All this talk of a foreign hand and Western oppression and conspiracy is nothing but arrogance and conceit clothed as education and learning. One really wonders if people would better tend their own house without this little learning, which is really a dangerous thing. Isn't it better that the mind be blank (and yet open) than full of these stereotypes?

... You know I have even heard from a retired Indian Army general-now-ecology advocate that the U.S. is responsible for the state of the soil in India because of the U.S.-inspired Green Revolution. And I have also heard from another Army man that we must keep U.S. products out because then we will become too "self-centered." That's an amazing observation if you've ever seen how people fight to get on trains and buses here and then take up more space than necessary, never mind the elderly. Soap operas and MTV are finding audiences and the economy is opening up—all with permission of GOI (Government of India)—but already one can see the day when America will be blamed for divorce, drunkenness, debt, social divides, slipping standards,

shootouts, and a host of other sacrileges—and this from people with a degree of education.

When will people face it, that if we give up traditions, it is not because we didn't want to. Indian traditions are sufficiently strong that in independent India we have no one but ourselves to blame for their perceived break-up. Indians are fond of observing that see, the U.S. has to have an enemy, doesn't know what to do without an enemy, etc. To me, it is obvious that any Indian with a half-baked education is the same way. It's time we drop the "arrogance." For another reason also: a country with such a rich heritage as India has no business wearing what looks to me like an inferiority complex in front of the rest of the world, but that is another question.

That was my experience in 1993 and those were my perceptions and my response as a 27 year old. No doubt some people felt I was "safe" to talk to. Wrong. If one knows better, it is a moral duty to correct. One has only to decide which battles to fight—*when, where, and how.* In general, doing so in a calm manner, not breaking the relationship and remembering one's own biases and the potential for misunderstanding especially in a different cultural context, one may be able to get the other party to see things differently as well as learn more about oneself. These are important conversations. *Travel does have the potential to be "fatal to prejudice."*

In the end, one must always see the human being.

Narrative: Transition Again

While I had already decided to go to graduate school in the United States, it was my father's health that made me leave India and return to the U.S. in January 1994. As for graduate school, a jobs publication for former Returned Peace Corps Volunteers advertised the new Shriver Peace Worker Program, hosted by the University of Maryland Baltimore County (UMBC), where one could enroll in graduate school while simultaneously doing "service" in a program helping an under-served community and taking classes to reflect on service, values, rights, responsibilities, privilege and so on. I decided to get a Master's degree in Teaching English to Speakers of Other Languages (TESOL).

In spite of having some superb instructors and a worthy program to contribute to, I dropped out after a semester—just as I'd felt at University of Virginia and completed a year there. I'd begun to think that perhaps I didn't function well above 30 degrees latitude, which is roughly the latitude of Houston where I grew up! I stayed in Baltimore and held three part-time jobs: teaching Spanish at an elite school called The Gilman School; teaching English with Baltimore Community College to Russian refugees; and washing dishes on the Spirit of Baltimore, a ship that cruised the Inner Harbor and outlying bay. I loved walking around Baltimore, where as part of putting Mali behind me, I also found the time to do a certain amount of writing of vignettes and stories.

I was told that people seldom drop out of a graduate school program. My reason for dropping out was more of a "pull" factor than a "push" factor, the pull being a Peace Corps Fellows program in El Paso, Texas, on the U.S.-Mexico border, where I could earn a Master's in Public Health (MPH) while doing an internship in the local health department. An MPH as a degree is something I'd first come to know about when I decided to visit the Mali director of CARE while I was in Peace Corps. CARE is a U.S.-based non-government organization (NGO) working in international development. I met the director at his office in Bamako out of a concern that they were not hiring local people when they were starting a maternal child health program in the district of Zantiebougou where I worked. Instead, they were bringing in people from outside, such as Bamako, and this was having a detrimental effect on the credibility and receptivity of people towards CARE. We had a discussion and I noticed his business card said MPH, which until then to me meant only "miles per hour." Learning what it was gave me the idea that one day I could be in his position and this was a good degree to get there. Getting the degree in El Paso also meant I could use my Spanish again and work on health issues that were more relevant to developing countries such as infectious diseases, which were more prevalent on the border than elsewhere in the United States.

Such was the initial draw to El Paso, a city that I moved to four times, spent 15 years of my life in, and both raised a family and immersed the ashes of my parents in.

1995 – graduate school

1997 – left and returned one month later for a job

1999 – left to get married and returned 9 months later for a job

2018 – returned to after reaching 8.5 year limit on Peace Corps staff employment

Sketch: Spirit of Baltimore

"I am meant for something better than this", he said to himself as he walked up the night street and away from the pier where the Spirit of Baltimore cruise ship had docked. It was late evening but still early, early enough for the late dinner crowd and the early party-goers on a Friday or Saturday evening.

"It's not that I am better than anyone else," he checked himself, "but I must be meant for something better than this." He still had on his "chef's apron" and "chef's hat" and salt and pepper trousers and black steel-toed shoes.

He thought of the other guys on the boat, as they called it, which was really a large passenger cruising ship, large enough to ply the harbor and its waterways close to the seaboard and back. Washing dishes, preparing salad, and placing slices of cake and pastries onto plates, then climbing the steps to the ship's first deck and mixing the salad with Caesar dressing and setting out the cakes and pastries on the buffet table. But his work was mostly below, in the ship's hold, and it was mostly dishes that came down fast. He would throw out the uneaten food, and there was a lot of it. Unbelievable amount of waste, just like at Bryant Halls, the athlete's cafeteria back at the University of Virginia.

He would collect the plates and silverware into racks and rinse both with a high-powered sprayer and then load them into the industrial dishwasher with its belts and hoses and soap and spray. He would remove the racks, set them out to dry, then stack them into silverware trays and portable dish dispensers. Even before that, while people were eating, he would tackle some of the larger cooking pots and pans and knives, taking care not to burn himself or cut himself. People had cut themselves before with knives but he had been careful.

His only near serious mishap developed from the habit of consuming a slice of chocolate cake or pie or lemon meringue off the plates that came down. Everything appeared untouched. Yet on one occasion, he was about to swallow a chunk of chocolate cake when he felt a large piece of glass on his tongue. He rotated it in his mouth in disbelief before carefully extracting it with two fingers. It was a large shard of a wine glass—almost "death by chocolate", he thought to himself later. At the time, he could only shudder at the thought of "what if."

He was meant for something different, it had always been part of the plan, a plan that always evolved. He tried not to make it appear whimsical but it could look that way. Here and there, bouncing about, a foot in multiple worlds, uniquely flexible in making a home and yet just a little out of place everywhere, too. It could seem just a question of time until he outgrew a place and sought to move on. The elation of arrival, of discovery, even of fitting in, would all give way and point towards an end, as though he wanted to follow the sun fading over the earth's horizon rather than remain in place.

He thought of his co-workers again on the Spirit of Baltimore, both black and white—though all black below deck except for him—and they were locals, Baltimore born and bred. It's not that as a human being he was better. It's that he had privileges, mainly education and exposure and even upbringing and the expectations that came with it, that sorted out a different horizon of possibilities.

"I am meant for something better than this", he heard himself say again, as he moved homewards along the docks as the lights of the evening shone across the Inner Harbor.

1995

Sketch: Reaching El Paso

The drive across the state, really just from South Texas to West Texas, would take 13 hours on good highways. He planned to break journey in Del Rio on the U.S.-Mexico border. Leaving his mother and father at home in Corpus Christi one sunny August morning, he set out on the long drive west, west, west in a big blue 1966 Chevy Impala, blue as the sky.

Headed for graduate school and an internship with the health department, this would be the start of something that would lead somewhere. He felt happy and free. He rolled down the window and looked at himself from time to time in the circular side view mirror, a vintage design feature of the old car, his birth year car.

He had never been to El Paso but for weeks, he had already been reading the El Paso Times at the library in Corpus Christi. He loved the fact that it was right on the border. The paper even gave news of Ciudad Juárez, the Mexican city on the other side of the Río Grande river, since both cities shared the same space, the same history, the same location at the southern spur of the Rocky Mountains. Two cities, two countries, two languages and cultures and ways of life—more similar than different, overlapping, not separated but joined by a river, joined at the hip.

It was the river, called the Río Bravo in Mexico, which brought people together and gave life to a region that was a sparse desert that lifted higher and more mountainous the further west he drove. The humidity and oppressive heat of the Gulf Coast slowly gave way to vast vistas, wide open spaces, rocky crags, and long tableland mesas. The land, the land, the land—so empty, so spacious, dotted with mesquite trees and sage bushes under a sky that stretched on forever as far as one could see. Here it was dry heat, cool nights, huge temperature swings between night and day. Even clouds were sparse and thin.

It occurred to him that he had never lived in a place quite like this, with such a sense of space. Towards the final approach, the highway cut between the volcanic peaks of Sierra Blanca and descended, winds blowing strong, and the far-off mountains of El Paso and Juárez could first be seen. As they grew larger and larger, the river unseen came that much closer to the highway, and the green fields of the agricultural communities of Fabens, San Elizario, and Socorro appeared. He would come to know each of them in time. Traffic became heavier and the highway widened. He saw turn-off to the Bridge of the Americas that crossed into Juárez, Mexico. Bridge of the Americas—how enchanting the name! All of it, and exits like Airway Boulevard, Piedras, Cotton, Montana, and Campbell were streets leading into neighborhoods he would come to know intimately from his work and living nearby.

In the evening, he drove up to the *mirador*, or look-out point, just below the "Star on the Mountain" that was lit up facing Juárez as though beckoning the people of the South. On the Mexican side, one saw *"Lee la Biblia"*, or "read the Bible", painted on rocks on the Juárez mountains. From the *mirador*, one had perhaps the greatest binational view anywhere in the world. From the University of Texas at El Paso (UTEP) and Mount Cristo Rey in the west along the river and the vastness of Juárez behind to the small section of buildings in downtown El Paso and the hospitals where one day both of his children would be born, and out to the sprawling East Side and down the lower valley where the border became harder and harder to distinguish the further one looked. The river—and once it really was grand—had even changed course in times past, leaving communities to wake up in different nations!

He found the whole setting absolutely enchanting. The sky at sunset was regularly awash in colors, too. It was a certain love at first site. He didn't know it then, but this would be home for 15 years of his life.

1995

Sketch: The Day They Met

The first time they met was a Saturday evening in Atlanta. He flew in late from El Paso, she picked him up. She was like the photo she sent him, leaning against a rail with the mountains of Vienna in the background. She peered at him wide-eyed, like seeing him for the first time. They did not hug or greet with the warmth and affection of people who know one another. That was what he had come for, to get to know her, after a few phone calls that indicated they might be what each other was looking for in a life partner.

He rode up the escalator behind her, a green bag for the weekend slung over his shoulder. They strolled through the huge airport and finally made it outside. It had been raining and a drizzle was visible in the street lights. They found her blue hatchback car in the garage and, as she drove into the city, rain began to pound the windshield and obstruct the view. It was still raining when they reached The Cheesecake Factory, a place he had never heard of and which was packed with people. They got a booth and the conversation stopped only to order and eat dinner, topped off with a slice of tiramisu which they both shared.

She had large inquisitive eyes, a voice as sweet as a Georgia peach, and mid-length black hair touching her shoulders. She didn't speak that much but asked direct questions and seemed to feel him out as she listened. For his part, he probably talked too much, liking the fact that a female was listening to him. Probably they talked about new things like what each other's work was really like, what her work and best friends were like, what his connections and travel and feeling for India was like, and maybe more about family in a guarded way for now and likes and dislikes in an expansive way.

He already knew she was divorced. It did not matter to him. No children were involved. Later, she would tell him the story in more detail. It was not her fault.

It had stopped raining by the time they drove home to her apartment, which she shared with a married couple who were also her closest friends in this southern city. He was shown her room upstairs as a place to sleep. He put his bag down, looked at the view of the carport outside and the clearing night sky, and slept contentedly until the dawn.

1998

Part IV

Householder

In ancient India, and even today to some extent, there is a view that life has four stages: *Brahmacharya* (student life); *Grihastha* (householder); *Vanaprastha* (seclusion or literally "forest living"); and *Sannyasa* (total renunciation).

I have written this memoir somewhat differently, with the stages: Childhood, Adolescence, Young Adult, and now Householder.

While every stage of life has its particular duties and is *equally important*, the householder stage of life—for those who enter it—is perhaps *the most challenging*. Or it can seem that way because one is so responsible to others in this phase. I certainly found this to be true, and yet had I to add a subtitle to this stage, I would write *"years of fulfilment."* The satisfactions balance the challenges and endure beyond the stage.

Times have changed, but traditionally, as the name of this stage suggests, "householder" starts with *marriage*. And a responsible career, if one does not already have it, since one must support one's family. And children. And a house and household, and with it financial obligations and "monthly bills". Debts and bills. And career advancement, which in the modern world, comes with its own many challenges, thus the struggle to balance family and career, home and work.

Marriage to Garima, 11 July 1998

Family also includes your parents and brothers and sisters, if you have them, not to mention your spouse's family and in-laws. And your grandparents. And the extended family such as your cousins and aunts and uncles and nephews and nieces. In time come your own grandchildren. And your parents—they become elderly, suffer health problems, go into a slow decline and more dependent stage of life. Family can lift you but also overwhelm you. And there is also your duty to society or your responsibility as a citizen and member of the community where you live. There is even planning for one's retirement, a "nest egg."

Marriage. Children. Career. Home. Family. Society.

At the same time, and easily forgotten while doing so much for others, there is you, oneself—one's own nature and needs and desires, one's own fulfilment and potential and destiny.

The householder, whether the husband or wife, is typically acculturated or socialized to put everyone else's needs ahead of his or her own. So there is the risk of losing oneself in the process, one's own dreams and desires. One's own happiness. Whether husband or wife, whether son or daughter or son-in-law or daughter-in-law or whatever the case may be, whether employee or even citizen, there come times when one must "*stand up for oneself*", be true to oneself.

Isn't one's own happiness and fulfilment important to meet the needs of others? Or must it always be sacrifice? What about "one's own baggage", one's own scars and habits of mind, patterns of mind, habits and behaviors—or is one fully mature already? Can one "serve others" if one's own needs are not met, if one has not learned to be happy from within? These are the questions that dog the householder, flummox the householder, but even those who do not marry or do not have children face the same questions.

It is not necessary to be a householder, or to go through every stage of life in anyone's design, in order to be a full human being. Some may not be "the marrying kind" and may be be better off without it. Definitely, being a householder brings unique challenges that can make or break you. And if it breaks you, you get back up, learn, adjust, and keep going one way or another.

Speaking for myself, my own life—and with it, my perspective on life and the space and circle of my affections—would be utterly different had I not gotten married and had children. Work tends to pale in comparison to *being there* for your spouse and children. There are certain lifelong bonds of affection, apart from obligations, that are engendered in the Householder stage of life.

Marriage: 11 July 1998

Purchasing a House: May 1999

New Job (AVANCE): August 1999

1st Child: 16 March 2000

2nd Child: 18 May 2002

Parents move in: November 2004

Mother's death: December 2004

New Job (Peace Corps) and Move to Peru: February 2010

Same Job (Peace Corps) now Mozambique: December 2013

Return to U.S.: July 2018

Father's death: August 2018

Son begins university: August 2018

New Job: October 2018

Daughter begins university: August 2020

Narrative: Finding a Career

El Paso and graduate school saw me take on more "responsible" jobs. The Peace Corps Fellows program came with an internship at the local health department. Soon I was in the field using my Spanish and organizing skills, supported by my professors, to supervise a team of VISTA volunteers conducting household surveys on the risk factors for hepatitis A in El Paso's outlying colonias. This was followed by a vaccination campaign. The association with the health department and the school of public health then enabled me to write a proposal to the Association of Schools of Public Health (ASPH) for the following year to study why some people completed preventive therapy for tuberculosis, which was more prevalent on the border, and others did not. Based on the results, I also worked with an artist from Ciudad Juárez to develop patient education materials for the TB nurses.

This did not directly lead to employment after graduation, and I was ready to leave El Paso, but before I did, a professor introduced me to the president of a new health foundation located in the same building as the school of public health. I left but one month later, she called me back as coordinator of a project that would involve nine communities, including two in New Mexico and one in Ciudad Juárez, to identify priority health needs and projects for funding. The following year, she gave me an assignment to interview the directors of 30+ non-profit organizations to learn more about them and their "dream programs." This assignment more truly awakened me to the vast work of non-profit organizations in meeting community needs in social services, health, and family support.

With an eye to moving to Atlanta to start married life, the association with ASPH then enabled me to get a fellowship with the Centers for Disease Control (CDC) to work on an international traveler's health project to reduce incidence of malaria, hepatitis A, and typhoid. However, the role did not work out to my satisfaction, and stirred by my wife's own layoff at work, I took an offer to work with the health foundation as a grants Program Officer and we moved from Atlanta to El Paso. Along with my wife's work at the diabetes association there, our salaries allowed us to qualify financially to purchase a house. My old nature, about not staying in a job if I weren't satisfied, led me to change jobs one "final" time, this time to AVANCE-El Paso, one of the non-profit organizations whose director I had interviewed the previous year and who was now moving on to something else. I would stay at AVANCE-El Paso for over 10 years.

The AVANCE headquarters was in San Antonio and AVANCE (roughy meaning "progress" in Spanish) was already nationally recognized for its model Parent-Child Education Program focused on mothers with children three years old or less. However, AVANCE in El Paso was not well known or on steady ground. I had no experience in fundraising but I was a good writer, analyzer, and organizer, and I soon learned how to plan and write grants to bring in funding. Later, with the help of an active Board of Directors, we instituted two large annual fundraisers. One was an art auction in collaboration with an art gallery and many artists and emerging artists who decorated wooden hearts that were auctioned off. The other was a free fundraising breakfast that allowed us to inspire attendees with testimonials from the mothers and children served in our family support and education program. They made one-time gifts and multi-year pledges. Both events lifted our visibility in El Paso. More grants and gifts and partnerships with elementary schools to host our program followed. Our tag line was AVANCE, helping young families break the cycle of poverty through early childhood development, parenting, and adult literacy.

Financial stability was elusive but developed over time along with growth and getting "the right people on the bus" and "the wrong people off the bus." Eventually, we began to receive a number of awards, including one of four inaugural "Immigrant Integration" awards from the Migration Policy Institute in Washington D.C. in 2009. All of our success was achieved on the basis of the program and vision of the founders of AVANCE, whose mission we had been faithful to rather than "chase the money" of whatever grants and funding opportunities happened to come along. AVANCE was a labour of love and extremely gratifying to me. As with Peace Corps, the people brought together by AVANCE shared a special bond, epitomized by a belief in the family as the first and most important teacher of children.

Sketch: An Awesome Responsibility

The first-time father returned home from the hospital, stepped into the house with his new baby boy in his arms, and suddenly had the unimaginable feeling that he, along with his wife, was completely responsible for the new life he held. The boy could break, he thought. He was so fragile. It was a sudden responsibility, tall and mighty, like no other he had ever known. He had stepped across the threshold of parenthood.

The baby moved and strained his eyes, looking for the light and finding his dad's eyes peering at him with a strange concern. His mother called anxiously from the kitchen in a pitch that was already familiar. These were his parents, the people that brought him into this world from somewhere he knew not where. He still had that that glassy look of unknowing in his eyes, as though he were between worlds, the one between his mother's womb and this earthly atmosphere, and between the vast unconsciousness of the mind and the consciousness of this world. The ache of arrival, the difficulty of discernment, the novelty of external sensations bore down upon this delicate and fragile human.

Kabir as a baby

The father, older now but thoroughly inexperienced, felt momentarily immobilized with unexpected thoughts. What if his son fell? Stopped breathing? What if they put him to sleep wrong or a sheet or blanket suffocated him? What if he choked on something he picked up not knowing what it was? What if an insect, spider, or scorpion around this house should bite or sting him? Even the dog, they couldn't really leave him alone with the dog just yet. The baby, in his crunched up miniature life was so vulnerable and yet so precious. It was an awesome responsibility of a different type he had never felt before. It was one thing to be responsible for your own life, for your part in a marriage, for your parents and extended family. It felt quite different to be responsible for a baby so utterly dependent on you as the parent.

The drive from the hospital to home felt longer than usual. His attention had been divided between the highway and the rear view mirror, eyeing the bundle wrapped up in the car seat next to his adoring wife. It was cloudy and unusually windy. The clouds would go. Spring would arrive officially the following week. For now, it was enough really to feel the rich blessing of parenthood. This moment would also change the lives of the parents forever, transforming the couple into a "family."

It was an awesome responsibility and the beginning of a love perhaps more "pure" than any other in the strength of its bond.

2000

Sketch: Oh Shit!

Smooth, grainy, and slimy, it seeped out of his diaper unbeknownst to the little boy who merely adjusted his pace crossing the street. Something wasn't right but it wasn't wrong either. His dad, cradling his little sister in his arms, held his hand and his mother walked alongside on a crutch.

They had just left the hospital in the beachside town of Puerto Vallarta, Mexico. The x-rays of his mother's foot were negative. She had sustained an injury when her toes slipped between two rocks as they were crossing a stream somewhere in the hills outside the town. She had exclaimed stoically, "I think I broke my toe." The little boy's response? "My toe is okay!"

At the time, his parents didn't laugh about it but only looked at him strangely and then at each other, smiling and shaking their heads. How could the little boy know better, he was taking care of himself rather well by his measure. And now he was crossing the street just fine as his dad looked at the brown something slowly sliding down his left leg and muttered, *"Oh, shit!"*

What indeed could be wrong?

2003

Sketch: Dora Exploradora

No rock on the path was too big for her. "Dora Exploradora", the father would say to motivate her, evoking her favorite book, *Dora Dora Exploradora*. And she bounded up the rocks in her path, following her big brother, born two years earlier, on the path uphill towards the cave.

She couldn't have been more than five years old and already she was so strong. Never one to be left behind, she came gladly and kept up gamely on these father-children hikes. Pride, and awe of the view, would shine in her gleeful brown eyes at a resting point. It was time for "dede" to take out the bagful of nuts, gummy bears, and M&Ms. Water was an afterthought.

Karishma as a child

On the way down, she would let her body go and run down the rocky trail in pursuit of her brother ahead. The father always feared she might fall going down and even imagined that it happened, but it never did and he loved to see her run. Once back in the car, they would grab a cheeseburger, fries, and soda in the drive-thru and pick up the same for "mama."

The high desert had its delights before the hot season, especially with the extra allure of any amount of snow on the mountains. It was an easy escape from the house. Hardly a light or stop sign, the majestic transmountain highway, a gravel parking lot, a rocky path, a zig-zag and downward look onto the highway cutting through the mountains below, followed by an ascent to the ridge and and long gazes into the horizon way out west. After a little rest, they would climb upwards and then follow a long traverse and take the ridge up to "the elephant." High up on one side, you could see the TV towers set against the deep blue of the sky, absorbing one in all the space and light and mystery of a mountain.

Sketch: On the Way to Ojai

It was a warm and sunny December morning in Santa Barbara when he went out for a walk. He walked by the boats lashed to the pier, by the shops that would be opening soon, by the park overlooking the waterfront. He thought of renting a car for the trip he, his wife, and two children were planning to make up to Ojai, nestled in the southern California hills, Ojai, the former home of J. Krishnamurti, a sage and seer he was familiar with from the books on his father's shelf.

Just then, his father called him on his mobile phone.

"Hear, Sanjay? Look, I'm sorry to tell you this, but your mother has expired this morning."

He stopped walking. He could say nothing more than "When did it happen?"

"This morning", his father said, "I went to her room at the usual time. She was quiet. She passed away some time in the night."

"I'm coming home. We were about to go to Ojai today, but I'm coming home. I'll be there as soon as I can."

His father didn't seem to express much emotion on the phone, but he had been the ever reliable one. The phone would not do.

His mother was gone. He had to take an extra round and look toward the hills of Ojai. His mother too had liked Krishnamurti, something about the 'sort of philosopher' and his white-gray wavy hair in his later years, his alertness, his attentiveness, his radiance, as though God were present through him. How strange that on the very day he had planned on taking his family to visit the special place where the sage had experienced a life-changing awakening, that his mother, so far from her childhood home in Switzerland, should pass away into the unknown, released from the illness which had made her bedridden and immobile these past many years.

The disease Multiple Sclerosis had already taken her from him, he felt, since she had lost the ability to speak for years now. She had barely been cognizant of what was around her. She died for me a long time ago, he thought ruefully, with his conflicting emotions. She passed away only a month after moving into his home, to which he had painstakingly built an extension to accommodate both her with her special needs and his father.

His grief seemed stuck. In fact, he would not fathom the full significance of losing her—of the heart-wrenching gap of a healthy mother to talk to in the tender years of his adolescence and early adulthood—for years.

2004

Vignette: Heart of El Paso

I was introduced to Hal by Sally, who had bought art from his gallery. At the time, it was a small place with a low ceiling and several rooms to hang art. It was set off the main avenue on El Paso's West Side and had limited parking of its own apart from the streets in the adjoining leafy neighborhoods to one side.

"We had better be prepared. He is not just an artist, he is a businessman," Sally advised. "He is likely to interrupt, but only if he is interested. So let's not waste his time."

They even prepared a few talking points, which ran more or less as follows:

- Thank him for meeting with us

- Introduce Sanjay as the Executive Director of AVANCE

- Briefly (very briefly) explain AVANCE's mission in the community

- Sally will propose an art-for-charity collaboration with the Gallery as a win-win

- Concept: *Toma Mi Corazón* ("Take My Heart") heart auction, wherein artists, emerging artists, and anyone who wishes will volunteer to decorate wooden hearts that will be auctioned to benefit AVANCE

- For the Gallery: good publicity and exposure, promotion of art at a community level, association with AVANCE's mission of educating disadvantaged children and parents

- AVANCE will assist by: distributing the hearts, organizing the labelling and display of hearts, obtaining corporate sponsors, alerting the media and doing publicity, staffing the event

"Ok, what does this mean for the Gallery?" asked Hal. "What do you want me to do?"

"Provide the space and invite artists to decorate a heart," Sally answered. "And I know you are very good with publicity, so if you could help advertise and promote the event, that would be great."

So began a collaboration that evolved into a deeper friendship. Where I was cautious, detailed, and meticulous, Hal was visionary. Where I rehearsed my speech, Hal improvised. We both focused on the big picture and pleasing people. We both noted shortcomings and oversights and made mental notes of doing better the next time.

Son of a hardworking Jewish grocer, he was a generation older than me. While still young, he took to art and music and a certain bohemian lifestyle (a "hippie"). He studied the great artists and paintings in Europe and returned to El Paso, the city of his birth, with a passion to capture the essence of a bi-cultural border city. His grandmother, of Syrian heritage, would take him across the border to buy fruits and vegetables for his father's grocery store, and thus emerged the painting "Mercado de Juárez", elaborated over 8 years, that would be the breakthrough to recognition. His paintings were rich in colour, long strokes, detail, and both the human body and the sun and environment.

It was his spirit that appealed to me more. A voice for peace, for harmony between religions, for understanding and respect between all cultures, and for the poor and outcast. Later, it was also his "veganism" that so naturally aligned with the values he placed on simplicity, naturalness, and a low impact lifestyle. In him, as I felt when I went away and returned on visits, I recognized someone who exemplified the heart of El Paso.

Sketch: Leaving Everything to go Overseas

It was November 16, 2009. He waited outside the interview room on the 8th floor of the Peace Corps office in downtown Washington D.C. He was there for a "final" interview, this time with the Peace Corps Worldwide Director and senior staff.

Less than two weeks earlier, he had come for day-long interviews, and only three weeks earlier there had been an initial phone screen and interview. But it wasn't his first time applying to be a Peace Corps Country Director.

He had applied in 2002, when he was too fresh, too inexperienced. He couldn't handle a question on emergency management, having been only an EMT on an ambulance and a soldier, and a Peace Corps Volunteer of course, during time of a *coup d'etat* in Mali. But he really didn't have the set of skills, maturity, and composure it took to be a Country Director, and they shouldn't have interviewed him.

Then he had applied again in 2005, again paying his own way to come to Washington D.C. and spend a day interviewing with many people. That occasion was infamous in his mind since one of the interviewers after lunch actually had to rouse himself out of a slumber and ask:

"As you know, the vast majority of your staff as a Country Director will be host country nationals. They may not have the same work habits as Americans. For example, they may have problems with punctuality, work ethic, and follow-through. How will you deal with this?"

Yes, American work habits—he had just been sleeping! The assumptions in that question—a dangerous arrogance, he thought, and that too in a Peace Corps interview, where to make such a generalization harked of the worst kind of ignorance. Regardless, he did not get the job that time, either. He could not surmise why and thought it must have been how he answered a question related to being careful in relations with the Embassy in order to avoid the assumption that Volunteers could be spies, always a concern he knew even if they did not.

In 2007, he updated his application to a full 36 pages, but didn't even get a call back. So it was on a whim that he re-submitted in August 2009 right before the school year started and the work at AVANCE got super busy.

He had let his Board chair know that he was applying, since he sensed there was a good chance he would be selected. He was right. Only a week later, he was called and offered the post of Peru, which was set to receive more Volunteers. They were impressed with how he had managed "growth with impact" at AVANCE. He could not really believe the trust and confidence they were placing in him to manage a large and growing post—were they right to place such faith and confidence in him?

His wife looked forward to going overseas, thinking a change would be good for their marriage as well as for the children. His father too, recalling their downstairs neighbors and family friends from Peru in the old apartment complex in Houston, was ready for a change since he was still living with them and would be going. When he told his 9-year old son, a big NBA fan, his response was, "Why not L.A., Boston, Cleveland?" When he told his 7-year old daughter, she said, "Why would I go to a country where the lake is called Titicaca!"

But now he would have to tell everyone in El Paso—the Board knew, but the dear staff, the team, everyone he had hired over the years, who had taken care of him while he took care of them, listening and supporting them in their jobs and their lives. AVANCE had been like a big family. And he had to tell the schools and the funders, plus AVANCE's donors. And AVANCE headquarters in San Antonio.

It was perhaps the largest turning point in his life up to that point, and there had been many. To take one's family overseas, to sell or rent the house, to sell possessions a family accumulates and put others in storage, to sell vehicles and pack up everything, not knowing how everyone would adjust to the new school overseas, a new house, new friends, new work environment, new climate, new food, everything. Peace Corps Washington had given him a "safe" choice, since living in Lima was not considered a hardship, certainly not relative to a country like Mali where he had served.

Upon arrival in Lima in early 2010, Kabir would start Grade 5 and Karishma would start Grade 3

What he said to people was, "Peace Corps changed my life when I was young, so it's an honor and privilege to go back as a Country Director and support the Volunteers to not only help the people of host countries like Peru but to learn and to grow themselves as a resulting of truly experiencing another culture."

Culture! Culture, it was. Culture had brought him to the border, the blend of cultures. Culture, the mix of cultures, had defined his life. Living in another culture, he knew, would be enriching also for his family. The whole idea behind Peace Corps was bridging cultural differences while being enriched by them. There really was no other line of work that he was more suited to, so he thought.

He had come to El Paso alone, not knowing anyone. The city had been so good to him. He was an El Pasoan now, through and through. The entire bilingual, bicultural vibe of the city had become his own second nature, had influenced even how he spoke English, how he switched from English to Spanish without a thought like so many El Pasoans. The border itself was terribly misunderstood by the rest of America who thought tanks must roll on the streets to stop all the drug traffickers and criminals when in fact El Paso was routinely ranked among the top three safest cities in America in spite of poverty and the rest of it. It was the rest of America consuming the drugs anyway. El Paso felt for the suffering of the people in Juárez, who could be at the mercy of violence between the drug cartels from time to time. But he defended the border and El Paso any chance he could as a place of law-abiding, hard-working, and respectful family people. Which it was.

Only five years, he told people, since Peace Corps had a "five-year rule" on staff appointments. He and his wife didn't even sell the house, he added, only rented it. Five years, *cinco años no más*, he said, I'll be back.

2010

Letter from Lima

September 25, 2011

Dear friends,

It has been a long time since I wrote. Leaving the "day-to-day" behind in Lima last week was rewarding and inspires me to send this note on another special part of the world.

A fair amount of staff time goes into what we call "site development", which means finding sites for the Volunteers, getting political support, identifying jobs Volunteers can do with local institutions, selecting host families, and anything else to prepare communities to host a "gringo." I got involved this past week since we are looking at placing Volunteers in a new Peruvian "department", or state, called Amazonas.

Amazonas is in the north where the mountains meet the jungle. It is the 10th largest state in Peru and larger in size than 64 countries. It has indigenous groups in the north such as the Ahuarun and Huampis, light-skinned and light-eyed descendants of Europeans in the south, and a majority mestizo population. Seven major rivers run through Amazonas, none of which is "the Amazon", but all tributaries to the Amazon which begins only in the neighboring state. It boasts a waterfall over 2,500 feet high "discovered" to the outside world only in 2002 and a number of spectacular pre-Inca ruins including mummies. Still, over 50% of the 400,000 inhabitants live on less than $3 per day, without piped water or sewage or roads to get their many agricultural products to market.

We didn't make it quite to the jungle but we found a great new area for Peace Corps Volunteers thanks in large part to the exceptional support given us by the mayor of Chachapoyas, the peaceful capital of Amazonas nestled on a ridge at 6,000 feet with a population of 24,000 people. Chachapoyas is also the name of one of 7 provinces in Amazonas and the mayor of Chachapoyas is also the "provincial mayor", charged with liaising with the mayors and authorities of over a dozen communities spread over many miles and mountains and connecting them to resources.

After flying from Lima to the coastal town of Chiclayo late the evening before, and then leaving at 5:30 AM and driving nearly seven hours, two Peace Corps program directors (both Peruvians, since there are only two Americans on the staff) and I reached Chachapoyas in time for the meeting with the mayor that our contact had set up for us. Our discussion with his aides was well under way when the mayor whose first name is Diogenes walked in, thin, fair-skinned, about my age, brown hair combed to the side, large brown eyes, and sporting a black leather jacket. He greeted us, sat down, listened to an aide brief him, and spoke rapidly and in a straightforward manner. Unlike most of his aides, he spoke Spanish in the dialect of the area and I had to adjust my ear and pay double attention. You could tell he was a man of action, and he offered to coordinate visits to communities that met our criteria and to accompany us the next day. We speculated that he must be glad to join us since political opponents of the regional government (not the mayor) had called a strike for the next day and there would surely be roadblocks and disturbances.

We left at 7:30 AM the next morning, going with the flow as usual but not fully realizing what awaited us or that we would be eating lunch at 5:00 PM and returning only at 9:30 PM that evening. We began our visit driving south along the Utcubamba river, descended from mountains, rushing with rapids, lined with trees, and as wide as a tennis court in places. The mayor told us about growing up in the hills, walking two days to get to school, and going back to visit his family on breaks. He then went to university and became both a teacher and the mayor of Magdalena, a small town we passed on the way. With the mayor calling ahead on his cell phone, we wound up visiting seven communities and their mayors, council members, and a few leaders of farmer's associations and women's groups. Each community ranged in size from 900 people to about 2,500 people not counting their various nearby annexes and outlying settlements.

We explained Peace Corps, stressing that Volunteers do not bring financial resources nor do they come with a pre-determined project "under their arm", but that they represent "human resources", are professionals, insert themselves into local initiatives based on their education and training, and establish what they will work on by first doing a survey and interviews to establish needs, priorities, and a dialogue on actions. We listened to the leaders, asked about the water and the number of children in school and the regularity of public transportation, etc. We noted a few of the issues our Volunteers could work on—— clean water and solid waste management in almost every community, helping a group of women weavers in one community, promoting eco-tourism, improved cook stoves, promoting "healthy households", combating child malnutrition, and in another community developing a master plan to conserve a natural area precious for its flowers, orchids, and birdlife and accessible 2 – 3 hours by horseback. The area as a whole is just steep, exemplified on our route where we saw a cow dead from having fallen down the hillside and, sadly, women grieving for a two-year old also dead from having fallen into an "abyss."

In each community, we also talked about what it meant to host a Volunteer and that Volunteers do not live alone but with host families who would receive the same rent from a Volunteer that they would for hosting a schoolteacher. More often than not, the mayors, who were all men, asked women leaders to identify 2 – 3 suitable host families that we could interview on a follow-up trip. *"Que bendito trabajo que me has encargado"*, exclaimed the woman so instructed in the first town—what blessed work you have given me, I will love to do it. Another talkative woman, short and stout with strong Quechua features in the poorest yet largest community some 17 kilometers off the road, listened to our criteria for host families, beaming the whole time, and you knew that she was thinking of herself as the "host mom" for the Volunteer. Everywhere, we felt interest, openness, graciousness, hospitality, humor, and warmth, and knew we had our new friend in the mayor of Chachapoyas to thank for it. We made no firm commitments but obtained letters soliciting a Volunteer signed and stamped by each mayor. These would be the letters to solicit the two-year visas for the Volunteers.

Back in the Peace Corps vehicle enroute to the next community, we discussed factors such as the work possibilities we could detect and the type of Volunteers needed in each community by their skill set, gender, and also their personality, proximity to other Volunteers and the ability to complement skill sets by working jointly on some projects, the distance from the main road and the regularity of public transportation (in the extreme case, one vehicle a day leaving at 4 AM), etc. We had a limited number of Volunteers to deploy way out here, but the next day, we looked at our options and decided to place 6 Volunteers in 5 communities (one married couple) instead of 4 as we initially contemplated. One community would have to be Chachapoyas where Diogenes had been of so much help to us. I thought to myself, how lucky these Volunteers would be to come to an area with enough leaders so ready to work with Peace Corps at the grassroots level. Time will tell, of course. The next day, we also got the nominal support we needed from the regional government, after waiting hours to meet with them since they were too tied up with politics.

On the way back to Chiclayo, we stopped by to see a few other Volunteers in the *bosque seco* ("dry forest") near Olmos, where it basically rains only once every 8 – 10 years or so, and then the entire countryside is deluged for weeks. Here was environment Volunteer John R., with a degree in wildlife biology from Seattle, working with a community of 300 people to protect the forest from loggers, to plant native trees and flowers in the plaza and to protect it from goats, to promote recycling, environmental education, and trash disposal at the school where he had also recently helped install solar panels so that people could recharge cell phone batteries and teachers could make copies without having to go to the next town. None of this was easy—we saw a truck full of logs in the next town and John told us the long, involved story of how the provincial mayor in Olmos had publicly committed to the rest of the solar panels and to the inverter needed, had his photo opportunities doing so with the media, but still hadn't come through. Since the people in his agricultural community had little time or money, the Volunteer was traveling back and forth to Olmos to hand-carry requests for approval from one end of the mayor's office to the other. Olmos of course had electricity while people in John's town lived with no electricity and one hour of running water daily. Ah, life in Peru and politics everywhere.

I never know if people fully read these e-mails and I don't send them often. If you do, take a good message here for what life is like in rural Peru and for Peace Corps Volunteers.

Cheers,

Sanjay

Sketch: *Fiesta Peruana*

"Whatever you do," one of two American staff in Lima told me early on, "Don't get in the way of Peruvians and a party."

That was advice I would come to heed.

At the end of a Monday, the health program director comes to my office and says, "Sanjay, staff are feeling stressed out, *mucho trabajo*, lot of work. So we have an idea *pero necesitamos tu apoyo*, we need your support."

"Ok, tell me", I say.

"We want to have a party—a *fiesta*—at your house."

"What—when?"

"Wednesday."

"But that's two days from now," I say, a bit concerned. "I gotta talk to my wife."

"Don't worry, *no te preocupes*, I already talked to her. She agreed, *está completamente de acuerdo*—she's all in."

"Oh, ok", I say uncertainly.

"You don't worry, we will take care of everything—the dance floor, the DJ, the drinks, the appetizers, the dinner, and clean-up—you just give the house and have fun."

"Ok!" How can I refuse.

"5 PM, they will set up the dance floor, 6 PM, we start."

Sure enough, it functions like clockwork!

At 5 PM, a little truck comes and parks in front of our house. Soon, they install a wooden dance floor in our backyard. They also unload tables and chairs and red tablecloths and white chair covers. They hang red and white bunting for decoration on the little roof over the dance floor that holds up the lighting needed for when it gets dark. The DJ, in his smiley face and tiny car, arrives and sets up the sound system. The safety and security manager from the office comes and sets up the grill. Staff begin to arrive from the office, catching rides in each other's vehicles, parking end to end in our small garage and driveway.

The safety and security manager from the office now asks for help in cutting the limes for the pisco sours—Peru's national drink concocted from a particular grape alcohol, lime juice, sugar syrup, ice, and egg whites blended together with a touch of vanilla extract on the top. A *brindis*, or toast, is held—*que se diviertan porque lo mercen*, may you enjoy yourselves because you deserve it, right Sanjay? Says the health program director. *Son bebidas espirituales*, she adds, they are spiritual drinks. Everyone smiles, laughs, drinks up. Pisco is a strong drink, and alcohol is not the point, only the initiation. The point is togetherness. Most take only one drink, only a few take a second drink.

The staff, a good 40+ people, are in their same clothes from the office. No spouses! In a moment, the music starts and the bold ones lead the way, dancing happily and extravagantly, in step and swaying to the music as though born to dance. Others follow. People are totally in the mood and free—dancing in lines, in a circle, in pairs, even just alone on the side, but in the rhythm. The appetizers are ready, dinner is cooking on the grill, the lights come on as it gets dark.

Just as people begin to get tired, dinner is ready. They all sit down at 8 person tables and the DJ changes the music to soft classical piano. After dinner, a few final dances—no wild finale like on special occasions such as a going-away party.

Then the health program director announces, "*Ya son las nueve*, it's already 9 o'clock—time to clean up!"

By 10 PM, everyone is gone, the dance floor has been removed, every last cup or plate in the back yard has been taken away as trash, the back yard looks exactly the same as 6 PM.

Next day at the office at 8 AM, everyone is on time, smiling, and happy! Photos are shared. People are cheerful. And ready to work hard and conscientiously!

I would think, where are the spouses?! It was only me and my wife. The staff all danced with each other, including our janitors and drivers, like we were one big family. They were mostly married with few exceptions. And, in Peruvian custom, EVERYONE shows up! One has to have a really big excuse to miss a party—it's considered solidarity that to do everything together. If someone didn't want to dance, he or she still came to hand out and accompany everyone. All costs were tracked, and the whole party budgeted beforehand—dance floor, DJ, etc. Cost were divided mostly equally, but with senior staff asked to pay a little more, so that lesser paid staff not pay so much. And money was collected from everyone within a day or two.

The party was carried out with the utmost efficiency. Neighbours would have to put up with all that music—just like I had to put up with their music other days. A good party reflected a certain attitude of Peruvians towards life. They couldn't understand young American volunteers talking about "stress"—they said, what's that? "We hear them talking about stress. And to us, it's like—that's life!"

Something similar was reflected in the rural areas that hosted Volunteers. When Volunteers were introduced to their counterparts as part of site visit in their respective regional capitals, an exercise would be facilitated in which the Volunteers being assigned to that region would talk about and present on five characteristics of American culture while their counterparts would do the same for Peruvian culture. Invariably, the young Americans showed they were individualistic and placed a a great value on personal responsibility while Peruvians showed the emphasis placed on solidarity and collective responsibility as well as on humility.

In this way, Americans began to be introduced to another way of life. They learned their way was not the only way, their values not the only values, and what they called stress, others simply called "life" and that was capable of being transformed into something joyous if everyone came together.

Sketch: A Dog in Cajamarca

The dog lay there in the sun, skin black as charcoal, body quivering. It did not move when the Peace Corps vehicle pulled up, a sure sign that something was wrong.

The regional coordinator driving the vehicle got out and approached the dog. He knelt down while the occupant of the vehicle who was the country director could only look on. The dog's belly moved up and down, it was breathing in rhythmically, its heart pumping away. Its eyes were placid. It knew something was dreadfully wrong. The dog was dying slowly, though young enough still. What had the dog done? What poison was this?

The houses around were silent. There was no movement except the breeze in the trees. It was early still. Some people must have gone to the fields, others to town, while others may have been sitting inside. It was a leisurely Saturday morning. The dog lay quietly in the equatorial sun which presently began to bake.

The staff member took out a water bottle, cupped water in his hands, and splashed it on the dog. No reaction whatsoever. Its placid, resigned, unblinking eyes looked straight ahead all the time.

"Shall we lift him out of the sun?" the coordinator asked the director. He nodded quiet assent. Instead of lifting him with his hands and having the dog's body crumple, the coordinator found a blanket and lay the dog on it like a stretcher. He cradled the animal, stood up, and lay it gently in the shade on the sidewalk in a garden. There was no change in the dog.

The coordinator and director moved to take care of their business in this little town. Knocking on a door and finding no one home, they proceeded to walk down the street. Returning some time later, they checked on the dog. It was the same.

"There is nothing we can do," pronounced the coordinator. He was from the area and knew these cases before. "The dog must have developed a taste for something it shouldn't eat, or maybe it has been a nuisance for a long time. They have poisoned it."

At least it was in the shade. Its breathing seemed deeper, more labored, its eyes more moist, more forlorn. The coordinator sprinkled more water on it. It would die like this. On a sunny Saturday morning in a small town once visited by the former president of Peru and where an American volunteer had once lived but which otherwise was like any other and held no claim to fame.

At least, the dog received an act of compassion before leaving this world. It wasn't much but it was an individual act, against the stream, done with kindness and gentleness and care. It was not just the shade and physical comfort, insufficient in itself, but the very act of caring that showed the better side of humanity to this poor creature often considered "human's best friend."

Sketch: Time Stood Still

He steadiest himself, hand on the hood of the car. He was still in his semi-formal office wear, briefcase slung over the shoulder. He had just crossed the street after jogging across the long bridge over the Potomac. If he did not hurry, he would be late to the hotel where his future Volunteers were waiting.

Holding on to the car, he suddenly felt faint. His eyes began to close. The blood in his brain plunged like a cascade. The mind seemed to fly away, his body gone somewhere he knew not where. Thoughts, images, recollections, dreams, the sub-conscious swept him up like a leaf in the wind. It was peaceful there, an open field somewhere, brightened by the sun, a green and yellow brilliance so dazzling, so peaceful… and where time stood still.

Where was he? What dream was this? It felt like minutes passed on the side of that busy street.

He opened his eyes, or had they been open all along? Probably. Only now he could see again. How much time had passed? A burgundy-colored car with large hubcaps and a huge windshield blew by like a silver bullet, glinting in the late afternoon sun and spewing emissions into the exhaust-filled air at a summer day's end.

He felt the weight of the black bag on his shoulder. He took his hand off the parked car in front of him. The moment had passed, the bizarre moment where his mind had entered a dream world far away and his body had stayed in this one. His pulse, his heartbeat, all seemed normal now. He must be on his way. They will be waiting for him. What a strange experience? What did it all mean, if anything?

He picked up the pace and yet seemed more refreshed now.

2012

Sketch: A Glimpse Beyond the Monkey Mind

"The mind is the forerunner of all things"—the Buddha, 5th century BCE

"We suffer more in imagination than in reality"—Seneca, 1st century BCE

It was as though he had never tasted dal and rice before. Slowly, he turned it over in his mouth, savoring the texture and flavor, softly chewing, then down the hatch it went. He hadn't intended to taste at all, he just suddenly began to taste it. It was nothing special, not home cooking, not a grand restaurant. Just simple food, the same as he had been having for three days already. This day, his sense of taste was especially sharp, and that was because his mind was clear.

It was Day 4 at a *vipassana* meditation center in Igatpuri, India, about 3 hours by train from Mumbai, in the hills. *Vipassana* means "seeing things as they are." The first three days had been spent focusing only on breath, on the nostrils, on the space just below one's nose, on air entering and exiting. It was not possible. The monkey mind ran away with his thoughts. His Volunteers, safety, risks, travel, sexual assault, adjustment issues, personalities. His staff, attitudes, conversations that replayed in his mind, what was meant, not meant. Peace Corps Washington, assumptions, misunderstandings, reports. His wife, children, and father at home—more misunderstandings, clashes, struggle, grievances, resentment, bitterness.

He also missed all of them. Why did he think only of the problems? What was he doing here anyway? He could be with his family who were on the beach in Goa right now.

He was locked away from it all for 10 days. No phone, no laptop, no Internet. No book or pen or writing pad. All checked in. No news, no conversation even, no glances even. Even though there were 300 males here meditating in 5 different dhamma halls, and another 300 females on the other side of a partition.

It was silence, "noble silence", time to observe oneself, starting with breath. With each day, the mind did slow down. And as Day 4 began, the instructor had said, "Now direct your attention from your nose to the top of your head, and slowly, as though a bucket of water is being poured over you very slowly, observe the sensations you experience, as you direct your attention downwards, behind your forehead, eyes, ears… and downwards… neck, shoulders, arms, hand, fingers, and back up… other arm… slowly, now chest, sternum, stomach… now back, spine, sides… pelvis, posterior, thigh, knee, calf, foot, toes… other leg… and back up… reverse the process… feel the sensations…"

And the whole morning had gone. He found that he was able to do about one entire body scan, head to toe and back, in about 20 minutes, estimating the time according to the length of the meditation sessions.

As thoughts abated, it was as though the senses became alive. On some days, he was more sensitive inwardly than other days. On these days, he could feel the vibrations, blood, pulse, a throbbing, an electrical sensation especially at his fingers, his lungs, his heartbeat, discomfort and pain too. Sitting cross-legged required some adjustment every 20 to 30 minutes or so, but he was able to manage.

On Day 7, it was smell. Walking out of the dining hall in front of the rose garden, he felt as though he had never smelt a rose before until then. It was unexpected and struck him as unusual. He lingered to be sure. It was almost overpowering. He had walked by them before but this day, for some inexplicable reason, was different. Then he walked by the latrines and the smell was equally overpowering! More than any other day.

Without thought—overthinking everything—the senses had become more alive. It was the disciplined days also. Woken up by a bell outside his window at 4 AM, basic toiletries, a walk to the meditation hall, meditation from 4:30 AM to 6:30 AM, followed by breakfast, bathing, and getting ready for the day, and more meditation 8 AM to 9:30 AM, a break, meditation 10 AM to 11:30 AM, lunch and rest, meditation 1 PM to 3 PM, a break, meditation 3:30 PM to 5 PM, tea and a snack, a break, a short meditation 6:30 PM to 7 PM, followed by a video discourse, a return to one's room, and lights out by 8:30 PM. No reading, no socializing.

One day, someone else had taken his chappals, likely by mistake. Or was it on purpose? Who took them? He had to take someone else's chappals. He began to inspect the chappals outside the meditation halls to find his own. He wondered if he should report or not. This one thing began to take his mind, to obsess his mind even. Two days later, he saw them, and quickly slipped off the ones he had and took his old ones back. He had no means to mark them as his, but he examined them more closely now, to always be able to identify them. How obsessed the mind can become!

On Day 9 in the morning, he felt a surge of energy, of something like small particles slowly moving together through his entire body. Any pain or discomfort was left completely aside. It occurred again on Day 10. It was as though for a full hour, he had become completely oblivious of time, completely attuned to the present moment, but to his body only—not a thought in the world, immune to any disturbances, just sort of entranced by a new energy within such as he had never felt before. No theory, no ideology, no complex method other than what Day 9 or 10 unexpectedly threw up and yielded by self-observation alone. On other occasions, it had not been there.

Sounds, sights, taste, smell—the senses had all been more alive than ever at some time or other during those 10 days. Simplicity, order, patience, observation, awareness, attention. Was it the result of effort? Or mere observation? Of following a routine. Of basic guidance. Of the sense of others in the hall also and their seriousness of purpose.

Mysteries of the mind, of the self we know so little about for most of our life. Because we don't know how and we don't take the time. We get carried away by the monkey mind only in our day-to-day. As though life is this external world only. And when things don't go right? We look within and don't know where to begin or how. When behind psychology, in the mind, all conditions arise. And what arises passes and comes to an end.

2012

Narrative: Moving on to Mozambique

By law, Peace Corps could extend the 5-year term limit for most staff to 7.5 years for 15% of its staff. Instead of two 2.5 year terms, the terms could be broken up to cover 7.5 years in two countries for overseas staff, but not more than 5 years in one country.

It was this very in-built flux that enabled me to get a job with Peace Corps to begin with. My bosses were content with me. While Peru had been good to me and especially to the family, Lima's weather was something I never got used to, being mostly cloudy and foggy with thin mist in the air ("neblinas") from May to November. And I still longed for Africa, especially after I'd seen the Africa regional director and Africa posts present at a conference. Making his presentation seem almost like a promotion, the regional director loved to say, Peace Corps Africa is "where the magic happens."

After I expressed interest in transitioning to Africa, I was given several choices. I was asked to give Mozambique serious consideration and to talk to the country director there. Portuguese was spoken in Mozambique and Spanish was the easiest bridge language to Portuguese. When I expressed concern about violence there, because I was aware of Mozambique's long civil war, the outgoing country director memorably told me, "But Sanjay, you're living in Lima, what are you worried about—Maputo is so much safer!" Ultimately, my wife and I decided on Mozambique because the American International School of Mozambique looked better than the other sub-Saharan Africa option that we were given.

Peace Corps had begun to take a toll on me. Concerns about Volunteer safety, issues with Volunteers and staff, variance in budget support from Washington, and especially bureaucratic procedures related to everything from hiring to budget management. Peru was considered the most complex post in Latin America but Mozambique was considered the most complex post in Africa, and that was saying something. I would deal with much more in Mozambique, especially transportation safety for Volunteers and visa problems with the government. In fact, nothing could be taken for granted, even flights and hotel bookings, even electricity. Tremendous downpours and cyclones were also a concern.

At some point, taking a cue from the Mozambican staff, I just accepted the baseline uncertainty of the operating environment and learned to relax and go with the flow while still bringing my best and most conscientious self to work every day. With Mozambique being so vast and spread out, and conditions so basic, Volunteers learned to be hardy and grateful for what they had. Their sites were bigger than in Peru and it was easier for them to find meaningful work.

After more than 20 years since my own service as a Volunteer, I was thrilled to be back in Africa. Mozambique was not like Mali in many ways, but I learned to appreciate the differences. Moving on to

Mozambique also meant I would not be going back to El Paso after 5 years. As it happened, the 7.5 years took us to my son's last year of high school in Maputo. Mainly on this basis—allowing my son to complete high school in Maputo—I was granted one final year, making for a total of 8.5 years as Peace Corps staff. By that time, July 2018, I would have to leave the organization.

December 2013

Sketch: CD Office

On the first floor of a two story building and basement, between the streets Avenida do Zimbabwe and Avenida Julius Nyerere, his corner office (Country Director office) held a sweeping view of the sparkling blue bay of the Indian Ocean. Some staff seemed to stop and give him a wide berth whenever he walked up the staircase. They greeted but averted their eyes until he made them feel at ease with a cheerful smile and broken Portuguese. *"Com liçenca"*, even his top Mozambican staff member would say upon coming to his open office door, waiting for an acknowledgement to enter.

Inside was a round table with several chairs and on one side, in front of a high-backed cushioned black chair, was his desk with computer, printer, inbox, and filing cabinets. Cloth prints in faded beige, brown, and orange lined the series of closets along one side of the room.

Countless calls he would take here, countless emails he would read and send, countless meetings with staff and Volunteers he would hold here. A black coffeemaker sat on one side, used mainly just to heat water for tea. He was too busy to make or care about coffee any longer. From 7 AM until 6 PM four days per week and until mid-afternoon on Friday and many a Saturday and Sunday, he made use of this chair and space to direct and manage a large volunteer program in the interests of the world's most powerful country, of which he was a faithful citizen himself. It was the peak of his career even though he hardly had time to glance at the sparkling ocean towards the east. Occasionally, the storm clouds blowing over the bay caught his attention and he wondered if he should make the walk home early or risk getting stranded or soaked.

In a cabinet by the window, he found framed photographs of two young Volunteers. At the bottom, it was engraved that these two Volunteers, one female and one male, had died in service a year or two earlier. The departing director had told him he would find this there. Staff had said they would feel uncomfortable if it was displayed in a public space. Instead, under the boughs of a large tree on one side of the office, fellow Volunteers and staff had decorated a wall in memory of the two Volunteers with the phrase, "The love they gave lives on", in the center. They had died when the vehicle they were in, just weeks into their service, had swerved off the road and overturned at a high rate of speed. The driver was intoxicated. Some passengers survived, some didn't.

From time to time, he would step around the roots of this hallowed tree and space and clasp his hands in prayer and bow in remembrance.

Maputo, Mozambique, 2013 – 18

Reflection: Africa gets to my Heart

I've spent almost 7 years of my life in Africa and have lived and worked in two countries on opposite ends of the continent, Mali and Mozambique. Others have spent their entire lives or stayed longer or know the continent better than I do and are more perceptive than me. But, as so many can attest, including a great many Peace Corps Volunteers after only two years living at the community level, there is something about "Africa" that gets to your heart.

I'm aware of both generalizations and what it means to romanticize a place or a people. This is satirized most beautifully and effectively by Binyavanga Wainaina in an article he wrote for Granta Magazine.

I can only speak of my own heartfelt connection and observations.

I felt it the first time I was in Mali, at ground level, something beyond Peace Corps and so powerful as though I'd been a Malian in a previous birth. I've said elsewhere I cannot thank the people of Mali enough. Mali is the debt I can never re-pay, only pass forward.

I felt it again in Mozambique and feel it still. Mozambique, where I stayed longer—4.5 years; I lived more comfortably—as Peace Corps staff in the capital; but I saw more of the country—more than most any American in country, certainly any American working for the government, and at ground level through the Volunteers with little of the show put up for outsiders.

Mozambique's independence leader and first president, the irreplaceable Samora Machel, had it right when he identified the three evils of his time: one, racism; two, colonialism; and three, economic exploitation. If it sounds like a Marxist analysis, it is, but as Samora said, *he didn't need to read Marx, he had only to read his own life.* Born in a farming family in 1933, able to attend only a minimum level of schooling in the Portuguese colonial system, a nurse by training, then a revolutionary, then the leader of the independence movement after Eduardo Mondlane, Mozambique's U.S. educated Ph.D., was assassinated by a bomb hidden in a book, and finally Mozambique's charismatic first president in 1975.

Since the colonial power had left a mere 1,000 high school graduates in the country, Samora appealed to people anywhere in the world who had socialist ideals to come to Mozambique and help build, educate, and develop the country. It wasn't long before apartheid South Africa and the former Rhodesia, working through disgruntled tribal chiefs, church leaders, and others in Mozambique, fomented a rebellion and directly bombed, sabotaged, and destabilized the new country, poor as it was. Samora turned to aid from the Soviet Union and to Marxism. In 1985, after the Soviet Union cut aid and Samora realized the fruits of Marxism in practice were few, Samora made a friendship with President Ronald Reagan of the United States. That is when American aid also began. But it did not stop apartheid South Africa from using a radio decoy to draw his plane, returning from Lusaka to Maputo, to crash into the Lebombo mountains on the South Africa side of the border with Mozambique. It was 1986 and Samora had effectively been assassinated and the country was still in a civil war that would end only with peace accords in 1992.

As Samora said, to understand Africa, at least from a development perspective, is to familiarize yourself with exploitation. Broadly over the centuries, it goes like this: slavery of human beings; ivory from elephants; gold, diamonds, rubies from the earth; other raw materials useful to industrial civilization, from aluminum, bauxite, tin, and copper to timber and of course coal, oil, and natural gas, to name a few. Then there is land that can be taken to grow and export cotton, sugar cane, cacao, coffee, rice, and so on.

Incisively, Samora also said, "for the nation to be born, the tribe must die." It is why he disempowered tribal chieftains and traditional authorities. Mozambique, like many African countries, is made up of a patchwork of 20+ ethnicities and languages, many overlapping with other nations since the colonizers did not demarcate borders based on what suited Africans but only on what suited their needs to control, exploit, and defend as much territory as they could from other European colonizers. For this reason also, with Mozambique under attack from a powerful and well-armed South Africa, Samora could not risk native language education and he chose to make Portuguese the language of instruction in schools to unify the country and construct a Mozambican national identity and not one based on Changaana, Makua, and so on.

I found Mozambicans tolerant in everything except politics. In one family, there could be Muslims, Christians, and animists without any conflict or even any need to convert one person to another religion. Even Volunteers who were gay chose to come out after a year and tell their students and most often the reaction was "that's interesting" mainly because their students knew little about homosexuality and, unlike neighbouring English-speaking countries, had not been indoctrinated by missionaries that homosexuality was "wrong" in any way. But in politics, there was little tolerance or political space. Elections and campaigning were not free and fair. Counting was fraudulent. The ruling party was all powerful. The opposition party could only get attention by firing at vehicles on the main EN-1 highway, effectively cutting the country in two and forcing military escorts for years on end.

Mozambique had a host of other challenges, to name a few:

- A high prevalence of HIV/AIDS, especially in the south where prevalence rates were over 30%

- A high prevalence of malaria, the fatal form falciparum malaria

- Over-crowded schools, with even 120 students in classrooms in the north, even when there were two schedules at school—a morning schedule and an afternoon schedule

- Minimum electricity generation, such that the better part of an entire province with Volunteers went without power once for 45 days due to a storm knocking out electrical towers

- Extreme vulnerability to floods and cyclones and droughts—one year I was there, there simply was no rainy season, the skies remained clear and the rain didn't come, and staff would come back from the field and speak of dead cows they had seen along the road in the countryside

- An under-funded, under-maintained national airlines with no domestic competition

- One helicopter in the entire country in case of emergency rescue

- Thousands of kilometers of dirt roads that became impassable in the rainy season—this was a factor to consider in all travel, whether by Volunteers or by staff, and it required great skill of staff to drive quickly on deeply rutted muddy roads and not get stuck

- An entire province with no traffic lights

- A half dozen psychologists in the entire country

- Police who might not be the police at night, rather the victimizer

- Unlicensed drivers of public transportation potentially driving while intoxicated

- A ruling party accused openly of corruption, especially after the April 2016 revelations of "hidden debt" pocketed by the ruling party resulting in suspension of foreign aid by the European Union and the IMF

- Heavy reliance on China for infrastructure such as airports, roads, and bridges, as well as for political support, at the expense of timber, fishing rights, land for paddy, and entitlements to natural gas in future

- A shadowy and mysterious Islamist insurgency, potentially connected to ISIS, that emerged along the northern coast after a series of spectacular attacks—one of my last acts in 2018 was to evacuate all the volunteers in Cabo Delgado province

Mozambique had a little bit of everything. It was harder being a Volunteer in Mozambique than in Peru, to wit:

- The risk of HIV/AIDS and malaria

- Much less availability of in-country transportation and it was unsafe to travel at night

- A knowledge of Portuguese was not enough to really communicate with most people in the country

Other tragic and difficult incidents for Volunteers in Mozambique during my time:

- Death of a Volunteer in a road accident due to an intoxicated driver

- Concussion to a Volunteer due to a fall from a cliff in the north of the country and complicated emergency evacuation to South Africa followed by surgery and convalescent care

- Concussion to a Volunteer due to a road accident in the south of the country and evacuation to South Africa followed by surgery and convalescent care

- Allegation of spying against a Volunteer in the north of the country for using a drone, resulting in his departure from the country

Further, while the average Mozambican displayed great warmth and benevolence to Peace Corps Volunteers, the ruling party after 2016, when the U.S. government began investigating the hidden debt scandal, became more and more suspicious of Volunteers, especially in Cabo Delgado and the north. This, in my view, eventually led to the "visa crisis."

And yet, a good percentage of Volunteers not only completed two years of service but they opted for a third year. Others stayed on in the country on their own. Others married Mozambicans after service and either stayed on or went back to the U.S.

Why stay? When you read about it and take it all in, what is it about a country—a land and people—that would make you want to stay? Women in particular also dealt with a fair amount of "unwanted attention" and harassment. And yet female Volunteers also loved the country.

As with Africa in general, it's not the government, *it's the people*. Too often, just as Chinua Achebe points out in his book "Things Fall Apart", the government goes on to imitate and adopt the same exploitative policies of the colonizer. With a notable exception in Mozambique: Samora Machel, who was incorruptible by nature, a true man of the people. Killed by apartheid South Africa.

From my point of view, there is also something about a country and a people that has suffered. I felt this in Peru, reading about Peru in the 1980s especially, and the war against Sendero Luminoso ("Shining Path") in the mountains and that also came home to Lima in the form of terrorist bombings, as Peace Corps staff could tell me. But it is even more so in Mozambique, where staff had personally suffered. A staff member had his baby sister stomped to death by guerrillas in the north ("you could see the sole of the boot on her face"). Another staff member in the south had been kidnapped by guerrillas. A staff member in the north had grown up as a refugee in Malawi due to the civil war. In a time of shortage of even sugar in the south, staff could recount having to buy candies and grind them to powder to obtain sugar. Various staff had suffered from malaria to the point of hospitalization and near death. Nor was staff immune to HIV/AIDS. Even professional staff had grown up poor owning only one pair of sneakers.

Because politics could get you killed, all staff seemed to have a basic "political awareness." This came as a bit of a surprise to me, but it was evident especially on long drives when it came out in conversation. One could only empathize with them, since political violence is something so many of us, including myself, rarely have to consider in our daily lives. Once I understood this, and the devastation of the civil war in recent memory, then I understood how much Mozambicans valued peace and reconciliation. The last thing they wanted was another war. When it seemed the opposition party was exploiting the use of violence and the death of innocent civilians for political gain, most people still felt there must be some validity to their claims, they are Mozambican brothers and sisters, and the ruling party should negotiate and come to some terms with them, which eventually did happen.

For me, Africa in general—Mali and Mozambique in particular—is in my heart. Experts in survival, placing value on peace and reconciliation, bearing relatively little rancor and resentment for the past, fortified by patience and endurance, naturally generous and hospitable, open and not clinging to tradition for the sake of tradition, expressing cheerfulness and optimism, in spite of the most hardships and the most challenging natural environment—I have only respect and affection.

Sketch: Talent Show

An evening towards the end of staff retreat. Staged after dinner in the restaurant, set amidst the sand dunes and a breeze blowing off the ocean. An IT specialist turned into announcer extraordinaire. A literacy specialist turned into a dancer, leaping and shaking with synchronicity the cowrie shell bands on his ankles and biceps. A cashier, though she may be a bit overweight, shuffling along to the beat of a traditional rhythm. Two staff from the northern office strumming a guitar and singing a song from the neighboring country that is sweet in melody and significant in meaning. A coordinator from the central office entertains with mathematical conundrums that stretch the mind. The lone Bulgarian national leads a group of Mozambican female staff in a Bulgarian folk dance. A senior staff member performs a skit with another staff member, one playing the program manager and one playing the Peace Corps Volunteer, who winds up getting forcibly sent home! The inside joke of it. Howls of laughter, shrieks of delight, rounds of applause. The American staff rock with laughter and shake their heads in awe and disbelief at the sheer abandon and raw talent in a different setting far removed from supervision.

A letting loose that is sorely needed by a staff that works so hard, so consistently, so faithfully.

It was the one time all year that we were all together—Nampula staff, Chimoio staff, regional program assistants from Cuamba and Mocuba, and the lot of us from Maputo. These were treasured times full of mirth and joy and conviviality. There was also something very African, in the naturalness that everyone displayed, beneath our civilized demeanors. It was as though the performances revealed a higher intelligence and awareness in comparison to the "performance" criteria of running a U.S. government volunteer program. Performance with sensibility, with art, with drama—as opposed to performance with protocols, guidelines, and outcome measures. They certainly "made it real"!

Notes to Self: Of Struggle and Dreams

August 29, 2015

To the deity of emotions,

On a Saturday, I feel that old fatigue: spent from another dizzy week at work, not having slept well, grateful to have a day with few external commitments. I can laze around at home if I like. And yet I feel those anxieties, like wet clothes washed up awaiting the next spin cycle—anxieties big and small, COS conference, USDH hires, a personnel issue, etc. And old longings in the background, still there, buried. And I feel a sense of loss, of a door closed, a turn that cannot be unturned, a truthfulness to self even that is no longer truthful. Moods. The mind. Memory. Writing to a muse—o where hast thou gone?

To the deity of memory,

Why did I think of you—a boy, bounding up the snow-laden path outside, up the mountain behind the hotel, under the boughs of the evergreen trees, a bushy-tailed squirrel here and there, the long flat marks of skis in the snow, a yellow sun coming up over the rocky mountain ridge and—stopping to trace an elephant on the snow embankment, a long trunk, wavy ears, small eyes in a large head, short front feet. In the snow. Oh why did I think of you? Outside the Tschuggen Hotel, Arosa, Switzerland, 1973. I was 7 years old.

To the deity of time,

What meaning has this life? It goes on and on. The minutes, on a divinely lazy Saturday, can be eternal. How does one become at peace with time? By releasing a hold, somewhat, on the things that press upon us, with all the weight of matter and meaning. By learning to live with a certain amount of imperfection, incompleteness, actions not taken. It will not all be resolved in a day or two days, or a week, not a moment or a month. One has to understand and adapt oneself to these external realities, recognizing what is outside one's control, at least for that day. One must learn to be comfortable with actions not taken, actions that may have been quite fruitless and are best saved for another day.

August 31, 2015

To the deity of dreams,

What mysteries. I dreamt of a visit to Bougoula, Mali—and a neighbor Bra I knew in Sirakoro—and of goats slipping through a fence, followed by horses, their wild brown manes rippling in the wind—and what many other things I dreamt of, seemingly disjointed, disconnected. I can make no real sense of it and can recall only the thinnest fragments. A mystery… that does leave me longing to get back to Mali one day and visit Sirakoro, a place I knew well, but 22 years ago.

September 13, 2015

To the muse of adolescence,

I was that boy who stuttered and stammered when called on. I remember it distinctly in Ms. McCain's 8th grade English class. The fear, the trepidation, the trembling, the speechlessness—planning what I would say if called upon. It was mainly fear of embarrassment in front of my peers. The fear of public speaking, of thinking before I spoke would persist with me for many years. Spontaneity was only in the mind, not in the words. I lived a covert life that way. And yet I paid attention, I was engaged, I was beginning to think. English became my best subject starting in 9th grade. I received top marks in writing. That would have been the year preceding my age 15 awakening, changing schools from 9th grade to 10th grade. By then, I disdained copying, anything unoriginal, and small talk in general.

To the muse of dreams,

Again last week, was it Sunday night. I dreamt of running naked, without clothes—and yet no need to be furtive or embarrassed, no one notices or pays attention. It seems quite normal. Was it only my imagination?

And was it Friday or Saturday night. Those fluorescent, brightly glowing, incandescently colored, triangular-headed, mechanical-like snakes—slithering in geometric patterns on the open ground at the edge of where the tent should be. I must pull down the tent flaps, I think, and prepare to do so. It is night, not long after dusk, and well before midnight, with the prospect, even dread, of a night that is just beginning. But they never cross the tent's border. They slither away slowly, geometrically, mechanically, lighting their way into the night. There was no real reason for alarm, no real reason to be afraid.

Sketch: Burnout

He found himself at the Global Leadership Summit of the organization he worked for. It was in the hills of Maryland outside the country's capital, Washington D.C. The weather was mostly rainy and gray and gloomy. It was fall and wet leaves filled the forest and pavements where the conference center was located.

But he had been feeling this way, gloomy and averse to socializing, for some weeks. Nothing could resolve it. Not a 4 week break in the summer, not runs on the weekend, not walking home for lunch. Something about work was relentless. Decisions, planning, listening, juggling, the occasional crisis intervention. Hiring, firing, reporting, representing, facilitating. He had a great team, to be sure, but it was quite lonely at the top. One always had to be up for one's people.

Something in his body seemed to curl, to slope in on itself, to go back into a womblike position. He felt like playing defense at times, like shrinking, like fleeing. He talked to his wife about it, but it was hard for her to understand. He emailed three higher-ups, and they understood but could offer nothing more than advice. They looked forward to meeting him at the leadership summit.

In normal conditions, he would be thrilled to get off the plane, step into the country he knew and embraced, and meet friends and colleagues. In normal circumstances, everything he liked about his job would give him pleasure. Meeting volunteers, meeting staff, making eye contact, affirming their achievements, encouraging them in their aspirations, lifting them with a word of humor. Representing the agency he loved and that had veritably transformed his life and worldview when young, whether to the embassy, the host country government, the partners on the ground in myriad localities, or to the new groups of trainees. It was an agency that prioritized human development in all its forms, both within the organization and in its programming in the field. The mission had that time-honoured sacred quality that few organizations had.

Strange then, and terribly discomfiting, to feel such little excitement or enthusiasm in his breast on the long flight from Johannesburg back home. What had changed exactly? Was it overwork? Was it a new human resources issue that smelled of wrongful termination? Was it family issues—the marital relationship, media-consumed teenage children, an aging father in ill health?

More than anything it was the work load. The telltale sign was that exactly the things that gave him pleasure all these years at work were things he now felt averse to. It used to be that the satisfactions outweighed the burdens, that what he liked to do was more than what he disliked. Now, he just felt a numbness to it all, an aversion even to that which he loved. Strange thing!

He went about the conference with this feeling. He didn't hang out long in the drawing room after dinner where the boss invited the experienced directors like him to pass on "words of wisdom" to the new directors. No, he was not in a mood to say. It would feel dishonest to say such things in this particular moment. He went back to his room. No one else was in the halls. He took a few shots on the indoor basketball court by himself to get over his feeling, but to no avail. He sent emails back to post on the lingering HR issue.

He made an appointment to meet his boss. The meeting felt sterile, unfeeling, insensitive. This particular boss seldom returned emails, never called him, only set up a desk officer to talk to him once a week. He was managing the most complicated post on the most challenging continent with the lowest staff-to-volunteer ratio. And this boss didn't recognize the toll it was taking on him. His words of praise went past him. It seemed so superficial. Besides, he had to appeal to the boss to speed up hiring, to understand why the staff retreat could not be cut from the budget, to understand the difficulty of working with a government in a country that cared less about its own people compared to what an aid organization like theirs did. The boss seemed to spend more time with directors he perhaps connected with more at a personal level, from what he saw as small, "uncomplicated", "easy to manage" countries though that was not true.

The next day, he had a lunch appointment with his old boss. There wasn't much privacy. They sat across a table under bright lights in the front of the large, high-ceilinged hall.

"I know you've been going through a rough patch. You tell me how it's been going," his former regional director said.

But he couldn't get the words out right away. It was even a little hard to look straight at his boss for long.

"Go on now, this is our meeting, tough guy, and I'm always here for you."

The warmth, care, and affection in his voice was palpable.

"I'm going through a tough time," he managed to say, "a really tough time, Carlos."

He felt a tear well up and his voice did just tremble. His old boss looked at him more closely, in the eyes, but he asked nothing so inane such as "Are you all right? Is there anything I can do for you?" That would have been far too superficial between them. The two of them had grown close ever since he hosted Carlos' visit to his former post. They had only grown closer on weekly phone calls in those days.

Carlos was a sensitive man with a keen insight and touch on management, always holding up his direct reports for the work they did. Everyone loved to work for him and he made everyone feel special. And it was known at headquarters that the Country Director of Mozambique was held in highest regard by Carlos, that he was his "favorite CD."

"You know, I wrote you," he said, still struggling to get the words out. "It's burnout, Carlos."

"I know it is, and I told you I've been through it myself, I'm still going through it."

And Carlos talked about his big job at headquarters and its innumerable demands. It was easy to listen to him. He spoke so calmly, in such measured tones, and yet with the empathy of a close friend and not a boss at all.

"Hang in there. You are one of our best, and unfortunately we overuse our best."

It was an old refrain. He had heard it said even in the military. *The Army likes to ride a good horse,* it was said, to the point of getting broken.

It felt better to eat something, to swallow, to drink the ice water with lemon, to share the table with someone who more than understood, who more than cared, who shared his makeup and soul.

He got through the conference… and the pain of no deputy director or other top American national at post for a few more months… and the difficulties of hiring and firing and volunteer management.

In the winter, he climbed Kilimanjaro with his son and seven other friends. He got over his burnout.

September 2015

Sketch: Humbled by Kilimanjaro

It was mid-afternoon already and the others had gone ahead. Only he was behind, along with an assistant guide, on the slopes of a great mountain, picking his way down the scree so as not to slide and fall. He looked up towards the sun and infinite sky, more blinding in light than blue in color. Walking down should not be so hard. Yet he was still in the altitude sickness zone and he had been walking all night, almost 14 hours now. Each step was heavier and more difficult than the last. The rocks seemed to tumble before him with every boot he put forth, creating a rattling sound that seemed to echo in the stillness of the surroundings so bare of trees and vegetation.

For some time now, he had resorted to counting his paces, resting, and re-starting—first one hundred, then fifty, now only twenty-five, only fifteen was to come. He leaned on the Massai walking stick he had bought in the foothills. He looked ahead. One of the assistant guides ahead was carrying his day pack for him, along with his own pack, and every now and then he would turn back to check on him. He must have been aware of his personal struggle, must have seen this before, and knew just enough distance to put between the two of them for comfort. He thought he could hear the guide still singing along, in English and Swahili, just as he had on the way up the giant mountain. In total darkness lit only by headlamps and frigid temperatures that became colder and colder, it had been so motivational to hear the guides singing, especially Bob Marley songs like "No woman, no cry" and "I shot the sheriff, but I did not shoot the deputy."

Aided by dozens of porters to get up this far, they were a group of nine, both parents and children, in addition to the lead guide in front and two assistant guides in the middle and back. At one point, perhaps only 500 meters from the ridge, one guide had to go down with the 10-year old of his friend, who also went down to accompany his son. Yet, even had they made it to the ridge, they still would have had to trudge another 1.5 – 2 hours over snowpack and in colder and thinner air to reach Uhuru Peak, the official high point of the near 6,000 meter Mount Kilimanjaro, Africa's tallest mountain.

Coming down, the other three boys in the group, including his own son, had "skied" down the same scree that was giving him so much trouble right now. Maybe he was using too much energy in just braking himself from skidding and sliding down, but he felt he had too little energy to do that without falling forward and going for a toss. It was partly age, he thought, and a more cautious attitude that comes with age, when one no longer throws caution to the wind in the manner of youth.

Anyhow, the others would be waiting for him at the designated campsite on the way down. And, at some point, below 4,000 meters or so, he should regain strength in denser air and any lack of oxygen in his blood should dissipate. He must simply pace it out, slowly, and keep walking. As the guides and porters never ceased saying in Swahili, as though it were a philosophy of life, one should go *"pole, pole"*—slowly, slowly.

He continued to marvel at the sight of himself and his utter exhaustion walking down and not up! How strange to think he had grown weaker on the descent instead of stronger. He gazed up at the sun and sky again. This is what it meant to feel *humbled by nature*. You test yourself, test the mountains, but nature also teaches respect and humility. It was no intellectual contemplation at this moment. He meditated on the thought and felt the feeling, vowing not to forget. One foot in front of the other had never felt so difficult. The mind felt clear still. Humbled by nature, this is what it felt like.

The slope slowly lost its incline. He could make out squat trees and a faint hint of greenery ahead. He challenged himself to stop less and pick up the pace and his endurance. He looked for signs of the others, but they were long since gone. The guide, lanky and standing tall and erect, looked remarkably unfatigued.

Eventually, the camp came into view. He rejoined the group. There was a sense of elation and exhaustion felt by all. Barely able to take another step, he dropped down on the bed. The rush of blood and sensations powered through his brain, leaving his mind with a warm feeling of relief, comfort, and satisfaction. He lay there, reminding himself of what it felt like to be humbled by nature.

January 2016

Sketch: Immeasurable Loss

The accident occurred on Good Friday morning. Two Volunteers got into the bed of an open back vehicle in a small town in inland Mozambique in southeastern Africa. They were headed to meet up with other Volunteers on the Easter weekend. The driver of the vehicle, inebriated, sped a bend in the road. One Volunteer jumped moments before the vehicle tipped. The other was thrown and died on impact.

One week later, leaving his family abruptly on their vacation in South Africa, the country director flew with the deceased Volunteer's body in a casket in the cargo hold of the Delta flight from Johannesburg to Atlanta where the casket was offloaded to undergo formalities. The director then got onto a plane for Charleston and rented a car. He was on his way to meet the parents and family members of the deceased Volunteer, "his" Volunteer, who had died on "his watch" and would not be coming home.

Some say there is no greater grief than for a parent to experience the death of his or her child. It does not matter how accomplished or not accomplished the child is. In this case, he was the proverbial fine young man, a budding scholar in physics, a student of the mysteries of the universe, and lover of nature and music and life. Whether or not he was religious, the director did not know, but he had been told his family was, the father in particular. He would face them now, and he had seldom, if ever, felt the mix of emotions in his breast and his whole body that he did at this moment, on the portal, with the door about to open. What would he say, could he say? What questions might he receive? He had thought about it, of course, but there was no getting over the anxiety of this moment. He too was a father.

Nervousness but beneath nervousness judgement and beneath judgement responsibility, at least a part of it, and beneath responsibility sorrow, deep like a wound. Then grief, for the parents most of all, and a step-sister, and the Volunteer who survived, and all the family and the Volunteers, and also the staff. The weight was overwhelming. He was the director by title and function. With a great sense of responsibility.

The door opened. They were expecting him. He was led into the living room. All rose and greeted him. He counted nine adults. He made sure to know the mother and the father. He was asked to sit.

He began with the customary words of regret and condolence, customary but so sincere. He allowed himself to absorb the quietness of the spacious room, with its tall ceiling and the bay windows and trees outside.

Did you know our son, was one question.

He had interviewed him in training only, recalled his face, his commitment to serve as a teacher. He had not really known him. But he was well respected, he was conscientious about learning the language, and by his qualities, aptitude, and interests, staff had selected him for that site.

Had you visited his site.

He had visited the province, visited other sites, and knew the Volunteer who had served previously in the site.

What can you tell us about the accident, we have heard about it, but you are coming from the country.

He recounted the details he knew, they deserved to know. He said their son was thrown from the vehicle.

Was he in pain, did he suffer, the mother asked.

Later, he regretted that he did not *immediately* say, to save the mother any more pain, that her son "died on impact", which he wound up saying and was likely, quite likely, it happened so suddenly.

What kind of training do you provide the volunteers about transportation, one of the family members asked. This was easier to answer, and he answered it to satisfaction.

"He passed on Good Friday", the father said, and we know he is in Heaven, in the arms of God now.

It was exactly one week ago. The hardest week of the parents' lives, a week of immeasurable loss leaving a family forever changed. Yet they could remark, with that grace and perspective made possible only by faith, that their son in fact was doing exactly what he wanted to do in Mozambique. He was happy to be a teacher and a Peace Corps Volunteer and was having "the time of his life."

All a parent ever wants is for a child to be happy and loved, his father declared, and he was both.

Dear Andrew had taken his talents, his guitar, his love of Nature, and his spirit of learning and inquiry across the oceans to serve as a teacher, humbly and in solidarity with people far from the capital in a country that was not his own.

Rest in peace, son and brother. Friend and Volunteer.

You are not forgotten.

2016

Sketch: Conch of Mozambique

He didn't see it since it was covered with sand. Stepping over it, his foot rubbed it and it revealed itself as a giant conch shell. He picked it up. It was white and near perfect in proportions, with a pointed top and fleshy pink opening.

It was his last day and last walk on the beach in Ilha de Moçambique, island namesake of the vast country. Was the conch shell telling him not to leave? Or to remember Mozambique? What a coincidence. It was not always that you found such a beautiful "caracol" while walking the beach. The sun was already high in the sky and felt warm on his skin.

He took the conch with him back to the hotel. He told his colleague Mateus who immediately interpreted it as a sign that he must not forget Mozambique. So when he told Mateus that he would leave the conch on the terrace of the hotel itself, Mateus insisted that he take it with him and that he himself would carry it. He had no choice and it made sense.

The conch made it to Maputo in his handbag, then to his bathroom there. A few months later, it was packed with newspaper in a box with other souvenirs and then unpacked on the continent of North America in a desert land on the U.S.-Mexico border. Thus it made it to El Paso and sat again on a bathroom counter. As a remembrance, as good luck perhaps.

Yet it had never been so much at home as it was in the Indian Ocean off the coast of Ilha de Moçambique. The blue waters of the bay, the white sand, the soft waves of the gentle tides moving it, and the creature who lived in it, along the ocean floor until one day it lay deposited in a bank of sand, only to be picked up by a passing stranger to be transported 10,000 miles away.

2018

Essay: The Enigma of Return

Enigma: a person, thing, or situation that is mysterious and difficult to understand (Oxford Dictionary)

"You can't go back home to your family, back home to your childhood…
back home to a young man's dreams of glory and of fame… back home
to places in the country, back home to the old forms and systems of things
which once seemed everlasting, but which are changing all the time—back
home to the escapes of Time and Memory."

– Thomas Wolfe, *You Can't Go Home Again*, 1940

I was headed for a fall and didn't know it. My ego was too big and I was not ready to be humbled by "home."

Family photo, Kabir's high school graduation in Maputo, 2018

I had been asked to apply for a job directing a large non-profit organization in Houston, but I was focused on El Paso. I reached out to El Paso's largest public hospital for employment, but it went nowhere after an email exchange or two. I had been asked to apply for a job with USAID building health clinics in Mozambique, but I did not apply. I had been told about a job as director of a country-wide development program in Tanzania. I researched, applied, went through different rounds of interviews, even discussed salary, then was passed up for an internal candidate. He was better qualified, I accepted that.

I found out about an opening as director of a non-profit working in the health sector in El Paso. This seemed perfect for me and was exactly what I wanted—that coveted "leadership role" job in my old hometown, just right for a Master's in Public Health, non-profit guy, seasoned manager and leader like me. So I thought. I researched, applied, even paid $2,000 round-trip travel and expenses to come all the way form Maputo and interview in person. The interview went fine. Influential people offered to advocate for me to their Board of Directors but I declined the extra push, thinking my own candidacy was good enough. Then suddenly I wasn't hearing anything. Runner-up again and again passed over for an internal candidate.

I sent out resumes here and there, including in San Antonio where my son would be going to university, but no bite. I would be going back to the U.S. without a job. "I have friends in El Paso," I told my wife and others, "they will help me."

After all, when I had left El Paso, an El Paso Times front page lead with photo of me feeding a child read "AVANCE director to head Peace Corps in Lima" with full story inside. And I was even one of 8 nominees for El Paso Inc.'s "El Pasoan of the Year" with a nice write-up. We had won a national award for "Immigrant Integration" from the Migration Policy Institute in 2009 and I had been invited by MPI to talk about our work at the Trans-Atlantic Council on Migration in Berlin that summer. And, in Peace Corps, I'd been given two of the largest and most complicated posts to manage and had taken in and supported over 1,000 Volunteers in the 2010s, more than any other Country Director in that decade. I was recognized in headquarters and served as Co-Chair of the Field Advisory Board in 2017, taking feedback from 65+ posts in the field, co-facilitating a board of top field staff, including host country nationals, and presenting recommendations to the Worldwide Director and staff at Peace Corps Headquarters in Washington D.C. My performance evaluation was strictly laudatory. Staff and Volunteers made me feel even more appreciated.

It was enough to make you dizzy, giddy, puffed up, ungrounded. And something of that sort happened. It went to my head. Ego.

I was headed for a fall, and the first sign was job rejections. Still, I had intention to stay in El Paso. I found myself writing the following on August 25, 2018:

I left El Paso in January 2010 and the United States one month later, following training in Washington D.C. for my new job as Country Director for the U.S. Peace Corps. Joined by my wife, two elementary-school age children, and my father, we then lived almost 4 years in Lima, Peru and about 4.5 years in Maputo, Mozambique.

*While I came home intermittently on visits every few years, now I have come home more permanently, to El Paso and to the United States. It is **the only place I can really call home**, having lived here 15 years prior to leaving. We maintained a home on the West Side, a mooring of sorts, also in the mind, feeding my own psychological needs for a deeper sense of home and place in a world defined by movement. The United States is where my parents immigrated to when I was not even two years old, leaving the Old World for the New World, and starting afresh midway through the journey of their lives. And El Paso is where my wife and I built our early married life and where our two children were born, my parents both died, and **I have a tribe of friends and people who know me and support me**. El Paso, known as an outpost in the high desert where the United States and Mexico meet in mostly friendly terms, has its own sense of a bi-national and bi-cultural self that I had absorbed and adopted to the point of thinking that in the Peace Corps, **I was representing not only the United States but also my adopted hometown**. And looking at El Paso's sky, and the mountains that so dramatically divide our city into east and west and hold along their rugged ridges the most spectacular showings of sun and light and clouds, my memory does yet stir and **I feel the years of an adult attachment to place.***"*

After such lofty terms, I then went on to jot down details of a series of irritants and indignities that are all part of the American scene today:

1. Being told we could not buy a more centrally located new house ("no job, no house financing") even with sale of our current house and regardless of a perfect credit history

2. Being turned down to rent furniture even for a few hundred dollars a month without proof of a job (then we found one company willing to rent)

3. We did get quick approval to get $20,000 financing for an auto loan

4. Having to go across the border to Ciudad Juárez for dental care, where it was $250 per crown compared to $750 in El Paso (Americans I met in Juárez told me a crown cost $950 in

Carlsbad and $1,250 in Santa Fe). I was also irritated by the behavior of the El Paso dentist who made no eye contact and just stood behind as I sat on the dental chair, looking at my x-rays and blithely reading out $5,000 of needed dental work.

5. Facing cost and insurance barriers to get a simple physical done with a doctor, which was necessary since the Embassy in Maputo told me they could not do it. First, I could not get a doctor's appointment for two months; then I got an appointment but was told I would have to pay a $1,650 annual fee to join the "MD VIP" program he was part of, even though I had Blue Cross Blue Shield, a very good insurance; then, I got another appointment, but was told my insurance had expired on July 16, the day I left Maputo and Peace Corps. I called up Peace Corps in Washington who told me lamely, "We apologize for the confusion, you are right, it does say in writing continuation of coverage at no cost for 60 days, but in reality it is only for 31 days after the end of the coverage period, so your coverage expired August 21, you can continue it by filling out the Continuation of Coverage form and paying the premium first."

Combined with the job rejections, it all felt like a rude awakening, a reality check, a humbling. No doubt I deserved it. Ego faces hard reality. Needs down-sizing. Re-define dignity and stick with that only.

The good thing was, on the trip I made to interview for the job in El Paso, I had stopped by the school near our home to see about getting my daughter into the I.B. program. This worked out. And my son had been accepted into a university in San Antonio with a full four-year scholarship. As a family, we had just made a road trip to help set him up in his dorm. We had now moved back into our old house on the West Side, including my father who had left Maputo a few weeks before us and had been staying in a motel. Our dog from Maputo had also made it safely to El Paso.

Then, on August 16, 2018, exactly four weeks after leaving Mozambique, my father passed away.

Sketch: Daddy, oh Daddy

The dog barked in the night. The mini schnauzer had been put inside the laundry room so that he would get used to sleeping alone. The son got up to check on him. Walking on the terracotta tiles of the corridor, it occurred to him that he heard none of the heavy breathing sounds from his father's room. The schnauzer was fine and he decided to check on his father.

He had said "good night" to him earlier that evening after placing a few saltines with peanut butter and warm tea in a flask on his desk. Lately, it had become difficult for his father to walk, which he was wont to do in the middle of the night to make tea for himself. Just the previous night, he had fallen hard on his rump. So the son had discouraged him, remonstrated with him even, not only for his father's sake but also because of the noise the struggling old man would make dragging his feet in the hallway and moving about in the kitchen. Every sound seemed to reverberate in the single-story house in a way it never had before.

They had all just returned from years of living abroad. His father, now eighty-eight years old, had spent the last 14 years living with his son and family. Since returning, his legs, especially the right leg, had become stiff and heavy with fluid due to a kidney problem for which a doctor in El Paso had just recommended dialysis. Diabetes, high blood pressure, quadruple bypass surgery—his father had seen a host of the treatments for the maladies of old age, though he was quite pleased with himself for keeping his blood sugar levels under control. He had ample records and charts for the past several years to prove it. He was a methodical man.

The son pushed the door open, haltingly, overcoming some obstruction on the floor. There his father lay, sprawled straight on his back, the left leg at a slight angle and the right arm with cane in hand. His brown sandals were placed neatly beneath the chair that was was still pushed in under the desk. His blue slippers were still by the bed. It was as though he wanted to go somewhere but reached for and could not find either his slippers or his sandals. The saltines were still on the desk, untouched.

Last photo of Daddy, August 2018, El Paso, Texas

His neck, which he had struggled to hold erect of late, lending him a sort of hang-dog look, was now extended fully, arched, blissfully free of tension.

More than anything, it was his eyes, wide open, staring at the ceiling, at the heavens beyond, as though perceiving space itself. Unblinking, gray black, enclosed in a thin elliptical dark blue ring, clear, so clear, so calm, so peaceful. His entire body lay at rest.

"Daddy, oh Daddy", the son said. His chest was not moving. The son placed his fingers under his father's nose and could feel nothing. He then placed a tissue paper in front of his nose but it did not move.

No movement—*no movement!* His father had passed—*passed!*

He ran to the bedroom and exclaimed to his wife, "Daddy is dead!" He then brought his daughter to their bedroom.

He called up 911, saying "Hello, I'm calling from 6840 Imperial Ridge, my father just passed away."

It was 2:40 AM at night. The dispatcher instructed him to begin chest compressions. Ten minutes went by trying to revive his dad, while the ambulance was on its way. When the paramedics came, however, defibrillator at the ready, he calmly stated in his objective way what the son already knew, "Once their jaw is set like that, rigor mortis has set in, there's no point in using the defibrillator."

His father's eyes had already begun to close somewhat but they were still very much open. The paramedic estimated that his father had passed away only an hour to an hour and a half earlier. Moments later, the police came. The son was asked questions, some it seemed to him to verify that there was no foul play. Then he was given time to "be with the body."

"Daddy, oh Daddy."

He lay down by his father's side, took his hand in his. He stroked his arm, kissed his forehead, and put his head on his father's chest. He wanted to lay next to him, but resisted the impulse. Kneeling on the tile floor, with his father's eyes still wide open with that faraway look, he said a prayer that he would never remember except to know that he apologized and he expressed gratitude.

Still kneeling next to his father, he used the mobile phone to call his father's younger brother and sister in Delhi.

Later, he recalled again how the mini-schnauzer had barked, which was unusual, but his dad had been close to the little dog, and it made sense. The dog knew.

His father—gone, at the age of eighty-eight. The reality of it began to sank in. Yet it was not merely a matter of grief, of self-grieving, because from his father's point of view, the time had come. He had told him the same, saying for weeks "I've lived too long" before confessing more recently, "old age is hard, but we must all go through it, so must I."

The very last evening, in fact, leaning on his side in bed, his father had said clearly, "Good night", which he didn't always, as though it were the last time and he had willed himself to death. Who knows how conscious, how much in his full mind he even was, when he got up for the last time.

Just the previous week, when he had gone to fetch his father at the Sleep Inn hotel, where he had been staying until they could move into their old house in El Paso again, the old man had been unable to remember him. Once in the car, he confessed, "You came into the room and I thought to myself, who is this? This is not Ranjit, this is not Viru. Who is this?"

Ranjit was his brother, Viru his cousin-brother.

It had become so difficult to walk, so difficult to keep his head up, so difficult to hear. In fact, he had declined spending hundreds of dollars on a new hearing aid, saying characteristically, "That's not how I act." He knew the end was coming and it was not worth it.

The day when he had picked him up at the motel and brought him home, they had gone first to the Red Panda restaurant for a bit of Chinese fast food. In the line, with his father in front of him, a Mexican-American man struck up conversation.

"Hey, is that your father?"

"Yes."

"I want to buy him lunch."

"Thank you, but that's ok."

"Because he reminds me of my own father."

"I'm sorry to hear that, really, but it's ok."

"Just allow me to buy him lunch, he reminds me of my own dad. And he passed away not long ago."

"Ok, thank you very much."

And the son let the stranger pay, which he did happily. It was a kind sensitive gesture of the kind humans are more than capable of, intuitively feeling the circle of life, the sanctity of life, the oneness and unity of life but also the transience of life.

The police left. The medical team left. The ambulance went away with his father and took him to the morgue for an autopsy. It was almost sunrise. His wife and daughter were trying to go back to sleep after a long night. He would call his son in San Antonio soon.

He wanted to take a walk, so he took the mini-schnauzer in the car, drove a short distance, parked, and went out on Lost Dog Trail. It wound its way in the foothills of the Franklin Mountains, amid the cacti, ocotillos, and creosote bushes. The sky was vast and looked so empty, so infinite. The high clouds turned pink and then yellow. He stared and stared at the sky, took in its vastness, its infinitude, felt his father close to him, and exclaimed to no one and everyone, "Daddy, oh Daddy" until he could feel the salty tears well up in his eyes.

All that his father meant to him, it was too much. In that moment, however, it did occur to him to be grateful for three things in the end: his father died at home; he was there with him; and he died in peace.

Now there were many things to do, and he must get back.

August 16, 2018

Narrative: Getting out the Vote

While abroad, I followed news and politics closely of both the U.S. and the countries I was living in. I would read the New York Times on my phone, or *El Comercio* and *La República* in Peru (usually in a Starbucks) and *O País, Savana,* and *Canal de Moçambique* (usually at Café Sol in front of my house) in Mozambique. On the one hand, I had to keep up with transportation safety and weather conditions relevant to Volunteer safety. But I've long been interested in news, politics, democracy, development, and civic action. In my mind, to ignore politics is to live one day under a government that is dictatorial and autocratic in one way or another. Democracy depends on an educated and involved citizenry.

Of course, I did not participate in host country politics besides discuss news and views with staff. Once back in the U.S., however, I was free to get involved. I could go door-to-door or make phone calls to get people to vote for a particular candidate.

I knew Beto O'Rourke when he was a City Councilman in El Paso. He had come to one of the AVANCE breakfast fundraisers and had made a donation. Later, he became El Paso's congressional representative. Now, in 2018, he was leaving his seat in the House to run for Senate, aiming to take away the seat held by the divisively anti-immigrant and conservative-libertarian Ted Cruz. I went to one of Beto's rallies, waited in line to introduce myself, and greeted him. Amazingly, when I said Sanjay formerly with AVANCE, he remembered me. I volunteered to help him and he immediately had me introduced to his campaign manager.

I had helped get out the vote for Barack Obama in 2008. Since El Paso is on the border with New Mexico, we spent most of our efforts on successfully "flipping" Doña Ana County from Republican "red" to Democrat "blue." This is because, in the statewide "winner-take-all" electoral college system, Texas was considered to be reliably "red" but New Mexico was a swing state and therefore an opportunity for Democrats. Obama captured my imagination—his unique background that I felt I could identify with, his grassroots community organizing work in Chicago, his votes against the Iraq War and irresponsible tax cuts, his advocacy for health care for all, and especially his ability to articulate a larger vision of America, of people coming together across party lines, his belief that you could persuade and convince people, by dint of reason and doing the right thing, to join you.

In Beto, I saw the same youth, energy, and vision. Plus, he understood the border: Mexico is not the enemy, migrants are not the enemy, and drugs are a U.S. problem not only because of drug traffickers but also because of the demand of middle America to consume drugs and because of foreign policy that has propped up dictators and oligarchs whose policies produce poverty and violence. Beto was also against "the wall" that Trump and the Republicans were using to hammer the border. El Paso had fences since 1995 and a wall since 2006 and was continuously recognized as one of the safest cities in the U.S. for its low crime rate including low homicide rate. Like most any one on the border, I did not believe in "open borders", as the opposition alleged. Border Patrol had an obvious and legitimate role to play. But also like most any one on the border, I was against the misunderstanding of border people, the border economy, and the militarization of the border. Xenophobia, paranoia, and discrimination were in the air.

I began to spend 6 – 8 hours a week or more going door-to-door for Beto with other volunteers, starting on the West Side but then spending most time in South El Paso. We used an app on our phones to identify registered voters. We also just ran into many people on the street and asked them to vote. My opening pitch was simple: *"Nuestro congresista Beto está postulándose para senador. El está contra el muro y para un mejor cuidado de salud. Por favor, dé su voto para Beto"*—"Our Congressman Beto is running for Senator, he is against the wall and for better health care, please vote for him."

I enjoyed getting out the vote and helping register people to vote, especially in South El Paso, one of El Paso's oldest neighborhoods which I knew from my work with AVANCE. It has a real community feel. The following anecdotes give a flavor of this civic activity and its value:

1. The elderly lady who said, "Of course, I am voting for Beto—I tell everyone—someone asked me what has he done for us since being a congressman and I didn't know what to say, but I said that our street used to be dark, with no lights, and I contacted his office, and only a week later, we had lights."

2. The elderly lady who said from behind a screen door, "I worked for Beto's family. I used to take him to the park when he was a kid."

3. The elderly lady who needed a walker inside her house and who was not sure if she was registered. When I could not find her name using the "am I registered" tool on the County website, we then moved on to other apartments. When we came back, she proudly pushed out her screen door and thrust out her yellow voter ID card to show us.

4. The man who got off the phone on a Sunday at noon and listened to us, thinking he could vote but not sure where he had placed his voter ID card. He said he had a driver's license, a U.S. passport etc. We went and talked to another man in a corridor. When we came back, the first gentleman proudly showed us his voter ID card that he had located.

5. The guy who came up to me on his bicycle on the first day of early voting, speaking to me in Spanish and brandishing his voter ID card—and saying yes, he had a driver's ID also and showing that. Even when I said he had everything, he then pulled his citizenship papers out of his pocket.

6. The high school kid walking down the street with his girlfriend who said he was registered and was ready to go early vote and even go back home and get his driver's license right then and there.

7. The guy who filled out the only extra voter's registration form I had, even though it was in Spanish, so that he could mail it that very day.

8. The girl on the west side who was idling in her car but who saw us and came out and asked for a voting application for her sister inside the house.

9. The African-American married to a lady who works for the County and who wanted to chat for 10 – 15 minutes and who said, "People leave a door-hanger on who to vote for and that goes right into the trash… but you are the first ones to come out here and ask me to vote for someone… and we like Beto and I'll vote for him."

10. The soldier who had just moved to El Paso who said, "I'm new here, I don't have a driver's license, but I have a concealed carry permit (gun permit)… I don't like Beto, but I hate Cruz… give me the voter's registration application so I can vote."

A minority were for Cruz:

1. The lady who said through the intercom, "I'm voting for Cruz because I don't agree with Beto on open borders."

2. The obviously disturbed guy who said, "Hell would have to freeze over before I vote for that bastard."

3. The hippie on my street who took one look at us, heard us say Beto, and slammed the door in our faces.

4. The guy running the grocery store on Campbell who said he was voting for "the red", pointing to his red shirt, and then when I asked if he minded to tell his why, he said, "Obama gave us that one year of stimulus funding and then he took it away."

Others wanted to give Beto advice or were ambiguous:

1. The lady who said, "Beto needs to attack more… this is Texas, and they will eat him up."

2. The African-American who said "as long as he doesn't want to bring in more immigrants, but yeah the wall is unnecessary, we already have a system that works."

3. The lady who said, "My husband is voting for Cruz, so I can't really take this information in the house."

Unfortunately, Beto did not win that year.

November 2018

Sketch: The Kindness of Strangers

I wrote this in March 2019. I had been volunteering 8 – 10 hours per week for months at shelters run by the El Paso non-profit Annunciation House and a network of 30+ churches. All of the migrants were legally in the U.S., having turned themselves in at the border and been processed as asylum applicants. Customs and Border Protection personnel had already verified that they had a relative with whom they could stay. They were issued paperwork with a date to report to a local court two weeks later.

Shelter volunteers like myself explained to them where they were, called up relatives for them, and took them to the bus station or airport after their relatives bought tickets for them. The shelters also offered clothing, meals, cots, and a shower. It was in my car that I got people to talk while I also offered advice on adapting to the United States. All of these conversations were conducted in Spanish.

...

Infinite kindnesses. As a young Peace Corps Volunteer in Mali, 1991 – 93, I was the recipient of infinite kindnesses from some of the poorest people in the world. Not merely a token sampling from the first harvest in a dry land, whether of mangoes or corn or peanuts. And not only the occasional live chicken or duck gifted to me by a poor farmer in another village and that I could not decline but had to carry on the back of my bicycle or motorcycle. No, I was repeatedly given an invitation to stay and pass the time; a hearty welcome, a broad smile, an inquiring concern; a friendly interest in me, my family, my country. And not only from my host community but from strangers in an outlying village, wayside town, or rickety vehicle. A stranger in a foreign land speaking their language, encountering customs and ways yet unknown to me, beyond what Peace Corps trained me, I could be totally dependent on the kindness of strangers in the most unlikely of places.

The following are brief portraits and translated extracts of conversations with some of the poorest people in the world who have come to the El Paso border, mainly from Central America.

I took a rail-thin Honduran farmer and father of four and his 17 year-old son to the bus station. They were bound for Los Angeles. I must have been older than the father although his wizened face, wrinkled by the sun and a lifetime outdoors, made him appear older. I had read that "the dry corridor" in the Northern Triangle had suffered four straight years of drought.

"And the harvests?" I asked.

"Just a grain."

"Were there times the family could not eat three meals a day?"

"Sometimes only two meals, sometimes only one."

There are children you look at and wonder how their small height can possibly square with being 13 years old on their paperwork. It is with the children in mind that migration is undertaken, not only to avoid prolonged detention in the U.S. but to seek a better education and economic opportunities for the children. Or just their protection from violence and the vicious surroundings brought on by the infinitely corrupting, multi-billion dollar drug trade passing through small and vulnerable countries.

"How far away was your son's school from your village?" I asked another Honduran dad of a 6 year-old.

"Three hours by foot."

"And the health center?"

"Also three hours."

"In your life, have you been to the health center once?"

"Only one time, when my wife almost died during childbirth and we had to take her there."

He worked part-time in the coffee plantations, where he was paid 130 lempiras ($1.25) a day. Coffee that surely winds up in the United States. That I consume. They were bound for small-town Virginia.

While the overwhelming majority of "asylum seekers", the category of their temporary admission to the country, are parent-child admissions, there are exceptions. One day, I was surprised to transport four Guatemalan men in their 20s, all married and who had left their wives and any children behind.

"Did you pay coyotes or a guide to come here?"

"Yes, but the coyote got us lost in the desert, so we left him after 10 days and spent another 5 days on our own."

"Where did you get water?"

"From ranches. We ate almost nothing."

I took them to exchange Mexican pesos for U.S. dollars, and they obtained a total of $42.75. Most migrants from Central America actually board their buses with zero dollars, so at least they had something. When they crossed in the middle of the street, I told them about jaywalking and needing to cross in the pedestrian lines. They asked to stop to buy something for their trip to Houston and so I stopped by the Walgreen's near the bus station in downtown El Paso. I had earlier given them advice to learn as much English as they can and one of the guys then asked me in English if I liked Coca-Cola. So now he pulled a Coca-Cola off the shelf and insisted on buying it for me. I declined but they all insisted. At the register, when the total of their purchases exceeded $42.75, I offered again that they remove the gift for me, but they would have none of it and quickly removed items from their side. Knowing how far they had come and how little they carried, this stuck with me and made me reflect later.

They were on their way to Houston, where I grew up as a first-generation immigrant and child of immigrants. Hit by Hurricane Harvey, Houston is now in full recovery, where 100,000 of the 300,000 construction workers are undocumented, working without papers, laboring in the shadows while building the nation's fourth largest city. To name just one industry in one city in one state in a country where 8 million of the 11 million undocumented are in fact working, filling labor shortages mainly in low-skilled employment that Americans of all ethnicities and national origins are simply reluctant to do.

"Everyone should have the experience of seeing these families and helping them," said a Latina from Miami to me in the bus station. She was also volunteering at the shelter. On another occasion, a middle-aged Anglo woman from Washington state had gone out of her way to stop by the bus station. It was already late in the day. She asked the staff about helping the migrants and was pointed to me.

"I just want to help, I can buy water bottles, diapers, medicine, anything."

A bit suspicious at first, I asked, "Are you spending the night?"

"If need be," she replied.

I told her how to contact Annunciation House, which was nearby, and I'm sure that's where she went with her admirable good will. Indeed, Annunciation House has coordinated volunteers from across the United States, including many Returned Peace Corps Volunteers, to help the asylum-seekers on their way.

The simple act of kindness that most sits in my mind was something I also witnessed in the bus station. I had taken a Honduran mother and her 3 year old daughter there. She had only been able to make two X's that came out as "+" signs in lieu of her signature to confirm receipt of the tickets purchased for her by her aunt in Austin. She had been quiet in the car while others chatted with me. She gave me the impression of being scared, petrified, almost immobilized with fear and uncertainty. She and I spoke to her aunt. While I explained the route and journey to her, her energetic 3-year old girl was wanting to explore the bus station and was by the vending machine, having already gotten into the bag of chips that another child had just opened. At that moment, a large African-American man in a wheelchair rolled up. One of his legs was the size of a tree stump with the mark of an infection that appeared to be in the process of healing. He thrust out a few dollars from the fingers of his hand, exclaiming in a loud voice, "I love children and this is to buy her some candy!" The Honduran mom was visibly startled. I quickly translated for her. And then it was my reward to see her features loosen at the edges and her face lighten up and grow softer in understanding of this unexpected but simple and magnanimous act of kindness. She knew now, in this strange but promising new country, that the kindness of strangers existed here also.

March 2019

Sketch: Unhappy at Work

Something had been building up, as though caught between the shoulders, weighing him down, and now seeking an expressive outlet. It was an exceedingly warm day, steamy even, the air laden with the heat reflected from concrete. He sat on a bench under the shade of an old oak tree, contemplating the latest turn of fate.

He felt his skills had begun to atrophy. That was the word. They were wasting away. It had been nine months now since the job he did for almost nine years had ended. It wasn't his choice, it was a time-limited appointment based on government rules and regulations. He worked for a government program whose mission he loved and he had been a part of as a young man, and it had changed his life at the time. He had gone back as a director of the same program. Even though he couldn't always get out to the field, where the development work carried out by "his" volunteers was happening, he more than satisfied himself doing the things that needed to be done. This meant holding meetings, directing, planning, reporting, counseling, representing, resolving, troubleshooting. Everything that is management and leadership in a complex countrywide program. The pace was fast, the people committed, the obstacles both expected and unexpected. It was as adrenaline-heavy as it was exhausting. He had even been through burnout on the job, but he had bounced back all the same. It was worth it.

Now his skills were atrophying. A small room in a small organization with a small budget. The organization was respected enough and the job paid well though that too was less than half of what he used to earn. Perhaps the job had potential and would develop over time. But he would never be challenged in the way he had been. He would never have the direct involvement in making things happen the way that he was accustomed to. He had to take this job because he needed the money. It paid more than another job that would have kept him busier and happier, but would have required a lot of moving about and taking the office on the road with him. But now he didn't have enough to do and he had too much time on his hands. He had taken this job with good faith and no intention to leave. Yet only months later, he was ready to move on. Somewhere he could use his management and leadership skills, he thought, erringly or not.

He sat under that tree, on a bench in front of the public library, ready to phone a friend. He was deeply unhappy.

Sketch: Permission to Leave

Sitting astride the mountain ridge at sunrise, looking both east and west, he surveyed the land. Towards the western horizon, on the long flat mesa that sloped down towards the river, he could see the shadows almost march down, retreating with the light of the sun. Soon, the rocky ridge of the mountain itself would be the shadow on the valley below. A river ran through it and further along marked the border, uniting and dividing two nations and three states, the creations of humans.

He looked down on the gap, Mundy's Gap, that allowed a trail to cross from the west side to the east side and vice versa. It was a pastime to walk up here, early in the mornings, sometimes with the dog, often with a warm coffee in hand. He loved the lay of the land and the way the mountain brought his senses alive. He had always had a close affinity to mountains. Without the mountains, he thought, he would never have made his home here.

But something was different today. For some time, something had been stirring in his soul. It simply was never his intent to leave. After years abroad, he had returned to the place and home where he helped raise his family and where he made his career and professional life. He felt wedded to this place, to this mountain, to the people he knew and who had helped him and whom he had helped.

But today, the mountains spoke again.

I give you permission to leave. You needn't stay here. If you love mountains anywhere, if you love Nature anywhere, then you love me. You have known me, treaded upon me, up and down and over my rocks and ridges, grasses and flowers. You have brought your inmost frustrations and hopes and prayers to me on many an early morning.

Wherever you go, if you love Nature there, it will be as though you never left me.

Therefore, I give you permission to leave.

It was unexpected, but came across clearly to him. He felt lighter even as he stepped down from the ridge, onto the trail at the gap, and walked down, hiking stick in hand, to the base of the mountain.

If he must leave, he could leave. If he go far away, he could. Looking east, he thought of India, the land of his birth, his forefathers, his spiritual home, as he called it. If he must, it was ok to leave, the mountains had given him permission.

Narrative: A Role to Play

I had said to my wife and others, "I have friends in El Paso, they will help me find a job." A friend did help me. I had first met him when he was assigned by the advertising and public relations firm he worked for to make a promotional video for AVANCE. Humble, cheerful, quirky, sensitive. He now ran a community foundation involved in large quality of life projects like the plaza theatre and children's museum but also in niche projects like helping children with special needs and people with low vision, according to donor wishes. He started me part-time and then full-time. For that I will always be grateful. It was just difficult adjusting to reduced circumstances. Not the kind of work I was used to, but we made headway on a few projects.

And then, on August 3, 2019, an armed and confused young man walked into a Wal Mart store on a busy Saturday morning and burst dozens of 7.62 mm bullets from an AK-47 in a mad killing spree. The death toll would eventually reach 23 and the wounded another 25, not counting the traumatization of hundreds in the store who witnessed the bloodbath over a terrifying 6 minutes as they cowered in the aisles and took cover under the tables at the store McDonald's. The fact that the shooter was white and had specifically come to El Paso to shoot "Mexicans" added an angle of premeditated prejudice that was a direct challenge to the binational way of life of the two border cities.

The community foundation along with another local foundation teamed up to receive almost $12 million in funds from across the country and overseas to support the grieving families and survivors. If I'd been wondering what my role in El Paso was, everything changed from this point forward. I helped coordinate the distribution of funds on behalf of a task force and worked directly with traumatized victims to refer them for counseling services and mental health therapy. Every day I was talking by phone and meeting in person victims of this mass shooting that had so traumatized the city as a whole. My knowledge of El Paso and position at the foundation, plus my Spanish ability and past work with Peace Corps Volunteers who were victims of trauma set me up to be "the right person in the right place" as far as this tragic and horrifying event was concerned.

Vignette: Victim Support

The lawyer looked at the photograph with discreet emotion. It was a picture of Jorge as a young boy leaning against his father's waist.

"Tell him his father was a very handsome man and he was a very handsome boy," she said to the foundation representative.

The three of them were seated in a corner of a restaurant across the bridge in Juárez. The lawyer was older and experienced. Her blue eyes, blonde hair and curls, and fair skin looked foreign on this side of the border. But her eyes and voice conveyed a genuineness and simplicity that belied the elegance of her clothes, red colored nails, and heels. It was the business attire common to her profession and more suitable to her executive suite in west El Paso. Due to the tight inspections of border traffic and shortage of customs staff, they had chosen not to drive across the bridge but to park in downtown El Paso and walk across.

"Tell him that no amount of money can ever replace his father."

Jorge's father was among the dead in a sensational shooting in El Paso just three months previously. He took out photographs of the maternal grandparents who raised him after his mother died. He said it was soon afterwards that his father had crossed "*al otro lado*" (to the other side), finding employment and building a new life entirely. His father re-married and fathered two more children, both boys. But it was not until he established legal residence there that he could return to visit Jorge just across the river. His father's new wife discouraged such visits. "*No es seguro*", she told him, *it's not safe.*

Jorge's wife had come in during the conversation. She lowered her eyes and seemed a bit unsure of taking a seat at the table, standing up and looking down before sitting down gently.

"She is my wife," Jorge introduced her, saying "I told you she is the one who makes the burritos that we sell to the workers at the *maquiladoras.*" The *maquiladoras* were the foreign-owned assembly plants set up on the Mexican side of the border where labor costs were cheaper, tax breaks granted, and worker safety and environmental concerns given short shrift. It was only one job Jorge had. As the rough abrasions on his large fingers showed, he also worked as a mechanic in a garage.

"It was my grandparents who raised me not only with love and care, but with values", Jorge said now with emphasis.

He described how three months ago, upon the death of his father, the FBI had given him permission to cross the border for the funeral but his step-mother had contacted the Mexican consulate to inform them that Jorge had once lived illegally in El Paso and had been deported and that granting him even temporary permission would be a risk that he stay on again as an "*ilegal*" in the pejorative language of the day.

"*Eso me dolió mucho*", he said, this really pained me, exclaiming, "I am not interested in the money, but the lack of recognition given to me as my father's first son, and how they kept me away from his funeral, that is what hurt me, that is my motivation."

While he could not cross, it was then that the Mexican consulate informed him about funds being collected for the relatives of the victims and gave him a phone number to contact the community foundation in El Paso.

The lawyer said, "Tell him not to be upset, but that he will have to provide proof that he is indeed the son of the gentleman who was killed. And the best form of proof will be a birth certificate."

Anticipating the question, Jorge took it out and displayed it on the table. His father's name and his mother's name were clearly listed on the certificate. His step-mother, with the help of her son, had already submitted an application for the death benefit that would be in the hundreds of thousands of dollars but which failed to also list Jorge as a son of the deceased. So she would receive 50% and her two children in El Paso would receive 25% each. Now, with ascertainment of Jorge's status, she would still receive 50% and the three children would split the remaining 50% or receive about 17% each. It was the job of the foundation representative to convey that information to the family in El Paso, whom he had come to know and had already informed of his visit to Jorge.

"I bear them no ill will. My brothers in El Paso should get their share, I want them to, but I should be recognized also. I would not take anything away from them, but I will show you how my step-brother threatens me."

He then showed the foundation representative a series of messages on WhatsApp laced with profanity, insults, and threats from a brother whose own story of being shot, losing his father, and still undergoing rehabilitation had been profiled in a leading national newspaper.

That was not altogether surprising to the lawyer. Walking back to the bridge, she remarked, "Now that was a good human being, didn't you think so? When you see all the hankering after money and the worst it can bring out in people, you are always gratified when you meet a truly good human being. That is what makes our work worthwhile."

The late afternoon November wind from the north whipped and blew about the dust from the surrounding desert. The lawyer had not come prepared for the change in weather and the foundation representative gave her his coat. But it was she who had provided comfort and respect to someone whose life had been harder than most and who only wanted recognition that he too was a son.

November 2019

Sketch: Easy Chair

He would sit on an easy chair in the living room. A couch, a table, another chair or two, a television with many channels to flip through. Mainly, however, with phone in hand, he would browse the Internet—New York Times, Facebook, articles posted by friends on Facebook, ESPN, gmail, WhatsApp etc. Time would fly by without his realizing it, until all that he read was just a mish-mash in his brain, one thing not so different than another, beyond recall or meaning, a boiled down soup that only left the mind's template numb.

His daughter was in her room, studying or passing the time on her phone or the laptop. This was her senior year and she could not afford to slack off. This would be her last year living at home. His wife was working now and often online at home, continuing her dream of being a life coach. His son was away, working as an assistant teacher in an AmeriCorps program.

By then, his wife knew of his heart's desire to leave for India and take up a teaching position in a high school. Something I've long wanted to do, he said. She knew that and said if it was his dream, he should pursue it. He had begun preparing himself—educating himself, passing a series of interviews, getting an offer, and so on. By year's end, he had even told his relatives in India.

His motives ran deep, something stirring in the soul, an inkling that this route would awaken those things that are part of the great mystery of life—self, soul, and service is one way of stringing it together. Because that life on the easy chair—isolated, unfulfilled, distracted, underemployed—was a disservice to himself and to life itself. One thing he knew: he could not sit on that easy chair and waste away, mentally, emotionally, socially. This is not living.

It took him some time to realize this and it came almost in phases. There was the discontent with work, "the lowest moment of his professional career", he told his wife; another big job in Colorado that he seemed perfectly suited for but again he was runner-up; there was the alienation from society around him, the thought that what apart from language and living in the same place did he share in common with people in the area—an increasing number of whom put such a premium on material things such as big trucks, big houses, and big guns—and with most of whom, given his own background, experience, and thoughts, he could feel little commonality. He would walk around the block, occasionally get a glimpse in people's garages, and be aghast at the amount of possessions squirrelled away, accumulated, serving no good purpose at all.

There came the one-year anniversary of his father's death. It was traumatic losing his father. His mother had died years before. He had no brothers or sisters. In this sense, he was also alone in the world. His relatives in India sent him WhatsApp messages acknowledging their thoughts were with him, but no acknowledgement came from his immediate family.

That evening, he woke up in the middle of the night, something he never did. He came out to the living room, sat in the easy chair, and flipped to a channel, somehow seeing an advertisement for the movie "Photographer." He had not even seen a Hindi film recently. It was set in Mumbai and appealed to his sense of the city, the city even of his birth—somewhat dark, somewhat funny, touristed places and non-touristed places, love across social divides of caste and class. What a coincidence, he mused, that on the evening of the one-year anniversary of his father's death he should be watching a film set in the city of his birth in the absolute middle of the night.

This was followed by an experience that he took to be a sign. He had gone driving north on a Saturday, intending to camp by the river in the bordering state. Enroute, he felt a keen sense of alienation come over him. "Alien nation", he broke the word down in his mind. He hadn't really used this word to describe his feelings toward society since he was an adolescent—a much younger, innocent, and more sensitive time to rebel against the world. At this point, he should be reconciling, shouldn't he?

Turning the car around, but thinking to find a better place to camp, he settled on somewhere closer to home. The following morning, he woke before anyone else in the campground and set out on a charmed hike on the trail that far exceeded any expectations he might have had— the brightening sky, the sharp peaks, the tall trees, the clouds creeping closely on the valley floor below. Huge outstretched old spruce trees that he just wanted to put his arms around, embrace, and gaze up into their circle of arms and branches.

He continued and spied a large red-tailed hawk perched on a branch on a leafless tree, with the stunning backdrop of the valley basin below and mountains in the distance. How close could he come? Close enough to almost see the raptor eye to eye. It noticed him. Then, with a calculated jump and spread of wings, it launched itself into the valley. In the silence and stillness, it made its way. How far would it go? And then it turned, made a half circle near the trail down which he had come, and returned, loftily and magnificently and unbelievably, to the branch on which it had been sitting! What kind of omen was this? The day was altogether mystical and so beautiful as to pull himself out of his body into a higher freedom of the mind and self.

Perhaps the path was now being laid. Again, sitting on that easy chair, the word "renunciation" came to him. This was a word that had great meaning to him as a youth, since it was tied to the Great Renunciation of Siddhartha Gautama, the prince who renounced royalty and eventually became the Buddha. Rather than passively read news articles that popped up on his feed, he searched for modern interpretations of "renunciation", of which there were very few.

It goes along with stage of life, however, and one traditional view is that the householder stage was nearing the end of course for him. Once his children were to leave home and be settled, the vanaprastha stage begins, where the aspirant deliberately lives simply, with fewer possessions, and shifts his view increasingly from family to society. For an old renunciate such as himself, with an old ascetic streak and a still living though dim spiritual sense, this made sense to him. After all, every day one could read the obituaries in the newspaper. Even then, he was involved in a project to support victims of a mass shooting. Do we ever know when our time is up, when we must depart for the next world, whatever that may be?

When he was younger, he wanted to live and work in the country of his birth. He knew about Teach for India, had even followed the initiation of the program there. A few days later, he looked it up and was delighted to find that they even took Overseas Citizens of India like himself as teachers. And he could teach in Mumbai. It all seemed a bit surreal: going back to teach in a respected program, that would include five weeks of training and a network of like-minded mostly young Indians wanting to help the underprivileged gain equal access to a quality education. He had a few weeks to send in the application and could change his mind at any time. Instead, as he dwelled on it, the idea shone brighter and brighter.

It was on a long drive back from Colorado, after having visited their son, that he told his wife about the prospect and his own motivations. He told her basically that he had always wanted to live and work in India plus teach, and that in fact she had even encouraged him to work for his old boss' organization working in India. That would have been the top job, but this was just as well, he said, even better, since it responded to his ideas about living simply and richly in community and as a teacher. He also wanted to grow spiritually. He did not know if he would pass the interview. His wife responded that if this is what he wanted to do, that if this was his dream, then she would not stand in his way because she believed in people acting on their dreams.

His desire to live and work in India was not a whim or caprice. It first gave birth in his youthful adolescence. It was on ground that was quite firm, being connected to India as his "spiritual home", that being due to the Buddha. It was this youthful spiritual awakening that had provided a light for him throughout his adult life, a light that seemed to be getting dimmer and not brighter. And he had wanted to be a teacher, going back to his youth and even more recently, as he reminded his wife. He did not think he could go wrong based on the durability of these aspirations. He thought now was the time—a low point in professional career, his wife's understanding, children leaving home, the need to do something for his health physically, mentally, emotionally, socially. Moreover, he had no debts and he could support both of their children with their college expenses. The opportunity opened to him like the door of Destiny herself.

Sketch: Storm in my Soul, Flowers at my Feet

Early Saturday mornings, timed to reach the Starbuck's drive-thru on Redd Road at 5 AM, he would proceed to drive up I-10 to Las Cruces until he reached the Baylor Pass trail. All his time in El Paso, he had never frequented this trail. It looked too open, too barren, too out of the way. But now it was time of COVID and every other trailhead around was closed. This was it. And still, his would be the only car in the lot at this time. On the other side of Baylor Pass, when the idea of India was seeding within him, was the trail where he had seen the red-tailed hawk fly in a long loop across the valley before circling back to its home branch. "Mountains of my soul", he thought.

It was spring and the yellow poppies were abundant this year, a carpet of color in the desert. The Baylor Pass trail was spectacular and he came to know every bend of it like the back of his hand. And he knew where to veer off and climb up, somewhat precariously, to a high peak to one side until the winds grew too strong. He could admire the dunes of White Sands in one direction and the shape of a peak above Aguirre Springs that looked like Ganesh.

COVID had changed his plans. How could he teach in the slums of Mumbai in time of COVID, a life-threatening disease, even more for someone in his 50s. It would be irresponsible, also to his family. Teach for India was adjusting, but now the 5-week Summer Institute to train new teachers would be online too! And teaching was likely to be online. If not, constant mask-wearing would be the order of the day. This is not what he had in mind being a teacher, plus kids in slums couldn't all be expected to have phones much less laptops, how would they learn? Teaching online and being limited in Hindi—not good for anyone. He needed to be on the ground.

He knew about Krishnamurti schools since a nephew had attended one outside Bangalore and he had visited it two decades ago. Now he went online to see if they were taking applications. He had thought that after the two-year stint with Teach for India, he could apply to one of these schools. Boarding schools would be different. One would not have to travel in and outside of school, limiting exposure to COVID. The schools were set up in nature, deliberately far from crowds. One needn't wear the mask all the time on a large campus. The teaching approach was based on inquiry as opposed to drill and memorization. With hope, he applied to the school in Rajghat, near Varanasi, called Rajghat Besant School. He knew Varanasi, plus steps away is where the Buddha had crossed the Ganges river enroute to Sarnath where he gave his first talk. He felt connected already.

Two weeks later, he had a phone interview with the director and then a second director. It went well. He could get in under the hiring freeze. He could teach geography and provide support to conversation in English classes, plus help start an enrichment class on current issues. Children and staff had dispersed but online would start in June. He was invited to attend online orientation.

What a light in the darkness! He would only miss the social justice component of the Teach for India program and that larger network of young idealistic teachers, something new and refreshing about India. Still, in Rajghat, he imagined gaining a community of like-minded people who could be expected to teach creatively as envisioned by Krishnamurti. And with room and board paid for, he would not have to worry about keeping house. Plus, they would wait for him until August, even September. And if he were serious about getting into teaching as his "third career", he thought, then he must also accept the fact that there could be some virtual teaching on the horizon.

Reflecting, as he did all along on these hikes, he felt the deep satisfaction of having raised and brought up two loving and giving children. They were his priority even though they had reached the ages of charting their own path and independence from the home. He felt grateful he had the means to contribute to their education, including financially. And, even though he and his wife were heading for a parting of ways, it was mutual and amicable. He felt glad she was blossoming again into a confident individual, more than himself in multiple ways, and that perhaps he had played some small part in contributing to her growth, at least not holding her back. There were things they must still do together on behalf of the children and each other.

He imagined himself like a tree. Many branches. Healthy body, healthy mind, healthy soul. All founts of well-being, and it must keep growing if it is to bear fruit. He felt gratitude coming down the path, the mountain of his soul. His heart was so much lighter, he could sing. Storm in the soul, but flowers at his feet.

May 2020

Part V

Vanaprastha (Post-Householder)

———— ❧❧ ————

As noted, I had decided to change my life not just my job. I opted for a "third career", which would be teaching as a way of giving back to society. No more administration, no more management. No illusions that way, no pretensions per se. Simply. Teaching. Facilitating. Learning.

It did not matter to me that family members thought I was going "backward." What is so great about their lives? I don't see it. What is noble about teaching? Everything. Who needs all the stuff everybody cares about? I don't. Do I have enough? Yes. Can I be in touch with my own children? Yes.

As I would often say later, without WhatsApp, I would not have made the choice to be away. Free texts, free calls. Sending and receiving photographs. This was not the India I travelled the length and breadth of in 1993, where one found an STD booth on opening hours only and hoped for a good connection, and people had no means of contacting you unless you told them the hotel number, and maybe you'd had to shift hotels due to a dirty room, poor service, or no occupancy. A letter to and from the U.S. could take two weeks then. Now a message took two seconds.

How could I come to India at all in time of COVID? Again, unlike the old days, the Internet allowed for up-to-date information, downloading of forms, calls with important people like the Indian travel agent in Oregon who managed to purchase my tickets in a tricky time. Flights to India were few, by Air India only, and billed as "return flights" for only Indian nationals and Overseas Citizens of India (OCIs). I'd had to get the permission of the Embassy of India in Washington D.C., who reviewed my information and OCI card and gave me an approval number which I had to give the travel agent. I also needed a negative COVID test no earlier than 96 hours in advance of departure and this had to be sent to the airport authorities in Delhi and an approval number received. All of the paperwork had to be presented to Air India counter staff in Chicago.

With my sense of the symbolic, and the importance I give to it, I booked August 14 departure from El Paso to Chicago, August 15 arrival in India, and August 16 arrival in Varanasi. August 15 was India's Independence Day. August 16, most symbolically, was the two-year anniversary of my father's passing and the one-year since I'd woken up in the middle of the night and chanced to see the film "The Photographer" set in Mumbai, the city of my birth. It so happened that my father also knew Varanasi since he had done his under-graduate schooling at Benares Hindu University (BHU) which is where he was on Independence Day 1947.

I had 3 suitcases, a carry-on, and a personal item, in airlines terminology. Required to wear a face mask, and afraid of COVID at the time like anyone else, I wore a face mask for pretty much the entire 14 hour flight from Chicago to Delhi. We landed in the middle of the night, as long typical for a great many international flights arriving in India. Airport staff was alert and efficient. After a screening and showing my paperwork, I could "quarantine at home." Passengers who had failed to give the COVID-19 test in advance to the airport authorities had to be given the test and be monitored for symptoms for 7 days in a government facility (bad) or 4-star hotel at their own costs. I managed to skip all that, be picked up by my cousin-brother, and go to a market to get a SIM Card and Indian mobile number.

Arriving by plane in Varanasi the following day, I was picked up by a driver from the school, taken to Rajghat, where I "quarantined" in a cottage at the Krishnamurti Study Centre across the lane from the school. The cottage was close to the banks of the Ganga, India's most sacred river, and it was in a forest or at least surrounded by trees, which in Benares one only finds a similar preponderance of trees at BHU. A touch of jetlag and the sacred mysterious quality of waking up almost alone in a forest led me to wake at 4:30 AM with the earliest bird calls, sit on a chair, often with a cup of tea in hand, turn off the lights again, close my eyes, and "meditate." Just listening to the birds, their different calls, any rustling or other sounds in the forest, perhaps one of the dogs, then the call to prayer of the muezzin from the mosque, bhajans from temples across the river, and routinely a loud "Jai Sri Ram" from someone whom I later saw was a fast and furious-looking walker huffing and puffing like an old steam engine on the lane just over the wall. Then, after listening in the dark, I would move to body awareness, starting with breath and other sensations head to toe, establishing the mind-body connection which is the basis of alertness.

I also began other facets of my new life: bucket baths, handwashing undergarments, rice and dal (lentils) with a sabzi (vegetable) for both lunch and dinner. Later, once I shifted to the school campus, I would have to get my own water from a water point and get my food from the dining hall (vegetarian only) using a tiffin box as long as we were under COVID restrictions. I could not go into the city, except for one occasion to buy a number of household items and necessities. I would go for short runs on Down Field.

Like everyone else, I sweat all day anyway. I had only a ceiling fan and floor fan in my room, no cooler or air conditioner. It did not bother me. I had the mindset to accept virtually everything exactly as it was, since I had come knowing to make adjustments and all my life I had made adjustments. Bucket baths and handwashing clothes were familiar to me from Mali and at least here I wasn't carrying water in buckets from a foot pump. While some teachers had better accommodations, especially those with families, I would have to think that a group of American career teachers could not live with this level of simplicity and modesty (not to mention salary) that Indians tend to accept as is, knowing full well the very different environment just outside the campus.

I attended and began to give classes online while simultaneously taking an online Krishnamurti Foundation of India (KFI) Role of a Teacher class with several dozen other teachers. The faces, the accents, the names, the places, the mindsets, the manners of expression, the sense of history all had an appealing familiarity to me. Day by day, my comfort increased.

And yet, I'd come at a very strange time—only staff children were on campus, students were all at home dialing in, many teachers were still off campus including the director who hired me, and staff meetings were also done online. In such an ambience, I only met the principal by chance, and behind a mask, when she was collecting her food from the outside counter at the dining hall. Still, little by little, I made acquaintances who all became friends. It felt good and I still had so much to discover, especially once we could leave campus more freely to take exercise (walking, running, and cycling in the rural area) and then once the children arrived in January and the rhythm of the school changed completely.

Narrative: Uplifted by Darjeeling

Being cooped up on school grounds in time of COVID was limiting, since my comfort with India over the years had come from getting outside safe "sterile" environments. I had a rare opportunity to get away for 4 – 5 days in the first week of October my first year. I went to Darjeeling, in the hills where my father had also attended boarding school for a time in the late 1930s and early 1940s. Starting in 2020, I regularly kept a sort of journal, the entries of which I called "self-assessments." Here is one.

Self-Assessment—October 10, 2020

"The Significance of Darjeeling"

Darjeeling was a milestone of sorts. On my own again in India. Self-navigation. Buying things, whether chai and snacks or basic needs or souvenirs, a haircut or a taxi. Walking, observing people, interacting. Being enchanted in a bookstore. Chatting in broken Hindi. Setting my hours and activities, all timed around outings, early morning runs, daily walks. And always Kanchenjunga behind the clouds and the mists, revealing itself to those with the patience and imagination to wait. A magnetic attraction, child to mother, silent sentinels of the valley those peaks, awesome and sublime.

I loved Darjeeling also for the sense of being at ease, at home, amid the mix of peoples in an extraordinary natural setting and mountain environment. Darjeeling worked its magic on me. Nor can I forget the darshan at Mahakal temple, the special Hindu-Buddhist syncretism characteristic of this part of the Himalaya. Another sublime experience, dazzled by the colorful prayer flags, the wooden prayer wheels, the hilltop shrine chants and worship, the trees, the cave even. The attitude of devotion that people have. Sure, it's a business too, and yet it is a remembrance of the divine in life, the higher self, the timeless aspect of the life that flows on to seeming eternity.

People were also very friendly. From the courteous staff at the hotel, including the manager who was up early the day I went to Tiger Hill; to the young men at Tiger Hill who wanted to save me the walk down by riding as a passenger on one of their motorcycles; to the barber and his dedication to doing a good job cutting my hair; to the bookstore owner who always recognized me; finally to the extra passenger in the drive back down the mountain and the chit-chat we shared in my broken Hindi. To cap it off, perhaps, the young Indigo Airlines attendant who gave me special attention to move through the long airport entry line, the bag inspection and tagging, even the e-pass supposedly needed for Varanasi, and then escorted me upstairs and through to security. Very kind she was.

Darjeeling is a town of some 150,000 made up of a dozen tribes from the hills, Nepali immigrants and their descendants, Tibetans, and Bengalis and other Indians from the Plains. Probably, huddled away, there are still those few Anglo and Anglo-Indian families, sons and daughters of tea planters and missionaries and government officials from long ago. They opened up settlement of this Lepcha land at the scale it has become, clearing the slopes to plant tea, bringing the railway, and establishing residences and facilities to make Darjeeling an attractive respite from the heat and other troubles of the plains.

I felt at home in Darjeeling. Whether it was Mall Road and the people of so many mixed origins and styles of dress who came to walk, stretch, and run, as well as pray; or the atmosphere, sublime and syncretic and peaceful of Mahakal temple; or the adulation felt for mountaineering's greatest heroes at the Himalayan Mountaineering Institute, which also goes for the statues of local heroes such as a poet, a social worker and activist, an educationist swami, and a mountaineer; or being able to navigate the shops and find what you are looking for and more; or just walking up and down the hills roads and paths, ever aware that you can drop in to Glennary's and sit on the terrace with a pot of Darjeeling tea.

I read Siddhartha on the plane. The old Herman Hesse book. Can you search so hard that sometimes you do not see what is front of your eyes? Can you be sensitive enough to the movements in your own soul that you change the nature of your quest—once, twice, three times or as often as it takes? Can you find a peace that is transcendent and that is not purely selfish and egotistical? I also read a memoir called "No Straight Paths in Darjeeling", which gave me a feel for Darjeeling's history and the reality below the surface of appearances, such as deep poverty in the hills and water scarcity in summer and long dreary rainy monsoon months. And naturally, I read the newspaper nearly every day, comprehending some of the local politics related to autonomy and other demands.

I found a place that I love, a place that I could go back to and rest my soul once again. Thank you, Darjeeling—land of the thunderbolt.

Narrative: A Sunday Morning

Since I live on the school grounds, and boarding school life has been ever so busy, I have not ventured more than a few miles outside of campus for the last four and a half months. Today was different.

Violent bursts of thunder split the night last night, followed by a tremendous downpour. At dawn, there was a freshness and clarity in the air. Cycling our way, the village lanes had already come to life with people, goats, and cows. We turned right, taking our beloved "buffalo route", following the paved, pot-holed lane through one village after another. Chatting away as the rice fields grew ever larger and greener, punctuated here and there by yellow flowers on vegetable vines.

The lane winds and turns and climbs to a bridge over a sacred river. The river is receding towards the end of the monsoon season, and the wind and water have flayed the sands on the banks into myriad geometric patterns. As the rising sun pierces the scene, we cross to our island destination and leave our cycles with an old man at a mill. The verdant green of the ripening rice stalks is striking to behold. We begin our trot down the lane, past houses and courtyards, people and cows and buffaloes. We veer right, overtake a line of women in colorful saris, and head straight for the Ganga. The sun glints on the water. The red shikharas (spires) of the Adi Keshav temple from whence we came are visible far upstream.

A mystical morning. The senses alive. An energy in the air. A transcendent, timeless beauty—the gift of being alive that we are prone to forget sometimes.

We run back with a renewed vigor, oblivious to time and distance. We hop on our cycles and stop once for chai and return home with a deep sense of satisfaction and contentment.

Coffee, almonds, apples, and pears never tasted so good.

16 miles round trip by cycle plus a 4 mile run.

December 2020

Sketch: Fresher's Day

Being a COVID year, children did not return to campus until late January 2021 and Fresher's Day had been pushed back to late March, a few weeks before students departed campus for summer break.

He told a friend, I refuse to get nervous about what I'll do for Fresher's Day. Younger new teachers seemed to be worrying excessively about what they would do. He would not say exactly what he had in mind other than that he would speak lines in several languages, "a journey of my life through languages", he called it. Or he might not. He wanted to keep them guessing. The event was postponed by a week, and in the last few days, he decided to keep it simple and make it interactive. Most importantly, at the request of several students, he determined in his mind to cap the presentation with a song in Hindi called *"Kabhi Kabhi."* They needed to know he could speak the language however reticent he was about it.

He lost no sleep over the event to come and he quietly missed rehearsal. He could not fathom doing it twice after all. This needed to have an element of spontaneity. He had typed out what he was going to do several days previously. And now, with an hour and a half to go, he handwrote the key points and transitions in his talk. Back in his room, he sang the song—melodious and sweet and easy to remember. He folded the paper in his back pocket, unsure if he would pull it out on stage. It was there just in case. Another friend said he couldn't sleep for four nights when it had been his year to present on Fresher's Day.

He saw he was in slot number twelve and he took a seat to enjoy the other performances. While waiting, he realized he was forgetting how he would begin, how he would transition, and so on. He pulled out the piece of paper several times to remind himself. His brain seemed to go into a form of electric standstill, a sort of paralysis. Now he was second-guessing the lines to the song. Was he missing a few words, an entire stanza? He glanced briefly at the lyrics on his phone to reassure himself.

He was tying himself in knots now. He decided he would not say some of the things he had written to introduce himself.

Then came the call to the stage: *Sanjay sir to share with us about Latin languages.* He bounced up the steps of the stone platform, received the microphone, and looked into the bright white lights that concealed the crowd of students and teachers in front of him.

Life has many twists and turns. I thought I would share with you a bit of my life through some of the languages I've been exposed to and learnt along the way.

I left India when I was an infant. We went to the United States and I grew up in Texas, a border state with Mexico. The language of Spanish was very much around me where I grew up, spoken by friends and neighbors. Spanish has always proven to be so helpful to me, and I later worked for four years in Peru in Latin America.

How do you say good evening in Spanish? Repeat after me—Buenas. Noches—buenas noches!

In university, I took two years of German at the request of my mother, whose first language was Swiss German. How can you say no to your mother's wish? You can't.

How do you say good evening in German? Say after me—Guten. Abend—Guten Abend!

In university, I took a semester of Hindi, but Hindi never came easy to me, perhaps out of the sense that I should know it, made worse when cousins in Delhi made fun of me, or maybe it was the script, but I learnt to read and write it. More on Hindi later.

After university, life took me to the country of Mali in West Africa. Mali is very close to my heart. I know you learn a lot from your professors, and you should, but I will say that I learned a lot about life from people who did not know how to read or write. I lived in a village of 800 people for 2 years, working on wells and health projects.

How do you say good evening in Bambara? Aw. Ni. Wula. Aw ni wula!

I also spoke French in Mali, especially with government officials and I had to write reports in French. How do you say good evening in French? Bon soir. Bon. Soir. Bon soir!

And finally there is Portuguese. More recently, for four and a half years ending in 2018, I lived in Mozambique, a country to the north of South Africa. How do you say good evening in Portuguese? Boa. Noite. Boa noite!

Now I'd like to say that you don't have to travel the world to be a global citizen, as perhaps you are learning to be. I was reminded recently of Socrates, who said he was a citizen of the world, and yet he never left Greece, barely ever left Athens. Clearly, being a citizen of the world is about thinking and perceiving—and has nothing to do with travel.

At the same time, we live in an era of globalization. India receives things and gives things. And I would like to tell you an anecdote followed by a song. There I was in Mali, West Africa, around the year 1992, and in a village market in the back of beyond, in a little stall with a grass roof, cassettes were being sold. What did I see? "Kabhi Kabhi."

Kabhi kabhi, mere dil mein, khayaal aata hai,

Kabhi kabhi, mere dil mein, khayaal aata hai,

Ki jaise tujhko banaya gaya hai mere liye

Ki jaise tujhko banaya gaya hai mere liye.

Tu ab se pehle sitaro mein bas rahi thi kahin,

Tu ab se pehle sitaro mein bas rahi thi kain.

Tujhe zamin pe bulaaya gaya mere liye.

Tujhe zamin pe bulaaya gaya mere liye.

Thank you.

The crowd erupted in resounding applause. Success! He returned the microphone and came back down the steps. Various people congratulated him. He paused to hear the introduction of the next "freshers" and then re-took his seat.

How he had tied himself into knots! But it all worked out. He had followed the thread of what he had written down, omitting quite a few little things, all the dross. He recalled a moment already well into his song when he was suddenly conscious of the trembling of his hands while holding the microphone. Yet, in the end, showing vulnerability is what had won him the audience and gave the whole endeavor its meaning.

March 2020

Sketch: Feverish Dream

It was too hot to sleep on the bed. The entire room seemed to be in flames. And this was at night and with the windows open. He moved his mattress on to the floor to a place that felt cooler since it was a few feet lower in height and still under a ceiling fan.

This was a fever that came in the night and it had so for over a week now. When the peak would come, he did not know. It made him dizzy. It seemed not to respond much to paracetamol.

The room was stuffy. He lay there, tossed and turned innumerable times on his side, which felt sore as did every muscle in his body.

He dreamt or was it a dream… that his position now was flat on the floor, with no mattress, and he lay slightly tilted toward the chair under the desk. It was an odd position to be in and he lay there perfectly still, peaceful even, oblivious to everything.

Then he felt the need to throw up the water he had just drunk. He got up suddenly and headed toward the sink. As he did, all the water came out in a stream onto the floor. But it was crystal clear and transparent, as though he had just drunk it, uncontaminated by him. So he grabbed the gray towel that hung on the chair and threw it on the water and pushed it with his foot. Then he lay back down and went to sleep, just trying to make it through the night.

In the morning, he found the towel on the floor. It was completely dry. He wondered how he could have slept angled towards the chair, since his mattress was in the same position and perpendicular to the chair. Did it really happen?

The dream was quite clear, especially about his position facing the chair at an angle, the clear water spiraling out of his mouth, and swiping the towel on the floor with his foot. It then came to him that his position on the floor was the mirror image of how he had found his father on the floor at time of his death! Only his father had died with his head by the chair rather than his feet, which were by the door.

He had never forgotten how his father's eyes were open, and finally at peace it seemed, after weeks of his head hanging from a neck that strained ever more. In the end, he appeared light and gentle, looking up far beyond any ceiling, as if the heavens had opened to receive him.

He had lain in the mirror image of the *death position* of his father. No other dreams were as vivid as this one, and his fever also seemed to have peaked, becoming less and less frequent every day afterwards. Then the episode was no more than a dream, a single incident in the experience of COVID.

April 2020

Reflection: Year One of a Changed Life

"Midway along the journey of our life
I woke to find myself in a dark wood,
for I had wandered off from the straight path.
How hard it is to tell what it was like, this wood of wilderness,
savage and stubborn (the thought of it brings back all my old fears),
a bitter place! Death could scarce be bitterer.
But if I would show the good that came of it
I must talk about things other than the good."
– Dante, "The Inferno", Part I of *The Divine Comedy*, 14th century

I reached Rajghat when I was 54 years old. I was aware also that at this age, my mother had been diagnosed with Multiple Sclerosis, which would become a 23-year struggle, and my father had been diagnosed with chemical depression, which put him out of work for 6 months. What would happen to me? Re-visiting my "dark wood" and path out, it could be summarized as:

Difficulty readjusting to America after years abroad,

Thrice runner-up in jobs I really sought,

Unhappy with the job I had,

Growing apart in my marriage,

Something stirring in my soul,

Sensing an opportunity to revive myself,

and what I thought mattered to me

(simplicity, nature, spiritual life, teaching, writing),

An opportunity in the disappointment and despair

of my enigmatic return to the United States.

Knowing I could fulfill ongoing family obligations

And that my wife and children were ok with it,

And with enough financial security

I had re-launched my life in India:

Teaching, living in community, running, writing;

Introspection, devotion, and inquiry.

I had changed my life not just my job.

I kept the equivalent of an electronic journal, with entries titled "self-assessment" that served as a tool and marker of my thoughts, feelings, and changes I was experiencing. I would occasionally wake up with "self-doubt" and a certain "nervousness" bordering on what I called "paranoia." A "vague disquiet", "nagging insecurities" I called it. Also a gnawing feeling of loneliness, admitting to myself, "I have not learnt to deal with loneliness" yet surmising: "Truth be told, I always will feel a certain path on the inside that I am walking alone because I have done so my entire life. I seldom even disclose that path to anyone, including even myself. Yet it is there. It has something to do with truth, honesty, being true to oneself, awareness, morality, insight, worth, and wisdom. It is dark sometimes but the trodding has that halo of light even when dull, foggy, misty."

And there was the other side of it. By December, I began to experience feelings of wellness, even more so in the new year, writing at length on 3 January 2021:

What a sense of wellness I feel today! Just as on New Year's Day. Something about going outside, walking, stretching, running, looking at trees, hearing the birds, catching the sun. And not getting too tangled up in the news and trivia.

I am also just overwhelmed with gladness to be back in Rajghat and my little flat here at R.R. House. Driving back… and seeing those buffaloes plodding forward just in front of our car as we drove through the gate – a "new familiar sight" that told me I was "home"! Greeted by buffaloes on the lane. I went right to making a coffee in my room and then to the TRC to catch a session on the Right to Information (RTI) Act organized by Citizen's Forum India. I want to be on top of what is happening in the country so that I can inform my students. I am aware of the gaps in my knowledge. Even to point the way, I need to know the signposts. Plus, I am just interested in democracy and people's movements and participation at the grassroots level, which can seem to me like the only level that really counts. At the same time, I am encouraged by developments in the field of renewable energy, whether large solar parks or enormous offshore wind turbines. Indeed, it would appear major corporations like GE and … investments by the Government of India … may yet provide a way to reduce fossil fuel emissions, provide cleaner air, and help us harness electricity from renewable natural sources. Still, I ended this evening on a note of realism, reading a book on "the unraveling of India", in terms of its inclusive and democratic values at time of independence, seemingly sacrificed on the altar of a chauvinistic and increasingly aggressive Hindu nationalist politics.

What can I say for myself as I start this new year? Far from my closest family — son, daughter, and wife (I could not say "ex-wife"). Closer to my father's family — his sister, his brother's family, cousins. Far in distance from friends though instant communication through What's App makes all this more easy to stay connected. Close to colleagues who may share some of the values I hold dear and who all aspire to "teach the children well." The students themselves are set to return in batches and life on the campus will take on a new vibrancy and rhythm.

I feel optimistic about the year to come. I have three and a half months, at least, of steady and strong teaching in front of me — whether inquiry into energy transition and other matters of geography or delving deeper into the Indian independence movement and other matters of more recent history. There is also my class teacher period, and the kids seem to respond to me, and there is my Latin American Song and Culture class that I have pioneered on my own and kids seem to enjoy amply.

I feel a growing contentedness in my soul. The restlessness of the year before coming here has all but evaporated. This is where I need to be, the work I need to be doing, the people I need to be doing it with. I am glad. I hope to harness the positive energy of well-being that exists, often just below the surface, and to apply it well — directing my attention and not directing it, learning and relaxing, being in the moment and reflecting too. Making the time to reflect, aided by writing, strikes me as just as important as my more mundane activities. I am grateful to be here and to the spirit of Life itself. God bless.

I began to write, composing nine "vignettes" in January and two reflections. I began teaching Spanish to two staff children on Sunday afternoons. I began playing basketball with the kids in the afternoons after they returned to school. I ate all meals in the dining hall now that the children had arrived. I rose early and walked or ran, bought books, talked to colleagues. In faculty meeting, sensing a scripted approach to teaching, I asked "Why do we study what we study?" I introspected, watched thoughts come and go, listened to "whisperings from the soul" as I called it, or in the way of Kahlil Gibran musing "has the soul crossed my path." March came and I could write: "Running life, writing life, social life, spiritual life – all better – and maybe I've taught the kids something."

. . .

In terms of teaching, I felt my load was too light. I had begun to feel I was "standing on the shores of the Ganga", watching the river go by when I needed to step into it. So I asked for more classes and was given the opportunity to assist and, to some extent, co-teach other classes in geography and history. I had to adjust to the reality of exams in senior school, which meant that all teaching ended in January, and revision (review) and practice for exams began. This was especially true for Class X and Class XII board exams, which in non-COVID years, the syllabus had to be complete by December. While I had some hesitation about teaching Indian history, when I hadn't grown up in India, I agreed to do it with enthusiasm. In the coming year, I would be given Class 12 Indian History and Class 11 World History while continuing with Class 9 Geography.

After my 11-day bout with COVID, I was lucky to get out of India and to be able to travel back to the U.S. I visited and traveled with my son in Colorado and my daughter in England. I also spent time in El Paso, where we sold our house. I lived for these trips over the next few years, what I called my "annual migration" to visit and spend time with my children, sometimes meeting up with them in third countries. Socrates had never left home when he said, "I am not a citizen of Athens, or Greece; I am a citizen of the world."

I began to feel more and more the same way.

Sketch: Beer at the Museum

It was light and airy where he sat in the café of the People's Museum in Manchester. Pedestrians, cyclists, and cars crossed the bridge over the canal. Olive green ivy grew down the walls on the far side. The wind continually played with the hair of a lady sitting on a barstool and devouring a sandwich on the terrace outside. On the inside, twin boys with blond hair and matching outfits sat across from their dad and in front of two mayo sandwiches too big to get their mouths around. A middle-aged woman with glasses sat in the opposite corner observing the scene like he was.

The beer, in its pint-size glass, tasted immensely satisfying. The thick octagonal sides of the glass, the amber color with a mild foam, and the coolness of the drink dribbling down his throat gave him a heady feeling. He had been on his feet for the past two hours looking at displays of working class movements and people's heroes. It was a heady tour through two centuries of struggle for basic rights, fairness, and dignity. Two items he purchased at the gift shop—a small poster on the struggle for voting rights in Britain and a condensed book by George Orwell titled *Why I Write*—rested in a bag at his side. He thought how Orwell, a favorite author of his while young, would have loved the stories told in this museum, full of the flavor of grit, perseverance, determination, and persistence. If this be "socialism", and a more fair distribution of the goods wrung from the sweat of the brow of the common people, then may the will of the people prevail.

He took another sip and another until his avocado sandwich on thick rye bread was served. The museum aside, it was spending time with his daughter in this city that leant him the light airy feeling of satisfaction. Seeing her and seeing his son earlier—two lovely children, now young adults, flowering in their different ways in different settings. His son loved the mountains and spent as much time as he could in them—cycling, snowboarding, climbing. His daughter loved the city, had even begun to stop on street corners to admire the contrast of old and modern architecture. His son focused on a heavy academic load and a double major in both physics and math. His daughter took a lighter course on disaster management and humanitarian response, in keeping with her desire to make the world a better place and of course to enjoy good food and company in foreign lands. She made friends easily and was not averse to a cocktail or two. That was a minor concern. He felt proud of her and happy that she was in a city like Manchester as opposed to a stuffy capitalist capital like London.

Indeed, it had been the most important trip of his life perhaps. Nine months without seeing his children. And the drama of COVID had complicated all his travel. The next day would be the flight home to India. He needn't even worry about the pre-departure COVID test, since results came by email the night before. It was all set, he could finally relax, reflect, and relish the surroundings and what would be his last beer for many months.

Sketch: Mission and Purpose

Now he was on the flight back to India, to Varanasi, to Rajghat and teaching.

"Yes, it was an important trip—perhaps the most important trip of my life: I saw my children." The exact thought and words came to him somewhere in the sky. Because thank God he had gotten out of India in time of COVID.

And then: "But now I go back to my mission and purpose." He felt it with such conviction that he said it aloud. Of course, so few were traveling to India during the pandemic that no one was in a seat nearby to hear him!

Teaching is what he wanted to do and Rajghat was the place to do it. Besides Geography, he would finally be teaching History, the subject he had dreamed of teaching going back to his own university days. That too, it would be Indian history, in which he had a sincere interest, especially ancient and modern Indian history. And it would be world history, which he would be uniquely qualified to do among the staff in Rajghat.

He only needed time to prepare and to build up enough confidence to overcome his own insecurities as a teacher. It was a career change, after all, and in mid-life. Coming into his second year, he already knew some of the children, understood some of their strengths and limitations, and felt content with the prospect of influencing young middle class minds and hearts. They were the ones to make a difference in India's future—India, the country he himself left soon after birth yet belonged to him in a subtle but enduring way. How right and fitting that he should give some of himself to some of the country's youth, though what difference he thought he could make, beyond teaching the subject matter, he was not entirely sure. Something a teacher does and says, even in non-teaching moments, has a way of rubbing off on the young, he thought. As long as you set a good example and are sufficiently free with children.

The whole process of teaching and learning, knowing and understanding, guiding and facilitating, studying and discovering had its mysteries. Yet, in one form or another, we all learn to be teachers in life, whether as parents, workers, or actual teachers or just among friends. The beauty of teaching surely is also learning oneself—whether that is about oneself or from the children or from the books. Learning and teaching go together.

With such thoughts, he knew his mission was grand and his purpose true. He himself would develop the skills, ability, and persona to be the teacher he wanted to be. It would just take time, sincerity, and practice. It would be a gift if he no longer have to worry about getting another job in the near future, especially at his age, if he could just direct his own path.

Was it hard work and good fortune that brought him to this pass in life? Maybe. Such was his *dharma*, or duty, as he saw it now.

Note to Self: Teaching History

Life has its twists and turns. Who would have thought I would be teaching Indian history to 12th standard students in India? Or even world history?

And yet I did aspire to be a history teacher for a number of years. It is why I obtained my B.A. degree in History and took some of the classes that would prepare me to teach history, although the certification program would have required an additional year at UT-Austin. That was back in 1990.

When I interviewed to work here at Rajghat Besant School, the director asked me if I could teach history. With national sensitivities in mind, I politely declined. An Indian brought up here and who has gone through the Indian school system should be teaching history, I thought, not a de facto foreigner like me. History can always be a contested area, especially in nationalistic times.

And yet, children here need to study a bit of world history and local teachers do not necessarily have that exposure or familiarity or comfort level, so it made sense that the Class X teacher welcomed my teaching the "Rise of European Nationalism" chapter. Nationalism and Romanticism, Women in the 19th Century, 1848: Year of Revolutions, and Nationalism and World War I were topics I took on, making presentations with gusto. With the chapter on Indian national struggle, I trod more carefully yet felt comfortable presenting on Mahatma Gandhi in South Africa, satyagraha in Champaran, and the Non-Cooperation Movement of 1920 – 22.

Unfortunately, history as subject for Class X and Class XII board exams becomes a feat of memorization and answering questions. The same material may be queried in a variety of ways. On the one hand, it is good that the children must learn the material closely. On the other hand, a sense of wonder, of curiosity, of larger questions related to meaning, purpose, and the present day falls by the wayside, a sort of collateral damage to the strong headwinds of exam-passing and servicing the state.

Now, I am asked to teach Class XII Indian History and Class XI World History next year. Both classes will have projects, with Class XII having to present their projects to an external examiner for a grade up to 20 marks and Class XI presenting to me for the same 20 marks. And with Class XII, I must finish the prescribed government (CBSE) syllabus by December latest, preserving January and February for revision and preparation for the Board exams in March.

In both classes, the CBSE objectives and basic syllabus is good and the textbook serves as a good framework. Why am I being asked to teach it? Is it that they have no other role for me—being full up on English teachers and Geography teaching in 11th and 12th requiring more technical mastery and a Master's degree? I shall stick also with Geography Class 9. But what expectations do they have for me in History?

To be clear on any matter of expectations, the director will be pleased if I do not follow the course of rote memorization but instead look creatively at supplementing the textbook, either through supplementary reading, presentations, or video; use a spirit of inquiry to help children to nurture a sense of intellectual curiosity and wonder, to think critically and analytically, to understand multiple perspectives and nuances, to develop the skills in verbal and written communication, and even to further their self-knowledge.

The inspiration behind the school, noted sage and philosopher J. Krishnamurti, thought history an important subject for human beings to understand themselves in a certain way. "You are the world," he said, suggesting many times that our conditioning is shaped not only by our individual lives but by our collective past as humanity, our sort of collective consciousness, the vast ocean of which is made up of the entire history of *Homo sapiens* over time.

I do not know if I am up to that lens or if that level will serve the students well. However, it is the sort of full glass view of which we are sure to have glimpses from time to time—"of all this, mankind is made—of such stuff, the consciousness of man, woman, human beings are made."

In taking history courses during my undergraduate years at university, with the aim of teaching history one day in high school, I would often ask myself what was the purpose of studying history. Why study the past? The "answers" I tossed around my mind were several as I recall. One had to with "appreciating the past" so as to value the present. That sounds too utilitarian and somewhat uninspiring to me today. It may well serve society and the state when such "appreciation" is linked to a more narrow concept of "heritage". But national heritage can degenerate into the slippery slope of nationalism and the dynamic of pride and prejudice, biases and hurts and wounds and grievances.

Another thought at the time on the purpose of studying history was learning from the past so as not to repeat the same mistakes, along the lines of the oft-repeated saying by George Santayana that "those who do not learn from the past are condemned to repeat it." Certainly, this has value. Nothing is more frustrating and hopeless to see humanity going down the same path committing the same mistakes it has always made, just in different ways. What are some of the mistakes—that led to war, death, and destruction, to unnecessary suffering in general? Or is suffering always redemptive, justifiable on some notion of progress or other, however skewed? Related to the concept about learning the lessons of the past is the dream, hope, and project of building a better society and a more just world. Peace and social justice and sustainable development, as some would have it.

Related to learning from the past, there is the idea of learning about "our human nature." This is also what Krishnamurti intended in the broader sense of self-knowledge and understanding oneself, given that we all share the same impulses and mental make-up that constitute human nature and the mind.

As to the purpose of studying history then, we may have:

1. The understanding of oneself… at the level of universal human nature and mind. This is perhaps complementary to psychology as a field.

2. The understanding of the present… based on an understanding of the past. Sort of a "making of the modern world" approach to history, i.e. how the past shapes today, socially, culturally, intellectually, politically, economically etc. Perhaps the aviso is that using recent history to explain the present, as opposed to treating the past more clinically and at greater remove and distance, also has the potential to make it more contested,

debatable, and political. Of course, this is not always a bad thing, and doses of such an approach are warranted.

3. Drawing lessons from the past… with its corollary, to build a better future. One is on safer, non-political grounds here and yet even positive goods such as peace, social justice, and sustainable development may be contested. Whose peace, whose justice, whose development? They are all necessary questions to ask.

4. Heritage, whether artistic and cultural, national and international, etc. The utilitarian, often majoritarian and subject to glorification, "celebrate our history" side is still contested ground. Whose heritage after all? What weight do we give achievements of one nation or group of people. What is achievement?

Alas, I digress, but it is to play with the waters, the ocean of history, of human heritage on its widest and grandest scale.

To sum up, what a strange, unique opportunity has fallen into my lap!

July 2021

Sketch: Stumbling in the Foothills of the Vast Unknown

It had been an exhilarating hike, full of local flavor and mountain vistas, and now he was utterly exhausted walking down. The clouds had risen soon after lunch, sweeping up from the southern plains to the ridge they were walking on. The moving mist was fascinating to watch. One could almost see the drops in the air and inhale the moisture.

The way down was still uphill in places and he and the guide had already stopped for tea twice to revive mind and body. It should have been easy but not so after scaling 1,000 meters since breakfast. In an atmosphere of the residual unpredictability that characterizes mountains, it had been a day of delights and surprises. In terms of view, even Everest had been in the clear and that too at mid-day, standing shoulder to shoulder with Makalu and Lhotse hundreds of kilometers away. And the ubiquitous Kanchenjunga was revealed from many different angles, each iconic, each mesmerizing. The distant snows glinted in the vagaries of light while shadows moved imperceptibly across immense valleys. One was reminded that nothing at all stood still even in the seeming stillness and vast silence that enveloped one when pausing to sit and rest in the wilderness.

Outside Chitrey, Mt. Kanchenjunga in the background,
November 2021

They were coming now to Chitrey. A series of bamboo poles bearing thin white rectangular flags could be seen through the mist. On the way up, an old man sitting on the ridge had remarked that they had been put up in remembrance of an old man, his friend, who died just last week. It was a touching act of humanity and friendship in a small place. Chitrey was just a handful of huts and a guesthouse and better known for the nearby Buddhist monastery where monks were said to be in meditation for years, some for three years, some for six years. This was amazing if true.

The inconsequence of time was captured in a plaque on a nearby chorten, or stupa, that wished happiness for all beings in their journey across the "vast ocean of time." On reading the various messages, he had felt that strange wave of recognition come up through his body, enough to make his eyes water for a fleeting moment—a strange yet familiar wave of recognition, given a long-held feeling of reverence that he had for the Buddha.

The place for chai in Chitrey went by the name of The Hawk's Nest. It was also a guesthouse but nothing formal. In fact, he wasn't sure if they were walking in through the front or the back. First they came to the kitchen, which doubled as a place for conversation with benches at right angles facing the stove and the shiny pots and pans suspended from the low ceiling.

The guide took a seat next to a friend in the kitchen while he moved into the adjacent sitting area. The moment he sat down, he could feel the blood rise in his legs and return to his brain, bringing on pure relief. In the room in front, he could see multiple beds and blankets, probably intended for a large group to sleep. Seated behind him and sharing the bench were two young Indian couples, drinking beer and looking at their mobiles. Two young men with Tibetan features, both in baggy pants noticeable for their quilt-like colored patches, attended.

The chai revived his body like medicine but it was the music on the stereo system that gave an added poignancy and surreal quality to the ambience. It was Pink Floyd and "Dark Side of the Moon", an album whose ethereal music and haunting lyrics captured moments like this and seemed never to grow old. It was followed by the long mournful notes of a lonely guitar and the song "Shine On, You Crazy Diamond" from the album "Wish You Were Here."

Something about this place felt so good! And so surreal, if by that word we mean both fitting and transcendent, relieving and reviving, haunting and stirring. He thought of the messages on the stupa, wishing that travelers "attain the goal they have set their hearts on." Even if for ultimate liberation, this implied desire and determination, while another message had exhorted the pilgrim to "subdue the mind."

With kilometers yet to go, they could not tarry long. It was early sunset time and the valley was filling with clouds. Another Indian couple was taking photographs of one another on the green grassy mounds at the head of the valley.

He thought about the exhortation to "subdue the mind." It made him think that it was less a matter of "control", since a repressed thought always bounced back. Subduing the mind must be more about wearing out our thoughts, like a bullfighter with a bull, bringing the bull to the end point of grogginess, fogginess, submission.

Is this what the monks in meditation just over the hill were doing with their mind? Watching the movement of thoughts to a weary cessation? In pursuit of higher Mind or whatever Way led on from there? Aren't we all travelers in a vast field of space and time?

And yet we must keep moving, applying the mind itself, applying the will, in a movement towards wisdom and understanding, compassion, duty, and fulfillment of purpose. And there is so much to enjoy and appreciate along the journey, with glimpses, vistas, and reflections to carry us forward.

November 2021

Sketch: Comfortable in One's Own Skin

He had never really felt comfortable in his body. At least not since the age of 5 or so. Back then, he could out-run all the children at school in a race, both blacks and whites. And he didn't break a sweat as easily as the others even in the heat and humidity of the Texas Gulf Coast. It was as though there was a unique and different something in his body and he wasn't sure what to attribute it to. Was it the unique dividend of mixed genes—Swiss and Indian? He could flatter himself. He even browned up in the summer sun more than others and received compliments for it from neighborhood mothers, so it was all a good thing.

Some of this changed upon adolescence. He wanted to be Indian for some reason, like his name, like his father, like his answers about his name and where he was born, his nationality and so on. But Indians were dark, or at least darker than he was. He only had one Indian parent, unlike his friend Sonu, who had two, and as a result had darker skin color, eye color, and hair color. Even the dark hair sprouting on Sonu's fingers and toes seemed to mark him as someone from India, like his own father but unlike himself

A certain fixation on his own skin color, and revisions of it in the mirror, took hold beyond adolescence until his mid-20s. By then, it was also personality quirks—being too shy, not being social enough, being nervous around women, not being confident enough—all this that he still carried.

To be comfortable in one's own skin, what does it take? To accept oneself fully, what does it take? To cease to want to look different, to just BE—what does it take?

One day, when he was 54 years old, admiring a recent loss of weight in a full body mirror, the thought came to him that he was now quite at peace with ageing. Ageing! In fact, it had been years since he felt so healthy, physically and mentally. His body felt younger or at least what a 54 year old body could and should feel like. He had not only lost weight, but his fitness had improved, such that running 20 miles was done in stride and with gusto and pleasure. The state of his body must also be a product of his mental state.

His mind, while not as sharp as he would have liked and in reality given to forgetting more and more bits of information, was somehow less agitated and more at peace than in years. He slept well and even enjoyed brief catnaps in the middle of the day. Sure, he could still doubt himself, be paralyzed in his mind with unreasonable fears. But moments of peace and contentment came to him from time to time, ever deeper and often after exercise. The movement in his mind would slow down, all his senses seemed more attuned to sense-objects in his environment, and his mind-body seemed to revel in an almost forgotten level of fitness. Ageing like this might not be so bad!

Here, in the midst of India, where he would always stand out for being paler than the rest, he no longer felt he needed to be anything other than what he was. And what was he? A middle-aged guy, of American upbringing and Swiss and Indian parents, more importantly of wide experiences in life and the world, an only child, a divorcee, a father, a seeker, a pilgrim. If he died tomorrow? In fact, something of him died yesterday. He was more aware of this now. Once again, he could understand in his own gut more and more of the inner life.

Skin tone, eye color, hair color—why should any of that matter in a person's self-estimation? It could of course matter to others, but they were foolish if it did, and who was he to change an opinion and why should it matter really? Surely, to be comfortable with oneself, with who one is in the basic matters, is the foundation of growth and learning. "In the basic matters" could mean "in the eyes of God" or "in relation to Nature." But not trying to be anything or anybody.

Sketch: A Day of Coincidences and Connections

Coincidence #1

He had set a goal of "talking to strangers" on his trip abroad. It was goal #4 after "meeting my kids", "running a marathon", and "climbing mountains."

Little did he know how soon such random conversations with strangers would occur. It was in transition at the airport in Istanbul where they began.

A young lady, cheerfully dressed like someone in a painting wearing a hat and carrying a parasol, stood in line for coffee. He actually got in a shorter line, but motioned for her to go ahead when his turn was called. She ordered. Maybe it wasn't what she wanted. He ordered. He had heard her voice, and the conversation began.

"American?", he asked.

"Yes, but I don't live in the United States. I live in Costa Rica."

"What do you do?"

"I'm a tour guide. I'm here in Turkey because I lead tours here."

"That's great. I'm from also from the United States but originally from India, where I live and work now." He paused. "I worked overseas for most of the last decade."

She looked at him quizzically.

"I lived in Peru and Mozambique. Maybe you've heard of the Peace Corps?"

"Yes! I was a Peace Corps Volunteer!"

"Really?! Where?"

"Panama, 2011 – 13."

"Wow, I was Country Director in Peru then. I know your CD at the time. Brian, Brian—his last name begins with an R."

"Yes!"

"Amazing—the PCV connection!"

"I know, it is already the second time on this trip that I have met someone who used to be with Peace Corps."

She told a story that he didn't really listen to. He could see she was young, vivacious, and with a vibrant personality.

"What are you doing in India?" she asked.

"I teach at a boarding school, History and Geography. I'm like the PCV again!"

"Wow, that's so cool. I love India, I've been there 4 times. I'm completing a course on Ayurveda…"

Receiving their coffees, and with places to go, it was time to bring the conversation to a close.

"What is your name?" he asked.

"Amanda."

"I'm Sanjay. Safe travels!"

"You too."

And neither remarked on where they were traveling to! And he hadn't told her he too had been a Peace Corps Volunteer—Mali, 1991 – 93.

He thought: What are the chances of meeting someone connected to Peace Corps—the organization that transformed my life when young—on the first "stranger conversation" of my vacation out of India in 2022??!!!

Coincidence #2

He had missed his flight in Istanbul. He thought the flight was boarding at 12:45 PM, and so he showed up a few minutes after boarding time. In fact, that was the departure time! They had asked people to board at 11:45 AM. Was it the one-hour time difference between Delhi and Istanbul that got him confused? Or the listing of boarding time as different from departure time? In any case, he felt a fool. It was clearly his fault. And now he was re-booked to leave for Rome at 5 PM.

Coincidentally, this was the time his daughter was supposed to leave the United Kingdom from Manchester—***the exact same time*** but several time zones away and from a different direction! An amazing coincidence. Even his daughter, who never talked about God, had to text him that God was moving in mysterious ways this day.

Coincidence #3

He had read about those people who miss a flight for some reason such as the original flight crashing, Heaven forbid. So was there some reason or purpose, besides leaving at the exact same time as his daughter, for missing his flight? It had cost him money too, and that too no small amount.

He boarded the plane and found his seat. It was numbered 25C. A moment later, a young African guy in ripped blue jeans is putting up his bag and motioning to sit in 25A. He makes way for him. The conversation begins.

"Are you from Africa?"

"*Je ne parle pas Anglais—Françias ou Italiano*", he says. *I don't speak English—French or Italian.*

He thinks for a moment and replies, "*D'ou êtes vous?*" *Where are you from.*

"*Je suis du Mali*", he responded. *I'm from Mali.* At mention of the word Mali, the older man could feel his eyes enlarge and lighten up and his heart beat faster. Air seemed to flow through him now.

"*Mali?! I ka kene wa?*" *How are you.*

"*Tooro si te. I ka kene?*" *I'm fine, how are you.* The young man responded automatically, as though unaware for a minute that he was speaking his native language to a complete stranger.

"*Je faisait deux ans au Mali*", the older man was so excited to inform him. "*Ça fait longtemps, plus de 25 ans.*" *I spent two years in Mali. It's been a long time, more than 25 years.* He wanted to say more, that he lived in a village, how to say "I lived" in French, he struggled to remember.

"*J'ai habiteé une petite village au sud, Sirakoro, a cotè de Zantiebougou, cercle de Bougouni*", he wound up saying in broken French. *I lived in a small village in the south, Sirakoro, next to Zantiebougou, in the cercle of Bougouni.*

Then he found it easier switching to Bambara.

"*I be baara ka Italie jamana la?*" *Do you work in Italy?*

From then on, it was mostly Bambara. The young man, whose name was Yaya Ballo, told him he was an agricultural laborer. He picked apples among many other products, depending on the season. Do they pay you well? Yes, he nodded. What are you doing on this plane, did you visit Turkey? No, I came from Mali, I got married three months ago. That is terrific. When did you first come to Italy? I left Mali in 2017. I went to France first and then Italy. You are from Bamako? Yes. How long did you study in Bamako?

Yaya's face actually began to open more with this personal question. Six years, he said, and then four years in a Koranic school. It is why, he said, he cannot write read or well in any language.

Is there anti-immigrant sentiment in Italy? Yes, there is some of that, he indicated, but moved his head as though to say it is not a big deal, perhaps to be expected even.

The older man recalled his own time in Mali and the proverb that was said to him, even as he was learning to speak Bambara.

"Yiri menna ji la chogo o chogo a te ke bamba ye." However long a log stays in water, it can never become a crocodile!

His new friend in seat 25A had to smile. *O tinye*, he said automatically—*that is true.*

The implication was that Yaya, just like the older man when he was in Mali, would perhaps never fully integrate in Italy. But then the older man added the twist.

"Nga a be mogow lasiran" But it will scare people! Yaya laughed and laughed, repeating the phrase.

He thought: What coincidence, what a joy, what a blessing to sit next to someone from Mali on the plane! It has all been worth it—this delayed travel, the extra euros. What a truly amazing, astonishing day of coincidences!!!

Unbelievable! He had a goal of "talking to strangers" on this trip, and it's like finding friends!

Essay: You are Running a Marathon

You are running a marathon by a lake outside a little town at the base of the Alps in France. You look at your watch and see you are 8 miles in and ahead of the pace you set for yourself, running a near steady 10 minutes per mile instead of the 11 minutes per mile you planned. Right alongside many others just like you. You are feeling great! Heart pumping, muscles churning, lungs expanding, oxygen flowing.

Slowly, a few motorcycles appear in the left lane and you wonder why. You are not clear in your own mind, consumed as you are with running. You see more motorcycles, clearly they are going somewhere. And then you see: a group of runners, a cluster moving towards you, long legs and long arms that even seem to be flailing at the air, struggling for advantage and moving your way at more than twice the speed you are. Could it be? Yes, these guys were at the starting line—and now they are headed back! You feel a pump of blood in your being, in your heart and mind, and you say out loud, "Oh my god, oh my god—already, already!" Disbelief turns to highest admiration and fervent cheer. You keep running but raise your hands now and begin to yell, "Go, go— *allez-y, allez-y!*" They pass you like a train, like a band of warriors on some plain—and yes, some plain out of Africa. They are beautifully black in skin color and the colors of their shirts and shorts offset and shine in the sun that much more dramatically.

Athletes! The true athletes one is honored to run the same course with on the same day at the same time. You keep running and do the calculation in your mind: you have run 8 miles. The marathon is 26 miles. They have run 18 miles. They have 8 miles to go. It has been only 1 hour and 20 minutes. If they have run 18 miles in 80 minutes, that is about 4 minutes 30 seconds per mile only! Is that even right, even possible? Even at 5 minutes per mile over the last 8 miles, they will finish in just over 2 hours. Indeed, the fastest finish is a little more than 2 hours (subsequently just under 2 hours! After this writing.)

You marvel at the human potential. What an inspiration! You even begin to run faster, to glide, to pass up a few other runners.

You hear the encouragement from residents and bystanders standing or sitting along the bicycle path that makes up the bulk of the race.

"Allez-y!" Go!

"Du courage!" Have courage!

"Super!" said in that lovely French accent, drawing out the last syllable.

"Tu vas très bien!" You are going great!

"Continue, continue!" said not as formal English but naturally and in an uplifting way in French.

"Tu es presque au but!" You are almost at the end!

Now, as a foreigner, you might think, are you talking to me or the person behind me? There is no one behind you, they are looking right at you! They keep up the encouraging words, clapping too.

Your whole body straining, you crack a smile at the edge of your lips and just say, *"Merci, merci."*

You have passed the mid-way point in the marathon. You are going good, still ahead of the pace you set for yourself. It is by one side of the lake only and now you have begun the return. You come to a stretch between trees shading the bicycle path. You notice the residents and bystanders cheering you on, and there is a little boy.

He is holding little yellow flowers in his hand. You glance to the side and see the field of yellow flowers. One part of your mind says not to pluck the flowers. The other part of your mind responds to this little boy with the flowers in his hand. He is handing them out to the runners who pass. They are bending down to grasp a thin stem holding up a fragile little yellow flower dancing on its head.

You bend down willingly, see the little boy hold out a flower for you, grasp it, and keep running. You attach it then, behind your ear. You look at your shadow in front of you and try to make out the flower in your ear. You run with love, with love, with love. You are touched.

You are slowing down without wanting to. Your body is stiffening uncontrollably. You feel your legs stiffen, your back stiffen. What do you have, what is the word for it? Strained disks? Slipped disks, two of them. But you are not out of breath, your knees are not hurting, your ankles and feet are fine. But you look at your watch and see you are slipping from 10 minute miles to 11 minute miles, even to 12 minute miles. Keep up the pace a bit more, keep it up, you tell yourself.

You dare not stop at a refreshments station lest you can't get going quickly again and it take minutes off your time. Now and then, you see some runners who are beginning to walk. You keep going. It must be mile 23 or so. Up ahead, you see a woman leaning on a man who is taller than her. He is not holding her but maintaining some space, with his hand in the small of her back. He is not necessarily consoling. He is giving words of encouragement and positive motivation. She straightens out and starts to trot again. You don't catch them.

Then, another mile ahead, you see the woman has stopped again. She is leaning on the man. A few other runners are clustered in that area. You approach. You hear words of encouragement. You hear a muffled sob. Surprisingly, a man nearby shouts, *"Ne pleurs pas!" Don't cry!* You are made aware of the tussle of emotions now. The man with her is also encouraging her. She is not limping, but she is struggling to walk. Her legs must be like wood. This is called "hitting the wall" in your body. The others don't shout but are encouraging. You are aware of everything because you too are struggling, struggling with stiffness, with mental resolve, with clarity of mind. You hear her sobs, you pass her and the group, but slowly. You round a bend and are aware that she is trying to run again. You hear the applause and encouragement. You keep running.

(Later, you congratulate them in the snack area warmly and sincerely. They acknowledge it with a smile and as much warmth and appreciation. Later, you reflect, no one carried her to the finish line, she had to find those extra inner resources of strength, grit, and determination.)

You cross the bridge towards the finish line, but it is too soon. The course leads you out to one end of the lake. You see you will run on one side of the flowers where your daughter took a photograph of you the day before. You come to a far point and notice a man laid out flat on the ground in the middle of the path. He is being placed on a stretcher! A fellow runner.

You keep running. You notice a man, with one of those group shirts that you recognize, fall to his knees, one knee at a time, helplessly. It could not be more than 500 meters to the finish! You keep running.

You are nearing the end. Your daughter will be there. You come round a corner and hear her familiar voice in an unusually unrestrained public cheer, "Yea, go, go, you can do it, yea, yea, that's it!" You look for her and vaguely notice movement along the sidelines.

You run up to the very end, wondering for a moment why you cannot run faster because you are not feeling bad at all, maybe not even tired, but oh so stiff, so unmanageably stiff. You notice the time clock, red numbers against a dark background, ticking and ticking, and you vaguely see your name and bib number and the flag of your country appear on the screen. You register 4 hours and 39 minutes in your mind. You are pleased. You can finally stop a few paces after the finish line.

You have finished, but the race is continuing and the attention is on all of the finishers.

(Officially, you have finished in 4 hours, 37 minutes, and 23 seconds—FIRST MARATHON).

Annecy, France—April 17, 2022

Verse: Pilgrims on the Everest Trail

Pilgrims on the Everest trail,

Come to glimpse the top of the world.

Marianna of Romania, resident in Rome,

Garrulous and free, an experienced traveller is she.

The Mexican-Italian trio of friends, a rousing reunion,

Not tea but tequila - "party first, climb later" is their motto,

A disco light and glass of champagne to toast friends along the way.

A data scientist from Bangalore, managing

A mid-life change of direction and aiming for the "Three Passes."

An RBS school alum and programmer from Patna, resident in Australia,

Thrilling to high peaks and high adventure.

A South Korea senior, 70 years of age, fit and fancy-free,

Re-living his glory days of summiting Everest 13 years ago.

Vidya of Rishikesh, talkative and open to the world,

The MBA returned from London on a fresh spiritual quest.

Nima, our guide, Sherpa born and bred,

Stopping for a smoke here and there,

And known to one and all along the trail.

By the bridge that crossed the Dudh Kosi,

On the path to Tengboche, father and son

Enjoyed a break and spirited conversation.

Views of America, the world, of culture, brothers and sisters,

Each on our paths - what are right views? what is teaching?

What is learning? When and how to give advice – if even then?

What is right action? What is our journey in life?

In a monastery in Tengboche, set precariously above the valley,

With mountains all around, a monk reads his ancient prayers,

Gurgling like the stream below, a path across a vast ocean,

There is a gem of wisdom in there somewhere.

The clouds rise up, a thick fog forms,

The air becomes moist, visibility near zero outside,

Trekkers come in out of the mist, and a woman, ever attentive,

Lights the stove in the dining hall and loads it with firewood.

Playing cards, chatting, and looking at phones, we pass the time,

With faith that bad weather presages good weather, that skies clear after a rain.

Opening the curtains well before dawn,

The giants of the world appear, looming ever so large,

Ama Dablam, queen of these parts towering over the valley,

Lhotse, her long ridge and a dreamy cloud forming like a halo on her tallest peak,

Even the lofty Everest, summit of summits, the great pyramid in the sky.

The first rays of the sun light the clouds like a sacrificial fire,

And they reflect it down on the highest peaks,

Dripping in magical hues of red and crimson and yellow,

What a light show up high, what drama in the pre-dawn sky.

All around – Tabuche, Shirtse, Kangtega,

Thamsherku, Kongde back down the valley.

Entranced we stand and stare at the marvel of it,

On the footsteps of the old monastery,

As the clouds swirl at the top,

Serenading these mountains majestic,

And the birds around us sing with the dawn,

And the sleeping dogs open their drowsy eyes.

There is a castle up the valley and,

With the permission of the gods,

We shall enter its ramparts soon

And greet the king and queen and

All the royal courtiers.

But not so soon! What message is there for man in this,

In this drama, this panorama, this awesome display of Nature?

Is there a message at all? Why are we transfixed, entranced, enchanted beyond measure?

Uplifted and forgetful of ourselves, our petty selves and concerns.

What have the gods wrought? What meaning is ours to make, or not make?

Only yesterday there was a veil over all this.

This is like meditation, he thought to himself.

Sometimes cloudy, sometimes clear.

The inner world reflects the outer,

And the outer world reflects the inner,

What a strange synthesis, to be one.

And is it always more clear after the clouds lift, after the rain stops

Like today, both inside and outside?

There is always hope, and sometimes but not always,

The greater the storm, the more clarity afterwards.

What is learning, what is growth?

Coming down, a little girl comes on to the path,

Takes our hands all of a sudden to examine,

Counting on the tips of our fingers, tracing the spaces in between.

We will miss the Khumbu Valley and its people,

Our heart is in these mountains

And already we have that longing to return.

May 2022

Sketch: Crossing Over

Had he "crossed the line?" To "the other side?" *Ya voy p'al otro lado*, the day laborers, visitors, and migrants used to say crossing the land border from "*México*" to "El Paso", his old home in the borderlands and itself a crossing point in the chain of mountains as well as for the great river flowing between the mountains. I'm going to the other side.

In America, he could feel Indian; in India, he could feel American.

He was born on a bridge, so to speak, brought up in the middle, accustomed to making his living between cultures, at times more one side, at times more another side. Ambiguity was his north, certainty his doubt.

Years ago, somewhere in the hills of northern New Mexico, while with a friend who lost himself in an evening gathering at some sort of hippie commune, he had felt a keen sense of alienation. He felt the urge to get away at once and struggled with himself. Every minute was suddenly longer, a torture, a temporary death, a sentence to live out. Yet his friend, who blended in so seamlessly, so comfortably, was happily occupied. He looked for the door but found only the bathroom to stall in. He exited and hid along the walls, hoping to be as unremarkable as a lizard in the desert. He walked outside and absorbed the starry night with a deep longing to be gone from there. Was it the crowd and their self-indulgence, the alcohol and the smoking, the substances, the hedonism? He felt his own foreignness keenly. He and they looked different, thought different, were different. He could not find the commonalities that night, nor was he bothered to look for them. He was not at ease at all. It was his own youthful insecurity perhaps.

While he could also think of moments like that in India, he was here now. And that moment long ago in America recurred to him now, because it stood out in marked contrast to the anchor of belonging he had felt in these mountains, the Himalaya, with these people, a group of 25 strangers on a trek.

He was old enough now to leave most insecurity behind or to recognize it for what it was, to just watch and observe. He was more like a citizen of the world anyway. The language spoken around him in India was not always familiar, not fully comprehensible. It did not matter. The cultural context, of music and songs for example, was familiar but still largely unknown, undeciphered. It did not matter. Games played on the trek were not something he frequently engaged in anyway, yet he played along to the group's delight and to let himself go. It did not matter. He still felt at ease. The trekkers, from many different parts of India, had all been brought together by the common goal of escaping the daily grind and enjoying a week-long trek in the mountains, marked by beauty, challenge, and privations. He felt he had found his tribe.

A week later, he went to meet a former Peace Corps colleague for tea in the country's capital. They hadn't known one another well, but they worked for an organization that changed the lives of its volunteers through immersion in another culture and a deep sense of service. They had both been volunteers in their own time and then were directors who had walked through privileged doors and held privileged conversations with ambassadors and all manner of host country officials. Lived in big houses, ate expensive food, sent their kids to elite schools.

And here he was, arrived by auto-rickshaw, he was visiting her at an expensive hotel whose opulence momentarily spooked him, appalled him, alienated him. It was the type of hotel where they had first met at a director's conference in an unnamed African country so many years ago.

Only now, in spite of the differences, he was somehow on "the other side", with few of the privileges they both had once enjoyed as expatriates. He was not an ex-patriate. He was an in-patriate, re-patriate, resident, a local though a different type of local. She, on the other hand, was the guest, visitor, foreigner—and at director level. Her colleagues were also guests, even the India-born colleague—his accent, his views, the limits of his knowledge all betrayed him.

Had he crossed over? He could indulge with equal interest the talk about U.S. elections, about politics, about people and places. They too had a global outlook, were not provincials. They could fit in the circle of global citizens, based on views, perspective, sensitivity, curiosity even. But not fate or destiny. That was divergent. His fate for the time being at least would not lead him back to the country that had formed him, that he had in fact served in multiple ways. He was now more on this side than the other.

Belonging to both, firmly to America by all his formative years, but the hold was less and less with every passing day. He went months, seasons, a school year without seeing or talking to another American. But his connection now to the country of his birth, to this land and people— where he now lived in community with people whose journey he shared, with friends he saw every day, where he still had family ties and where ancestors had served the government and fought for independence—his connection here grew more steadfast every day. He held both countries in his heart—indeed he had all his life—and felt no compulsion to choose. But he was more on this side at this stage, where he needed to be, where he wanted to be. At least for now and for the foreseeable future.

November 2022

Essay: What do I teach when I teach history?

At the beginning of the 2023 – 24 term, I asked my Class 12 students, why do we study History? They responded with the usual and a little more:

1. "Not to repeat the mistakes of the past"

2. "To understand human behaviour"

3. "To understand the present, why things are the way they are"

    To go a little deeper, I said that History is not just the study of the past but also the study of change. I then brought in what a Class 11 student had said, can we just study History out of a pure interest in the past, can we love History for itself? Have you ever thought that the ancients might have known some things that we don't, for example might their philosophy and feeling for life have been more profound than ours? Perhaps that was a stretch, but students then added two other reasons:

4. "To appreciate how our ancestors lived", alluding to our forbears not enjoying the comforts we enjoy today

5. "To understand the distortions of history that have been made for political purposes"

The last comment caused me to say that none of them had said "heritage", but heritage is also a reason for studying the past and, that alongside the triumphs and inspirations, one must avoid the exaggerations and distortions that come when pride in heritage becomes the focus of history.

And then we commenced with the Indus Valley Civilization.

This is what my notes tell me, as I look back on the year and wonder, as I do on a weekly if not daily basis, what have I really taught anyone today or any day? Today, for example, was a typical teacher's day on an exam-driven week nearing the end of the term: a Unit Test on USA and Australia in World History, followed by a video on the topic of "being Japanese" from the perspective of Japanese minorities; a review of the Unit Test on rights and citizenship in Political Science, followed by opening the chapter on secularism, which starts with the outdated narrative that "every political party professes to be secular"; and then distribution of a sample test to those same Class 12 students quoted above who will soon be appearing for their Board exam. As I grade the Unit Test on World History later in the afternoon, I go through the usual reactions of a teacher: pleasure and satisfaction at the in-depth answers and well-chosen words of a few students and disappointment at the glaring mistakes and misunderstandings of others who I thought were grasping the content.

Ideally, teaching history involves teaching students to think critically about both the present and the past. Children should learn to read the textbook narrative critically and to understand the basis of the text in historical evidence such as ruins, inscriptions, historical texts, linguistics, and even DNA evidence as well as the works of historians. But apart from all this, even as we move from evidence to interpretation, I still wonder on a deeper level, what do I teach when I teach history?

Some would say, I merely facilitate the learning of the student, but that strikes me as too idyllic. Why then can they not learn on their own? As seen from any student who leaves our residential school and goes home for a time, they cannot absorb the feeling of history, having missed out on class discussion. They did not have the teacher or their peers to question the text, to question each other's assumptions, to look deeper, to bring new information by writing on the board, to cover a few things that our text does not cover, to challenge ourselves. Whether this is called teaching or facilitating is a matter of words. One must go beyond the assumption that all the teacher has to do is get out of the way of the child's natural penchant for learning. If the teacher does that, then the child will learn by following their own wayward interests and inclinations. What they will learn is anyone's guess, but they will not learn the subject, and maybe something else, too.

Again, having given ample thought to how I teach my subject, what exactly am I teaching? Recently, a guest visited the school and posed this question—why study History—in our faculty meeting. Thinking about it, I said "to understand our human nature." In that way, History helps with self-knowledge, too. I gave the example that one thing you find repeatedly in history is one party attempting to dominate another party, and this suggests that in our human nature, there is a recurrent will to dominate. All of us have violence within us. Some of the best questions in history, I said, relate to motives. It is what makes the chapter on the Mongols so compelling. What were the motives of Genghis Khan to leave his little corner of the world and set out on a vast project to establish the largest empire the world had ever known up until that point? And further, once you go beyond the brutality of conquest, a reputation that was surely deserved from the point of view of the victims, we then learn about how the Mongolian Empire changed a large part of the known world. Security of the Silk Road, expansion of trade, a policy of religious tolerance, and more.

Once we learn this, I then have my class wrestle a bit with the question, was Genghis Khan a brutal conqueror or a great unifier? The answer, arguably, winds up being both. So do you think the violence is justified? I am always relieved if a student says, like this year, "No sir, I just don't see how you can justify that amount of suffering, no matter what good comes out of it."

The risk of asking this question is that students don't know how terrible war is, how utterly destructive it is, even though the NCERT textbook has source material that says Genghis Khan commanded that "in the exaction of vengeance not even a cat or dog should be left alive." Yes, it was a kind of "total war" in the 13th century, well before World War II which is often seen as the marker for the kind of warfare that would not spare civilians. The reality of war, however, in all its barbaric cruelty and bloodletting and numbness is not something they can even imagine.

Still, what am I teaching, just the subject? I hope not! I had no interest in history myself until Class 11, when I had an unorthodox teacher who would question the assumptions of students in the class on topics that weren't in the syllabus. It was 1983, after all, the year that Israel invaded Lebanon—a pattern that sadly repeats today, although it's Gaza now. A good number of fellow students were Jewish and repeated simplifications they undoubtedly heard at home, such as "the Palestinians left in 1948 and they weren't coming back." Voluntarily? The teacher would ask. And the questioning of assumptions began, even on controversial topics of religion and identity and even at the risk of a student relaying what the teacher had said to his or her family at home. For the student would never have the knowledge of the teacher, neither the breadth nor depth of understanding, nor likely would his parents have it regardless of their level of education. This teacher would also mimeograph supplementary reading assignments and ask us not to answer a set of questions on it, but to come back to class and each of us had to ask "one intelligent question" about the assignment. What he meant by "intelligent" had more to do with critical reading or mindful reading and the "why" questions as opposed to questions with a ready answer.

History requires study, not only in terms of knowledge, but in some training of the mind—borne from understanding evidence and bias and correlations, from the habit of comparing and contrasting societies and civilizations and nations across time periods. The conversation this teacher had with a student or two in class on a subject that did not concern me, like Israel and Palestine, nevertheless had me looking for more in my high school library and checking out the first history book I ever bothered to read, bearing the title The Fertile Crescent, on the Israel-

Palestine conflict. I still remember the laminated brown book cover. To my astonishment, I discovered that there were claims to a land that dated back not a few decades but thousands of years. It was that conflict, in fact, taking place in real time then, that taught me "historical thinking", or taking a current issue and thinking evaluatively in terms of history.

But what am I teaching, besides the miserable memorization for exams, besides the awful repetition of violence—"man's inhumanity to man"—that sadly makes up for a good amount of human history? Our World History textbook just in Term Two covers "confrontation of cultures", "displacing indigenous people", disease, slavery, death and misery on a mass scale, industrialization, colonization, the pollution of the environment, war and genocide, world war, decolonization etc. The greatest advances in science become the greatest threat to the world in the form of the nuclear bomb. But aren't advances in science and medicine, art and culture the true legacy of humankind, that has made our lives better, what we have salvaged after a run of perhaps 250,000 years as Homo sapiens on a planet that can barely contain us?

Today, humanity confronts problems it never confronted before in its past. The spectre of climate change. Mutual destruction. Sustainable living. Mental health. And, if it can be argued that war is less than it was, it can also be argued that hatred is more than it was. The common person who merely followed orders as a soldier in times past is today both the victim of and participant in the vast cesspool of "social media" that feeds on the pride and anger that in times past only the rulers and religious leaders and elites were "privileged" to have. Social media has magnified and amplified the dark side of human nature, even as it has connected people across the globe in matters of empathy, good will, and beneficence.

It then comes as no surprise that I have often thought, paradoxically, that what I hope we learn from History is to be free of history. Through the process of studying History, can we slowly lay aside our pride, prejudice, pettiness, fear and so on? Can we check our tendency to violence, to self-aggrandizement, to absolutist thought and feeling? Can a sustained, in-depth holding of the past teach us to respect it but to be free of its excesses? Is the importance of moderation, reasonableness, compassion, peace, tolerance, and inclusion something we can take from history, even if it means understanding human frailty, which is surely a lesson of history? Humility—but in these nationalistic times? Who will stand up for it—who will correct the aggressive leaders and manipulators who aim to drive us into a single view of the past, absent its complexity, its discrepancies, its nuances? It is a tall task.

You're swimming on the surface, I found myself telling my students this year, go deeper. Question the assumptions. Ask why. Listen to what each of us has to say. What do you think?

At the end of the year, it is rewarding to see the students more excited about History. Their sensitivity to depth and complexity, their knowledge, their written and verbal communication skills have all improved, in different measure for each student. Are they better human beings? Maybe, but the field of action is not theirs yet. One can only sense that they are more thoughtful, more intellectually curious, and more sceptical of blanket statements about the past. As my old teacher used to say, "I hope history teaches you to develop a healthy skepticism."

November 2023

Sketch: Chamber of the Heart

From the moment he walked into the eastern gateway of the temple complex, he was entranced. It had come upon him all of a sudden, without conjuring it up or being aware. Without any volition, his hands folded together of themselves, at his heart, in prayer mode. What was it—recognition, familiarity, a strange feeling of being at home?

What was certain was the awe and wonder that came over him. He had been here before, many long years ago. He walked further along, captivated by the brightly painted lotuses on the ceiling and the strange mythical beasts that made up most of the sculptures that lined the hallways. These enormous beasts (*yali*) had the head of an elephant with trunk and tusk behind it protruding downwards like a sword long, curved, and smooth; the bulging eyes of a crab; the mane of a lion, the back of a horse, the belly of a crocodile, hands like a crocodile's clutching the elephant trunk, and feet either like a crocodile or the sharp talons of an eagle.

Had he left his senses, was this a science fiction fantasy? He was not one given to blind faith or blind belief or going through the motions of devotion. He liked to keep his feet on the ground, so to speak, but he also did not believe man was the measure of all things and the visible world was the only world.

A guide interrupted his reverie, advising that he would wait 3 hours in the long line of devotees but for 1,500 rupees the guide would get him past the line. He said he was not interested and the guide shrank away disappointed. Instead, he meandered over to the right, passing a throng of people in an interminable line that snaked between tall columns.

He walked down a long hallway, with people coming towards him as though they were leaving. Then there were hardly any people. Through an opening, he could see the early evening sky again. It was getting dark but one could hardly notice it in these vast chambers that gave one a feeling of being underground.

A man sat meditating alone in front of a small locked shrine. A woman dropped a yellow white flower beside a lingam, that rounded black stone that, paradoxically, represented the shaft of light in which Shiva had emerged from the earth. Further ahead a family was praying to another deity in the corner of the great temple complex.

These were people of faith. That is why they came here, to worship the gods, to attain all their blessings. Devotion he could understand but faith is not a word he thought a lot about. But if what was meant by the term was a sense of the sacred, of something intangible, vital, and essential, beyond the reach of the most powerful microscope—if it meant a small but palpable sense of some other unseen world, then he too had faith. He had always felt that he was part of a greater whole than his small self might think.

Numerous signs said, "This way to exit", but he did not want to leave just yet. Another sign said, "No foreigners beyond this point." That is where he went, crossing a portico into another chamber of this vast complex. Where people were coming out, he aimed to go in. He entered yet another inner chamber and saw a queue of devotees. They were a diverse lot, older women in bright red sarees, and some in short hair which struck him as unusual; many young and bare-chested men in black lungees, with a string of prayer beads around their necks. The older devotees, sometimes with their spouses, moved slowly and deliberately. Young couples, too, with their young children, had come to visit the famous temples of the land. Everyone came together here, leaving behind daily life with its monotony, distractions, and anxieties, carried along by their faith and converging in the bowels of one of the largest temples in South India.

View of the *gopurams* (temple towers) below which the deities reside, accessed through multiple chambers

A *pandit* in a green-embroidered white lungee, the sacred thread of his kind looping across his pale bare chest, saw him and motioned him to get into the line. Perhaps this was all the official encouragement he needed to join the throng of worshippers and he quickly identified a rupture and moved seamlessly into the queue. They shuffled slowly past a giant statue in black stone of Shiv Natrajan. It was adorned in white cloth and garlanded with flowers. But this Shiv was not the focus of worship, and the line moved forward to the garba griha, a dark inner chamber that he could see was illuminated only by a few flickering *diyas* (earthen lamps). Two privileged devotees sat cross-legged in front a large black lingam on which white and yellow fabric was draped.

Hands folded at the heart, he paused for a moment. It struck him that this inner chamber, the sanctum sanctorum, was reflective of the inner chamber of the heart. In fact, the whole temple experience was symbolic of the outer reflecting the inner, external life reflecting internal life. God was abundant in Nature, yet God was also within. Here in some inner world, where one might not know whether it was day or night outside, hot or cold, sunny or rainy outside, a deity resided, timeless and without form, and we could see him or her only with our hearts. Sages and mystics had said to see with the heart, the greatest of all faculties, and not the mind. This is what the word "*darshan*" meant, to see the god within, and to hold that sight, reside with it, recognize it, carry it with you when you walk away. A moment of calm, of peace, of fullness, of indivisibility where conflicts, both external and internal, are resolved, even if only for a moment, so that they are seen anew, in a different light, a different and godly pair of eyes, godly for their freshness.

A pandit smeared ash on his forehead and stuffed his open hand with flowers of red, yellow, and white and a small packet that contained more ash. He wandered back out of the chamber into the hallway, admiring the sculptures, marvelling at the yalis, those mythical beasts holding onto their elephant trunks looking like swords, at the brightly painted lotuses on the ceiling, and at the busty female goddesses, their thin waists lined with jewellery. It was mesmerizing, enchanting, and deeply symbolic in an ancient way.

He came out now, into one of the external chambers where the worshippers could look back again on the inner chamber. On either side of this portal stood two enormous statues as guards, in a commanding posture with leg held high and arm crossed holding a flame. How strong, how confident, how infinitely serene and powerful appeared these enormous dwarpals or door guards. In front of them, and facing the sanctum at this distance sat an enormous statue of Nandi the bull, serenely, pacifically, attentively. Other sculpted figures abounded. Devotees moved about with folded hands, some sitting on the floors, cross-legged in adoration or meditation.

Not wanting to leave, he too stood about, absorbing it all, strolling around, stopping and staring, before slowly making his way out. Unlike people who had shed whatever faith they had been brought up with, he in his mind had not ruled out the existence of things that he thought science could not measure anyway and the rational mind could not perceive. Faith had to be approached through experience, and the experience was by nature subjective and not objective. He found nothing wrong in this. One had to keep an open mind and heart. Science itself needed to maintain such an open outlook, on the basis that all knowledge is incomplete and the scientist himself or herself is forever a student of the universe.

He found himself back outside and it was evening now. A long line of people stood waiting to have a darshan of the main deity, the fish-eyed one, the one time three-breasted goddess with the green parrot on her shoulder, the namesake of the temple and who was once a mere local goddess. He walked by a peepal tree where numerous rocks had been lodged next to the trunk and engraved with intertwining snakes, ancient entreaties for fertility. On the lower branches hung little yellow crate boxes with miniature lingams inside them.

In a corner of the complex, some people stood in front of an elephant with his mahout. For a fee, this ancient and intelligent animal was made to bless devotees by patting them on the head with his trunk. But its sensitive eyes, in reddened eye sockets beneath long eyelashes, looked terribly sad and tired of this repetitive human game. When do the demands of devotion become excessive or commercialized? What about ancient ideas of the divine—what have they to tell us? How much do we perceive and reflect?

January 2024

Sketch: Sunday Cycler

Early on a Sunday morning, a teacher cycled away from the school where he lived. He pedaled across a small bridge and up a lane that wound between the tall trees on the bank of a great river. He came upon the familiar road where the shops were still shuttered and a few people huddled in tea stalls while others squatted around small fires on the road.

It was dark still and his mind began to churn. He would teach only one more year anyway, he thought. By then, the textbooks would change and history as a subject would become mythology, a canvas of the religious imagination, a projection of national pride, the triumph of politics. Instead of waiting another year, why not head to his favorite eastern Himalaya hill station now and write the book he had always wanted to write? After all, children at school were too often inattentive, disrupting class with their chatter or even interrupting to talk over him. One can never achieve depth in the classroom, he thought. The whole world was becoming more and more coarse and superficial. But isn't this why he got into education in the first place?

Something was stirring in his soul, something that he had not felt since four years ago, when his own children had left home and moved on to university. At that time, he had made the momentous decision to leave his career to take up teaching in a residential school. Now, the school itself was in difficulties. Admissions were down, teacher morale was sub-par, and there was a sense of not living up to the vision of the school's illustrious founder. More immediately, there was the very real prospect of the smallest class sizes ever. He only felt committed to the batch that would be taking board exams next year, and he should see them through. Perhaps he should drop his favorite subject, World History in Class 11, and go back to Class 9, where he would be more assured of a decent class size and wouldn't feel he was wasting his time. He liked the idea and filed it away in his mind, deciding to let it rest and see if it still made sense later.

He crossed the train tracks and came to an intersection where the vendors of apples, bananas, grapes, and oranges were setting up their carts. He turned onto the main road, went past the flyover and autorickshaw stand, and came out onto the broad tree-lined avenue that was the entrance to a different sort of town, still scented with the past. A monk in maroon robes and shaven head walked up the street. The trees were taller and his mind registered the sudden sense of space. He cycled past an inconspicuous museum set back from the road and thought to himself how it displayed the national symbol of the entire country. Amazingly, it had been picked out of the earth a little over a century ago during an excavation of the ruins of the monastic quarter across the road in front of the great stupa. Covered in dirt, rainy season after rainy season, buried for centuries, forgotten, yet retaining its unusual polish and gloss, a gem in the rubble, the lion capital.

Further ahead, he parked and locked his cycle, greeted the chaukidar, and entered the enclosure. In front was a tall narrow building made of brown sandstone. A group of female pilgrims in yellow robes could be seen inside. Likely, they were from a foreign land, somewhere in Southeast Asia. Only worshippers were allowed into the shrine at this hour. To the right stood a white marble statue that had been erected just last month in remembrance of a king of old who had spread the message of dhamma far and wide. He had been dedicated not to the conversion of people to any one religion or philosophy but to the cultivation of virtue and humane conduct among all sects whatever they may be, seeing that they all sought liberation, just in different ways.

Signs lined the path to the shrine with the sayings of a revered ancient teacher who had inspired the old king and whose image in gold was the focus of the pilgrims' devotion. Purification of the mind, freedom from suffering, the way of inner peace and compassion for all—these were the themes of the great teacher, the Awakened One. The last sign exhorted people not to go by what others had said in the pursuit of truth, but to find out for oneself, to test out any theory and accept it as true only if one had found it to be true for oneself. It was not the first time he had visited this place and he had been familiar with the multiplicity of sayings since his own youth. Only last year, he had brought a group of students from the school here.

He came to a memorial on one side and removed his shoes. Immediately, he saw the larger than life figure of Gautama Buddha seated on a dais with the five ascetics who became the first disciples. He was mesmerized, however, not by the calm eyes of the Buddha but rather by the face of one of the ascetics, so full of emotion, dripping almost with tears of gratitude. Yet, what despondency, what despair, what grief had he suffered—or perhaps his look was meant to represent what all of humanity experiences. The eyes downcast, the brow protruding, the cheeks thin, the lips brittle, the veined hands in prayer pose.

The ascetics all sat in reverence in front of the Enlightened One and his eyes so serene, hands in teaching mode, calmly elucidating truth, the mysteries of the mind and human existence. A large coloured parasol sheltered the circle of ascetics and the Buddha, and above stretched the boughs of a peepal tree. A sign said this tree had been planted as a sapling of the original bodhi tree under which the historical Buddha was said to have instructed the five ascetics.

After entering, the cyclist had been dimly aware of how his hands had come together almost instantly in contemplation and reverence. He stood now with his eyes closed. Opening them, he felt his senses more alive to his surroundings. He made a parikrama around the fence which enclosed the tree. He was aware of a lone devotee reciting a mantra in front of an incense stand. He observed a caretaker monk who removed leaves from the display and lit the diyas in front of a glass case enclosing an idol of the Buddha. He sat down, crossed his legs, and closed his eyes. He observed his breathing. He felt inside for his heartbeat. He became aware of the movement of his body, of veins and nerves and tissue. Of the sensations in his head. And back to breath. Other devotees had arrived and he was aware of the movement in front of him. Birds sang in the tree and a train whistled in the distance. A momentary calmness descended upon him.

Some time later, he got up to leave and soon found himself cycling back to school. He recalled again the look of that one particular ascetic who seemed to bear the burden of the world in his downcast face. It then occurred to him that not once while he was at the memorial had he thought of his particular troubles. In fact, it was as though they had rearranged themselves in his mind and acquired a new perspective. His mind had cleared. And it did make sense to go back to Class 9. He would ask the principal. He no longer thought of leaving the school for the time being, which perhaps is the only time that counts.

March 2024

Narrative: Japan Interlude

Committed to my students and doing one more year in Rajghat, I also gave my resignation a year in advance. In my mind, I would be 59 years old the following year. Feeling the mind changing, and with a long-held goal of writing, it made sense to me that my 60th year must be dedicated to writing the book I always wanted to write. Of what I would write about, I conceived at the time:

Not a traditional memoir—'I, I, I'… rather, a pointillist, impressionist painting of moments that make up a life—give life meaning—in my particular experience (my life's meaning) but also my observation of people and places… interspersed with narrative and reflections, even quotes, but I am not so sure—even symbols… basically make art out of my life… this is the groundwork, all I really wish to plan—it is the form I will use to execute something new out of the human spirit (I sense Faulkner)… that is how writing must begin. Maybe my imagination will lead to something more."

I imagined Gangtok, a hill station in the Indian state of Sikkim where the Indian side of Mt. Kanchenjunga is located, as the setting for this writing sabbatical. I had visited twice before, made a few friends, and liked the cafes and walks. As importantly, I had identified three schools where I could volunteer, and had visited two of them and knew a parent whose child went to another.

And then… Japan intervened. Changing my future plans.

As usual, before embarking for the summer break from school, I jotted down a few goals: see kids, meet friends, trek in the Himalayas, immerse myself in a new country (Japan), and visit family in Delhi. Elaborating, I wrote:

I want to renew the mind—its cutting edge sharpness, insight, and vigor. Renewal. After a long phase of school, and its ups and downs. Reflection. Release. Room to grow. Somehow I see the Japan part of the trip helping most with this—some actual solitude.

My itinerary to Japan, what I then referred back to as "23 days in Japan", was as follows:

15-18 May – Tokyo (Asakusa neighborhood)

18-20 May – Fujiyoshida

*** side trip to Lake Kawaguchiko

20-28 May – Kyoto

*** side trips to Kifune and Kurama, and Uji

28-29 May – Hiroshima

29-31 May – Setonaikai National Park (Hiroshima Bay)

31 May – 2 June – Amanohashidate ("Kyoto by the sea")

2-4 June – Kyoto

*** side trip to Mt. Otoyama

4-7 June – Tokyo (Ueno neighborhood)

My method would be immersion, like Peace Corps. This meant: staying in ryo-kans (family-run inns); using public transportation (trains, buses, metro, ferry) and avoiding private taxis; walking, hiking, and cycling; rising early, beating the tourists, and going where the tourists don't go; informing myself regarding top sights and off the beaten track sights; reading on sites on culture, and on history, plus reading Japanese fiction; learning some language; taking up calligraphy; keeping a travel diary; and trying to feel the places where I would be, emotionally and with my whole being, and not just intellectually.

It meant not following a lot of outside news, but truly immersing myself in Japan and its culture. It affected me profoundly.

Sketch: "Forest Bathing"

"I loafe and invite my soul,
I lean and loafe at my ease, observing a spear of summer grass."
– Walt Whitman, *Song of Myself*, 1855

For the sake of sending to friends, he snapped a photo of his shoe on the forest path. Moving a step or two ahead, he heard a scampering off to the right of the path. A small deer came into view. It appeared not to see him. He stopped in his tracks, keeping still as a statue. The big black eyes, the nonchalant chewing, the sound of twigs breaking with the light movement of limbs.

He felt his own heart beat, his lungs breathe in and out, his muscles tighten and loosen. It was as though his every cell were alive, in tune with his surroundings. The deer moved out of his vision, followed by a larger animal, perhaps the mother, with deeper rounder eyes and the same alert but casual and peaceful look. As the deer stretched its neck to pull in fresh leaves, he took several steps closer. The deer seemed to be aware but did not care. Slowly, it moved down the hillside. Another hiker came upon the scene and immediately took a photo.

He came upon a shrine in a forest grove. He absorbed the ancient primeval stillness of the place. It felt as though the trees spoke, the gods were in the air, the kami must be here. Kami was the Japanese name for the spirits thought to inhabit everything and everywhere. With no care, nothing to worry about, nothing in the mind—no companion, no conversational interlude, an alert mind and senses—he felt a sharpness of perception. Walking slowly, sauntering, lingering, looking at the trees, at the roots spreading out on the ground, gazing up and down and away from the path. Listening to the birds chirp, the sound of water flowing somewhere, the occasional leaf blower or chainsaw in the far off distance. In wonder and awe. Feeling heartbeat, pulse, breath. The path was his and his alone. Solitude, silence, the majesty of trees, the grandeur of the forest and a hillside, even more so when it was dotted with shrines. Reverence, the feeling of the sacred filled the air.

It had taken time to get to this moment. He had woken up strangely that morning, thinking his laptop wasn't charging when it was, unable to figure out how to turn on the water in the shower, getting on the early bus but then missing his stop and having to run to the station. He had almost missed the train that took him away from the city. He was the only one to exist the second to last stop. It was in the middle of the forest and he had to walk a long way on an empty road next to a stream, below massive cedar trees on the hills, to get to the famous Kifune "lantern temple."

No one was there. He had the place almost to himself, save for a caretaker who came around scattering leaves with a leaf-blower, disturbing the silent solemnity of the shrine and the forest. Later, he said a prayer for everyone close to him, starting with his children. And then started the walk crossing from Kifune to Kurama, unexpectedly bathing in the majesty of the forest.

Sketch: No Translation Required

The structure, set in the center of a small lagoon, was remarkable for its proportions. There was a central building with long eaves that jutted outwards and a high roof in the middle, on either side of which perched two small but gallant golden phoenix birds, breasts facing outwards. This building, with a very large opening that faced the lagoon, was flanked on both sides by two raised platforms that seemed inaccessible and appeared to serve no purpose other than amplifying the sense of evenness and balance of the structure as a whole. Each platform stood on stilts and also supported a miniature tower with long eaves. The entire structure, called

Phoenix Hall, was made of light brown wood except for the olive green roofing tiles and what looked like paper shutters.

Numerous tourists had arrived early on a Sunday morning. Entrance into Phoenix Hall cost extra and was organized in groups of fifty. While waiting for his group, he snapped photos and toured the adjacent museum. It began with a short video in Japanese but with English subtitles. The Emperor, it read, wished to re-create Paradise on these grounds, a paradise that was called the Pure Land, the entrance to which the devotees might imagine themselves "sitting on a lotus held by the bodhisattva riding on a cloud". The entire structure, in fact, was built to resemble a bird spreading its wings, ready to fly. And the each of the two birds atop the central tower was a phoenix, made of gold such that they "glittered in the fading sunlight."

The words and the image struck a deep chord in him. No wonder, he thought, many of the tourists were elderly, and he too was feeling his age. What a beautiful vision of the entrance to nirvana, according to belief. When it came time to enter the main hall, the tourists or pilgrims, as it were, were asked to remove their backpacks and place them outside with their shoes. No photos were allowed. The guide led them inside, where a magnificent wooden Buddha statue, known as the Buddha Amida-da in Japanese or the Buddha Amitabha in India, was seated prominently, looking out on the lagoon, with far-sighted eyes, eyes that saw into the future.

He felt his hands fold in prayer position as he looked up at the eyes. He beheld the thin lips, the long ears, and the fingers partly clasping one another and nearly forming two hearts. Everything in proportion.

The guide continued speaking in Japanese for many minutes while he stood there, eyes on the Buddha, dimly aware that others seemed not to be folding their hands. He did not consider himself devout at all, but it was moments like this, where he felt he was in the presence of something sacred and transcendent, that he needed no translation, no explanation, no posturing.

Precious lord, I know who you are—you are familiar to me—I have known you since my youth—you have been with me always—I need no translation.

Nor did he need to reflect on what he felt, when he had felt it first, before, last, why, what, and so on. There was no need to analyse. The moment was brief enough. The time in the hall was limited to less than 15 minutes total. He stood with hands folded for some time, sensing his heart beat, his blood circulate, his pulse beat, his breath move in his chest, every cell in his body alive to the moment. After some time, he put his hands down. He was the last out to walk out. He felt surprisingly refreshed, uplifted, and grateful. Everything outside appeared brighter and every face more beautiful.

May 2024

Sketch: No More Hiroshimas

He had been climbing for some time. It was light out but early still. When he took the path behind the temple, a group of elderly persons were still in their morning routine, moving their arms and twisting their bodies ever so ponderously, as though shifting a great unseen weight in the air.

The path was steep and narrow, cloaked by the exuberant growth of tropical vegetation and towering tree canopy. His mind was exceptionally clear, fresh and bright as the morning sky after the previous day's rain. He rested for a moment and noticed little white flowers on the ground. With that sense of elation, almost ecstasy, he composed in his mind:

"Flower petals on the forest path,

Like little white lanterns,

Still have a fragrance."

And what was that fragrance, that delicacy, that perfume, that intoxication? Life itself, it could be nothing more. He walked a few steps further, and he was reminded. Out loud, he said, "because this place has known death."

He had come here for that reason, actually—Hiroshima, August 6, 1945. He figured when planning the trip that he could not visit Japan without visiting the place where the first atomic bomb was dropped, wiping out a city and causing vast death and destruction. At first, he felt compelled to visit because he was an American citizen who had served his government, represented his government overseas even. But then he thought, my relatives weren't Americans at the time, so why does it involve me? That was not quite right, and in him the thought came that he must visit, must confront the reality of a horrific act of violence, because he was a global citizen. Everyone must confront violence, the logic of violence, the impact of violence. And it could not be in theory, it ought to be in close personal terms.

He was remembering his visit to the Museum of Peace the previous day. Soon after entering, people gather in a circle around a map of Hiroshima on which a video is transposed, and the viewer becomes the bomber, witnessing the release of the huge bomb from the belly of the aircraft. One sees the bomb fall through the air until a point above the city where it explodes, delivering a shock wave, generating enormous heat that builds into a vast fireball that radiates out from the hypocenter in orange and red colours to a radius of at least 2 kilometres. He watched it twice, and then felt a lump in his throat, in emotional anticipation of seeing and experiencing the consequences that the Museum would depict in gory detail.

Eyeballs popping out,

Skin peeled and hanging,

Swallowing black rain…

That you thought was water to quench the thirst you felt from your burns, he thought. If the heat and blast didn't get you, the radiation did. If you survived, your days were always numbered, your life was cut short in pain and suffering 1, 5, 10, 20 years later. You were the walking dead.

You were only a child or a civilian, or maybe even a soldier asked to fight for your country which was now being invaded—and you died ignobly, not on any battlefield resisting the enemy, but you simply vaporized or crippled like in the most unimaginable sci fi drama.

He could not stay and contemplate every story of the suffering of the innocent. Instead, he found himself asking himself, was there no warning? Why Hiroshima?

There was a guestbook. He picked up a pen and wrote:

"I'm sorry, people of Hiroshima and Japan, for the atomic bombing—it was not right, innocent civilians, it was not right—it was the outcome of the brutal logic of war, of numb hearts and a dead conscience, the worst single atrocity in history—no more Hiroshimas, our promise to you, no more Hiroshimas."

Whenever he felt mental and emotional stress and trauma, it seemed to build up in his back. So he had taken a seat in the Museum and looked out over the green grounds of the Peace Memorial, beyond the cenotaph and to the A-Bomb Dome. It was a murky, drizzling kind of day. Using his phone, he searched for the answers to the questions he had. No, there was no real warning, and certainly not of an atomic bomb. In fact, even scientists confessed later that they thought most deaths would come from the heat and the blast and they under-estimated the deaths that would come from radiation.

Criminal, he thought. No idea of the consequences. No demonstration of the bomb first. No fair warning. Why not demonstrate the bomb on an island off Tokyo Bay? And not at 8:15 AM rush hour in a city. It was all designed for maximum death and destruction. The imperial government also needed time to respond, absorb the gravity of this new weapon of mass destruction, and decide to surrender. Certainly, the second bomb in Nagasaki was not necessary, nor did the one in Hiroshima seem necessary to him now. But the logic of war, and its self-serving indifferent rationalizing, brought it on. It wasn't a question of

Japan being guilty or not for its own crimes in the war. It was a question of a new and untested weapon that no one even knew the effects of, had under-estimated the effects of, and on a largely civilian population. The war had been concluded in haste and selfish, despicable and dishonorable fashion, all to avoid an invasion of the mainland and yet at terrible cost.

The death of innocents! Screams to heaven each and every time.

There must be a stop to violence, an end to the self-satisfying justifications, starting with ourselves and our relations with each other, each and every one of us. In thought, language, and deed. Humanity must evolve and the bomb, the product of science and psychology, showed that.

He reached the top of the mountain. A lone old man was already there. He looked old enough to have been alive at the time of the bombing.

He looked over the re-built city, like a phoenix risen from the ashes. He envisioned where the bomb had been ignited from almost 600 metres above the city, again for maximum death and destruction. Total war, complete immorality. No other words. Japan itself was a different country and people today.

Walking down, the path diverged twice and he was not sure which one to take. He had to backtrack until he had a proper sense. Further down, something caught his eye to the right. Images. Figures carved into stone. Looking Indian in inspiration.

He moved closer and was taken aback to see the figure of Ganesh on mossy stone. Ganesh, the remover of obstacles, the god of good tidings, the first to be worshipped. It was quite possible that the stone pre-dated the bombing, since a sign at bottom said the bomb had not affected the mountain due to both distance from the hypocenter and the terrain itself and its elevation. He lingered for a bit in contemplation. What an amazing discovery he chanced to see!

Close to the very bottom, he came to the Mitaki-dera temple, now bathed in sunlight and backed by blue sky, its vermillion colors looking absolutely splendid and vivid, the colors of Life.

May 2024

Dialogue: "We are Friends!"

In a small sushi *izakaya*, one of those cozy six-seater restaurants. And in a small place, Amanohashidate, on the Sea of Japan facing west towards Korea and China.

"Where are you from?"

"I live in India. India."

"But your face is… European."

"My father is Indian, my mother is Swiss."

"Ah. Because Indian people are having different face."

"Yes. But my nose is Indian."

Bringing a smile.

"And you, are you from Kyoto?"

"Osaka", he says. "She has a second house here. She likes to fish."

"Oh, very good", I say.

Her plate of sushi comes out. She may be his wife.

"Too much", she says.

"It looks good", I say.

"Maguro", he says.

Hmm…

"Tuna", she says.

Ah…

"Oishii", I say for *delicious*.

"Oishii."

I reach for my bag and pull out my Point and Speak Japanese phrasebook.

"Sakana", I say. *Fish.*

Hai, yes.

"Ah *tuna—maguro."* I see it and say it now.

Hai, yes.

"Maguro suki," I try out, wanting to say I like tuna.

"Maguro suki"? He repeats with a smile, noticing my book.

His plate comes out. It's a fish with a large head and fat body. Its body is battered and fried but its head is left uncooked.

I look in my book and try to say "fried"—*"itameru"* in Japanese, but it is not understood. I try *"ageru"* for deep-fried, still not understood. I wave it off. Not important.

He says *"tai"*, but I don't understand.

My plate comes out.

"Maki sushi?"

Yes, I say.

He orders tuna sushi with the chef. I think it's for me.

Moments later, I am served two tuna sushi, *maguro sushi.*

"Arigatou arigatou," I say. *Thank you, thank you.*

"Maguro sushi", he says.

"Maguro sushi, yes."

I taste it.

"Oishii."

"Welcome to Japan!" he says.

They will go night fishing, he says.

"Sugoi", I say—the word for *"cool"* or *"amazing"* coming to me.

He smiles and says, *"tanoshii."* Tanoshii, I repeat. *Fun.*

I am tempted to get sake, which I notice is 600 yen for hot and 1000 for cold.

"I would like the sake please", I say to the chef.

"*Hotto* or *tsumetai*", he asks.

I think I get what he is asking, but I am not sure about *"tsumetai."*

"Which one is better?" I ask.

The chef tries to explain but what he is saying is a little complicated. The man and wife break in, and say *"tsumetai"* is better.

"Tsumetai?" I ask.

Cold, cold, they say.

Ok, I will have cold.

But the kind man takes the opportunity to get a bottle immediately from the chef. He opens it and pours it into my glass to the brim.

"Arregatou arregatou," I say. *Thank you thank you.*

"This type, top quality", he says, pointing to the bottle. I try to memorize it.

I say I am a *sensei* in India, a *teacher*.

What subject, she asks.

History, I say.

Oh.

I also teach some history of Japan, I say, Meiji era.

Secondary school? She asks.

Yes.

I teach in Varanasi. It is next to the Ganges river.

They understand river, and talk among themselves.

I take out my phone and show them where Varanasi is, between Delhi and Kolkata, which is familiar to them, and I point out the Ganges river, and I show them the photograph on Google associated with Varanasi. He asks to see my phone. He and his wife look at the photographs. They recognize Varanasi now.

Beautiful, they say.

It is close to Sarnath, I say, Buddha's first sermon. This does not seem to bring any recognition.

He says many Indians were in Miyajima in Hiroshima taking many photographs. I do not know about Miyajima, but I know *"ima"* means island. I say I was on Ikuchi island. Setonaikai, I say—she corrects my pronunciation, Setonaikai. I did cycling, and I make a motion that looks like running, unfortunately. Then I say, cycling again and "Shimanami." Oh, Shimanamani, they say—the long cycling route across Setonaikai national park brings recognition for them.

"And I went to Hiroshima", I say. I point out a photo of A-bomb dome and of Mitaki-dera. He recognizes A-bomb dome and says "bad" and explains to his wife where Mitaki-dera is. I point out the view from the top of the mountain above the Mitaki-dera shrine. He explains to his wife. I also show Mt Fuji on my camera and mention Fujiyoshida, where I was.

Do you want any more food? He asks.

No no, I say, I am full.

"Would you like more sake?" I ask.

"No", he says, "we go night fishing," indicating the time has come.

He sees the fish in my book, and points out *"tai"* for *sea bream* and *"hirame"* for *flat fish*. He asks if I know *"suzuki"*. I don't. He tries to describe it. I don't know. I look it up. *Sea bass*. Will you fish for sea bass tonight? No. In deeper ocean only, I think he means. He shows me photographs of large fish he has caught, including a *suzuki*.

We enjoy the sake.

"We are friends", he says and gives me a fist bump. I give him a high five in return.

He steps out to use the toilet.

She asks how long I will stay in Japan. I am here for three weeks, I say. Oh, that is a long time. Yes, I have not come only as a tourist, I try to say, looking for the words, I have come to study Japan. Study, yes, they understand this.

India is very hot now, 45 celsius. Even 50, she says, aware of the heatwave. Yes, too hot. But isn't it always hot, she asks. Yes, true, but this year, even more hot than normal. She nods. He returns.

It is time for me to go also. Thank you. I will come back to Japan, I say. *Matane*—see you again. Good luck fishing. Enjoy your stay in Japan.

I stepped out and the evening sky was amazing, simply amazing.

Reflection: Thank you, Japan

On 6 June 2024, reflecting on my trip, I wrote as follows:

"I'm not sure I've ever had another trip like this to Japan. Only my 'discovery of India' trip long ago, over an extended period of time, 1993. Then of course Peace Corps Mali, 1991 – 93. In terms of sacred moments in nature—times like early morning walks in El Paso's Franklin Mountains or Las Cruces' Organ Mountains; that time, walking in the Alpujarras in southern Spain, in 1992; some walks and hikes alone in the Rockies of Colorado, like by Telluride. But not all the time.

"A lot, a lot happened here. I feel like I've recovered something in my soul. Revival, rebirth. Reminded. Above all, I think it was the trees that spoke, like deities in the trees—Yoyogi Park, Sengen jinja in Fujiyoshida, Fushimi Inari in Kyoto, Kifune, Mitaki-dera, Otoyama and Iwashimizu Hachimanga. The trees, the mountains, the sea. The people. The city life.

"As I said to friends on WhatsApp just two days ago, Tuesday, from the bullet train as I left Tokyo:

"'This country has affected me deeply. I had the vague goal to seek some renewal on my Japan trip, but I didn't know how. And yet I feel rejuvenated. I kept a daily journal. It is all there. Something about the totality of the experiences—the order, the beauty, the climate, the Shinto shrines and Buddhist temples, Mount Fuji, the gardens, the city vibe, readings on Japanese culture, literature, and history, journaling, cycling and running, mountains and sea, walks and the ease of public transportation everywhere, people's kindness, cafes, and a favourite bookstore in Kyoto, and taking up calligraphy.

"'Even visiting Hiroshima and reflecting on that horror, but seeing how the Japanese people responded—'no one should suffer as we have, no more Hiroshimas.' Peace.'"

I also reflected on some individuals I'd gotten to know in my reading and site-seeing, including Basho (the celebrated 17th century poet and wanderer), Shokado Shojo (a famous 17th century Zen monk who lived on Mt. Otoyama and to whom the bento box is credited), Lafcadio Hearn (perhaps the greatest interpreter of Japan to the West in the Meiji era and late 19th century), and the 21st century author Hiromi Kawakami whose book *Strange Weather in Tokyo* I loved.

Continuing, I concluded:

"The other observations about myself on travel, solo travel—these numerous moments of ecstasy: my emotional response to the place and not only intellectual; I think my whole being responded to Japan; being alone was important to feel it, to reflect, even to do calligraphy; being alone, I could also change plans, follow my whims; being alone, I could also observe my body—heart/pulse, lungs/breath, cells/sensation throughout the body—and this enabled me to enliven my senses and perception—to respond not only in my mind or not only be driven by bodily needs—but to respond with my whole being.

"And I credit Japan with being a highly stimulating place—the trees, the mountains, the sea, the sky—the shrines, the temples—the cities and culture of respect, politeness, and kindness. Thank you, Japan."

It so happened that on the day I left Fujiyoshida, it was cloudy and drizzling. So instead of going out for a run as planned, I walked slowly, umbrella and 7-Eleven coffee in hand, around Sengen-jinja, the shrine and trees at the base of where the Fujiyoshida trail begins, the most popular trail ascending Mt. Fuji. Coming back to where I was staying, which was an inn that used to house pilgrims who had come to worship Mt. Fuji, I found myself packing in my room. On my first night, I'd had a full-on view of the volcanic mountain with its sublimely proportionate slopes, so conducive to painting, so soothing to the eye. I'd slept parallel to it on my futon and could make out its outline in the darkness, and I drew comfort as though from a presiding deity.

Now, as I was packing, I chanced to look up. At that very moment, the clouds parted, revealed the mystical peak, and covered it again, and it continued to rain. Then I heard three rumbles. I could not believe my eyes or ears, as I was kneeling in front of my backpack putting my things away. What was it? As human beings are wont to think so thought I: am I being saluted at departure? Am I being called back? I still had all of Kyoto and Hiroshima in front of me. I was less than a week into my trip.

It so happens that day was May 20, the day that I left Fujiyoshida and reached Kyoto. And it so happens that I reached Hiroshima on 28 May.

Post-script, April 2025:

As of this writing, one year later, I have a ticket to leave Delhi at midnight on 20 May, destination Kyoto. And a reservation to reach Hiroshima on 28 May. And plans to live and work in Japan.

I barely scratched the surface and I can sense the depths. The culture and that sense of the sacred pulls me forward.

Short Meditation: Ganga in September

The river in September has this magical quality. She rises, falls, and rises again, bringing down the water and silt from the plains, hills, and even mountains far away. If you scoop up the fresh deposits on the bank or the ghats, it is like holding history in your hand. And when you let it go, your palm sparkles with bits of feldspar and quartz left behind, and you think of the high Himalaya. From whence has it come, who will here proclaim? How near, how distant?

I have looked at the river this month and asked myself what might it teach me. Early in the month, when I felt I had forgotten that life and love are in constant flow and flux, I thought again of non-attachment in these terms: "Allow everything to flow through me. Not stagnate in a pool of the past, a backwater. Let love flow and move on, move downstream. Not linger… I need to move on from the past… or move with the past… just let things flow through me again, like Ganga."

And, since then, I have felt better—not clinging, letting go, feeling free. A sense of renewal.

Since then, as the rains picked up, and the river began to swell, I wanted to feel its energy from time to time. I would walk across the Malaviya bridge in early morning, and later I would run across. The river forms almost a tide coming around the thick round concrete posts under the bridge. How strong, how fast the current, plunging as it comes around and down, exerting a backflow, a whirlpool, a riptide. She is happy this time of year, not stagnant, reveling a bit in her ancient sense of a lost wildness, her former un-contain-ability, all that time before the era of dams and diversions of the river for irrigation and so on.

It is mid-September when suddenly the river rises dramatically in 24 hours. There has been much rain upstream, and it can take a week from Delhi to reach here. I was on a train crossing the Malaviya bridge, exhausted from school, when suddenly my eyes opened and I recognized Namo Ghat and the copper metallic sculptures of hands folded in prayer.

Hands of devotion, in adoration of the river, now surrounded completely by water, with the ghat totally submerged. I sit up sharply, in awe, feeling the connection with the river I have grown to love over the past few years and which has soothed and comforted me time to time.

What is it about the river? Sunrise in the east, and a flame across the water, that follows you wherever you go, like the light of God, the external mirroring the internal. God never leaves you, God seeks you even as you seek God. And moonlight in the west, in the early morning, fading away as the sun rises, having traversed the sky at night, a watchman (or watchwoman) whilst we are asleep.

Tuesday mid-month—oh what divine weather! It has been raining since the depth of night. I hear it outside, but most of all I hear the leaves, the branches outside my window, pushed to sway and sing together, like music to the ears, softly and yet soulfully too. The very air feels different. The rain and breeze together, here in the forest at the junction of the Varuna and Ganga rivers, at this time of year, feels like a caress, a kiss, a departing embrace from the retreating monsoon. It is as though we spend the day under a loose end of her sari, as she leaves us for the season, promising to return, leaving us with her best memory of the year.

I walked in the rain of the morning, across the bridge, and down by Namo ghat. "Surging, swirling, lapping—our enormous lively Ganga", I texted friends. The energy of the river, the rain, and the breeze—the lowering of temperatures, the sheets of rain, that divine wind—it was all a tremendous cocktail and heady dose that carried me through the day with the most warm and positive thoughts, with love of life, gratitude, and a smile and good cheer to spread.

It is the day my Class 12 history students must present their projects. The windows in the classroom are open wide, and the breeze moves in and out, and the shutters bang against the window from time to time. One's senses are especially alive, the students' voices are especially lovely today, their honest manner of presentation laudable. They took it seriously, and I feel proud of each of them.

By weeks' end, the river subsided a bit. A final magical walk was due. It was then I stopped to pick up a handful of the alluvial deposits. And I also paused to admire the flow of the river at ground level, like a sea she appeared, almost a tide rippling outward. And closer to shore, she overturned her waters, with such gentle and inviting sounds, like water music. How the water swirls, flowing this way and that, like a dolphin or seal flipping its fins, only here is a great river turning itself, showing itself, revealing itself to one and all, to those that see and worship her from the banks. It is water that is all pervasive, that seeks every lowly spot, that blesses the lowly first.

Can we not all learn to be as soft as water, to show and reveal ourselves, as freely and naturally as Ganga, not only in September but year-round?

September 2024

Reflection: Tackling Prejudice and Nurturing Values

"The point is that something, some psychological vitamin, is lacking in modern civilization, and as a result we are all more or less subject to this lunacy of believing that whole races or nations are mysteriously good or mysteriously evil. I defy any modern intellectual to look closely and honestly into his own mind without coming upon nationalistic loyalties and hatreds of one kind or another. It is the fact that he can feel the emotional tug of such things, and yet see them dispassionately for what they are, that gives him his status as an intellectual."

George Orwell, "Antisemitism in Britain", *Contemporary Jewish Record*, April 1945 (written in February 1945)

I have written elsewhere about bias, prejudice, and stereotypes. In my last year teaching, I reflected on a few observations at school and wrote the following.

...

Is it enough to be friendly only to one's own friends? What about those who are different than us? Whether that be a different religion, gender, nationality, class, caste, colour and so on.

We live in politically charged times, when politics has moved into the space of religion, fanned by social media, running roughshod over facts let alone sensitivity to others.

As a teacher of history and political science in senior school, it cannot but concern me to witness in my last few years:

- An entire classroom's desks scrawled with either *"Jai Shri Ram"*, *"Sanatani Hindu"*, or *"Hindu"* for a whole year (which I requested to be freshly painted when I took the room this year)

- The phrase *"Jai Shri Ram"* written on the classroom bulletin board on return from Diwali break, which then inadvertently greeted a new Muslim teacher who taught at Jamia Islamia when the slogan was shouted in attacks on students and teachers in anti-CAA protests in the year 2019

- In a discussion on "Religion in the News" in Culture class with Class 9, that looked at threats to the respective minority communities in Bangladesh and in Sambhal, Uttar Pradesh, the back row in the Lecture Theatre erupts in *"Jai Shri Ram"* after I tell them that the crowd marching to survey the mosque was shouting *"Jai Shri Ram"*

- In the same discussion, in talking about how to keep communal harmony, one boy declares "final solution" since we had just got through studying Nazism

"Final Solution" was the euphemism given by the Nazis to their plan to kill all Jews. Knowing the boy's sense of humor, I suspect he said it spontaneously just to get his fellow students to laugh, to make himself look smart, and to go with the crowd. While I normally provide plenty of latitude for questions and comments, at that moment I said, *"That is not appropriate, this is far too serious a subject."* After class, I asked him, *"You wouldn't have said that had my co-teacher been here today, would you?"* He nodded that he wouldn't have. My co-teacher is Muslim.

This is a large part of the problem. We have no Muslim students to speak of at the school. Had we only 10 Muslim students, in a school of 220, things would be different, I am certain. Besides a handful of Muslims on staff, including contract staff, we see Muslims daily crossing the lane that divides junior school and senior school. To wit, over the wall of our sports field is a dargah and a mosque. According to the 2011 census, 28% of Varanasi's population is Muslim. Hindus and Muslims have been economically dependent on each other for centuries, particularly in the weaving and sari industry. Yet we have no Muslim students. And, when asked, hardly any children have friends who are Muslim.

I point this out, as someone who grew up in the United States and went to public schools that had every race and ethnicity—whites, blacks, Latinos, and Asians. We got to know each other as people first. So when I learned in schools that blacks had once been slaves, I was shocked. How could my friends, their ancestors that is, have been slaves? It made no sense to me.

Going back to Rajghat Besant School where I teach, those are just a few incidents and observations. There are many others. It is the nature of teaching History and Civics/Political Science that brings it out. But more than this, it is what is in the news, what is in the newspapers in the hostel, what is in social media and on YouTube at home, what extended family, friends, and neighbors talk about at home, what politicians drum up and serve for us to consume, veg and non-veg alike.

In that discussion in Culture class, I might note that I had prepared slides and links to two videos, one on victimization of Hindus in Bangladesh and one on the most recent attempt to convert a mosque into a temple in Sambhal, which also explained the Religious Places of Worship Act of 1991. This is Class 9, so it was not surprising that no one had heard of it. Moreover, I had prefaced our discussion with the following slide:

- Sensitive topics require sensitive and respectful discussion

- We must raise good questions and seek facts, understand different points of view, be willing to adjust our point of view - not just take sides

- School is about questioning and learning even as we are developing our values and points of view

- We should always be prepared to look at any issue freshly

The class did serve to educate and it also served to show that young minds have formed more than we think. Once topics like converting a mosque to a temple are raised, it is all emotions and *"Jai Shri Ram."* You can hear it in what is said and read it in the faces, gestures, and side comments. And yet, it is about 1/3 of Class 9 who lean politically one way, including sons of politicians, 1/3 who are against communalism, and 1/3 who are neutral or indifferent. In Class 12, it is different. By that age, it is possible for students to support a particular party and yet condemn the communalism the party is a part of.

On an earlier occasion in April with Class 9, as we were learning about the Election Model Code of Conduct, I showed the video of the Prime Minister's rally in Rajasthan in which he said if the opposition won, then a certain group whom "you know by their clothes" and who are "infiltrators" will "come after your *mangal sutras*" (Hindu woman's wedding necklace). The children heard the speech and were stunned, even those who were enthusiastic about *"is baar 400 paar"* (meaning this time, over 400 seats in the 543 seat lower house of parliament). One boy whispered to another in Hindi, *"This is a mistake."*

Why are some children able to perceive harmful rhetoric and others are not? How is it that identities form so strong so early?

I have a student in class who, knowing hardly more than the little we are made to learn about the Constitution in the textbook and whatever I supplement, says he wants to be a politician and that, if elected, he would change the Constitution. How is this? When he does well on the test, I tell him, you have all the right answers, but you don't really believe this, do you, you want to change the Constitution, right? He smiles.

This particular boy was out of school for weeks just at the time we studied Hitler and Nazism. He declined any offer of assistance, did poorly (2 of 20), took a re-test, copied and was caught cheating, resulting in final adjusted marks (4.5 of 20). As it was, I had reason to be concerned about other students. Just before the last day of studying Nazism, one boy informed me that a number of students in his hostel admired how Hitler "made Germany great again" and how he conquered Western Europe in his famous blitzkrieg or "lightning war." He suggested we have a debate on Hitler, for and against. I said, let me think about it, thanks for telling me. The first thought in my mind was, well I'm not surprised, but *how really is it possible? What are they not seeing?* I had made clear, with emphasis, that the supporters of Hitler wound up dead on the battlefield of Stalingrad, for example, the largest battle ever in history, with one million dead in seven weary months, the fields littered with corpses, and the Germans lost.

Together, over 3 weeks meeting 4 days per week for 40 minutes each class, we learned about Germany after World War I, the Versailles Treaty which punished Germany for the war, the rise of Hitler and the Nazis, why they became popular and how they instituted dictatorship in place of democracy, aggression at home and abroad leading up to World War II, a war in which 60 million died including at least 12 million Germans and including the "extermination" of 6 million Jews and 1 million other "undesirables" in concentration camps. We had taken the time to enquire into such questions as: *Why did Hitler and the Nazis target Jews in particular? Why did people, including educated people, follow orders to kill even innocent civilians? What was education in Nazi Germany like? Is it easy to get people to hate other people—if not, how did the Nazis do it? What are the techniques of propaganda used then and still used today? If you were afraid to resist the Nazis openly, on fear or incarceration of death, how could you still have resisted them? How do Germans look back on Hitler today, with pride or shame or something else?* Much of what we talked about I had written on the blackboard plus given daily homework assignments and notes that I checked at the beginning of every class.

So I decided to approach the request for a debate in a particular way. The following day, I first wrote the proposition, *"Hitler was a great leader"*, on the board. I then asked the children to define leader—and we could appreciate that the word leader is used not only in politics, government, and the military, but also there are business leaders, sports leaders, religious leaders, school leaders, and so on. Leader is not a title, it is a description that is earned. What then makes a leader great? Children listed many things such as listening to different points of view, being inclusive, recognizing when you have made a mistake, being effective at getting things done, leaving a place better than it was before, and so on. So then, was Hitler a great leader? Silence. No one had listed that a great leader was someone who made powerful speeches, targeted violence at the minority community, and conquered territory. So the answer that he was not a great leader seemed too obvious. We then had a short debate anyway on whether Hitler was good for Germany or not. In the end, I emphasized again to children that Hitler led Germany to devastation. Or didn't he? What does social media say?

In that discussion in Culture class with Class 9, at one point, I posed the question, do you think of yourselves as Indians first or Hindus first? "Hindus" said some, "Indians" said others, "both" others said. Then a girl in the front row said, "Sir, human beings first." *She got it!*

Children are a reflection of their parents but also society. Society is a product of history. And we need to be faithful to *all* of history, not just one community, people, or nation. Children who come to school must also expect to have their pre-existing beliefs on history and politics to be challenged, whatever side they come from. Face history, face yourself. Understand the past to free yourself from the past, not repeat it like a blundering fool. Such is education, such is democracy.

January 2025

Reflection: A Running Odyssey

Training for long distance races is like meditation for me, especially anything 13 kilometres or more as a training run. It's as though the narrow noisy chaotic stream of morning thoughts widens into a larger channel, slowing down, rippling, allowing one to focus and observe. Like the Ganga river next to me. Sometimes a thread will emerge or an idea and it sustains me through the run, but I keep looking at the paved lane, the dogs, the buffaloes, and the people, whether in tea stalls, barber shops, or paddy fields.

I run in Rajghat and environs. Rajghat is on the eastern edge of Varanasi, fronting the Ganga and wedged between the city and the villages. The villages are accessed by a narrow bridge across the Varuna that is fit for pedestrians, cycles, and auto-rickshaws but not for cars, thus suddenly reducing traffic while still near to the city. By late March, the heat already makes running difficult and by June, the humidity doubles the challenge and neither heat nor humidity relent until late September, allowing for only a short training and running season, October to March.

Conscious of my age and with it a tendency to put on weight, I run mostly for physical fitness but I am keenly aware of the connection between body and mind. In my school days in Houston, Texas in the 1970s, right from elementary school there was something called the President's Medal of Physical Fitness with the slogan "Healthy Body, Healthy Mind." This struck me, probably since the connection was not something I'd thought about until then. Today, I recognize it's significant in so many ways. For one, I know that without physical energy, I don't have mental energy. At the same time, it takes mental discipline to drive the body forward until it discovers its own momentum.

On 21 November 2024, I signed up for three races in what I consider my Rajghat running season:

- 15 December 2024—Tata Steel 25 K—in Kolkata

- 5 January 2025—Chennai Half Marathon, which I later upgraded to 32 K ("20 miler")

- 2 February 2025—Kolkata Half Marathon (21 K)

I am a teacher and my ability to run longer distances is usually confined to Sundays when I don't teach. In October this year, while on Diwali break, I already hit 18 kilometres on a training run, which usually takes me 3 – 4 weeks to build up to. In November, however, I had to cut back for such reasons as Diwali travel and suffocating pollution in Delhi; a conference hosted by the school, where I took visitors on long walks and put aside running; and a week-long spell of low-grade fever and weakness where I could not run. By 21 November, I was having doubts about being ready to run, with another conference taking me away from Rajghat, but I signed up anyway with the agreeable thought of it all.

Every runner knows his weak spots. With me in particular, I am aware of a weak left knee and a stiff lower back, which is a result of two herniated disks in my lower back. In fact, an extremely conservative doctor in Peru once told me, in 2010, to stop running altogether and take up cycling and swimming instead. He had no idea what running meant to me and I blew him off. One can always run slow, slow jogging it is called, and overcome most any inconvenience. Cautious medical advice takes away all the fun of living and seems to ignore the mind-body connection—that we need our cherished physical activities as much for the mind, which then generates a sense of well-being that then anticipates more of the same. Running in fact has an impact on body, mind, and soul, and it takes all three to get through a challenging distance race where you push and stretch yourself to the limits of time and place.

As I picked up my training again, from 21 November on, I began to feel good. I would text a few friends and former running partners of my progress, ending with the upbeat phrase "all systems go." I felt just a little indomitable then, blissfully oblivious to my age, an overripe 58 years old. Little did I know what was in store for me.

On Friday the 13th, as luck would have it, I flew to Kolkata with only hand baggage and as I walked with my bag slung across my right shoulder, only minutes from my Airbnb studio flat, I felt something tweak in the shoulder. Strange, I thought. I was cautious for the rest of the evening, almost favouring my shoulder as I walked about. I got a haircut at a favourite barber shop on Park Street and paid extra for a head, neck, and back massage. Going to bed, there was a time at night when I felt I had finally found a rare relaxation position on my left side and I was able to nestle in comfort and peace. In the morning, however, no sooner had I risen from bed and walked around a bit than I felt an excruciating pain, like lightning, shoot through my body from right shoulder to left side. I groaned, even let out a scream, and fell down on my bed. I found it difficult even to reach across the bed for my cell phone.

I lay there for a time, in shock at my circumstances less than 24 hours before a 25 kilometre race, my first big run of the season. My back was killing me at that moment. One thing I know about my back is that it needs movement, however slow and gentle. So I got up, moved slowly to get my clothes and shoes on, and gently went down the stairs, appreciating the many film posters as though for the first time. My intention was to amble slowly to a nearby Nature Study Park that I always find soothing.

First, I stopped at the chai point on Russel Street right outside my place. I noticed my senses were quite sharp. The mind, beholden to the body's vulnerable condition, knew no errant thoughts at that moment. I took in my surroundings, noticed the tree roots blending into the buildings, the early morning activity on the street, and an attractive young woman with a cute smile and suitcase crossing the street to drink chai with her two male companions. I found these sights comforting. An elderly graying woman who must live on the street asked me for a chai, so I got her one. She was very grateful and gave me a sweet smile. The chai was so good I got another for myself.

I then began my slow walk, vaguely remembering the directions. Everything—the trees, the streets, the old doors, the bricks, all called to me with a certain "decadent Calcutta charm"—everything looked so beautiful. I came to Shakespeare Sarani and the familiar tea drinking, kachori eating corner. I then came to the park, still feeling weak, stiff, something not right. At that early hour, I observed a physical trainer shouting out "one—two—three—four" in cadence to his female trainee as she went through a series of stretching exercises. I observed an old man with a long beard and a gaggle of aging women. I then stood behind a bench in front of the large pond and slowly began stretching, first rotating my left arm in front of me, then my right. I stood up on my tiptoes, going up and down, stretching out my calf muscles. Everything was connected to the spine. I extended my arms. I did some core strengthening exercises that I had used years ago to get over back pain. I could see the pond, the birds, the reflection on the pond, the ducks. I could hear the sounds of the birds and the people. It all was incredibly beautiful, more than ever before, as though in my pain and coming slowly and ever so prudently out of my pain I was on some higher plane of existence.

Compelled to pay attention only to my body and taking in my external environment had the effect of inducing a wondrous calm over me. I took a round of the park, a photograph of the regal but simple statue of Rabindranath Tagore in his robe on the other end, and in my new state of wonder and relief, I wandered over to the Shakespeare Sarani corner for kachoris and chai. I then walked further away to my favourite Artsy Coffee & Culture café. I was the first customer. Beautiful melodies of classical piano resounded in the café and I sat down on a couch, pulled a version of Tagore's Gitanjali off the shelf, and deeply enjoyed the first 12 poems, finding in them the very high quality of spiritual realization in which they were no doubt composed by the great poet. I lingered in a temporary state of mental revelation and emotional ecstasy before exiting and having the good sense to buy myself a tube of Volini pain relief cream on the way home. I stood on the street outside the little medical shop, lifted my shirt, and immediately applied the cream to my chest, lower back, and neck. I then walked slowly back to my flat. The sudden pain and crippling sensation had been pushed back, but would it return?

I thought to finish the Tata 25 K race in about 2 hours 50 minutes. But I had done it 3 years before and finished at 2 hours 43 minutes, so that was on my mind. I felt the need to prove to myself that I was at the same level of "fitness" even though we all naturally slow down with age, especially without consistent training. And what about the "joy" of running? Shouldn't that count more? Aren't the two related—both enjoyment and performance? Friends texted to remind me to enjoy the race.

I got up at 4 AM, ate half a paratha and some curd from the night before, drank a cup of Nescafe, tanked up on water, and walked the 2 kilometres from Russell Street to the starting line in the Maidan by Dufferin Road. A friend and former Rajghat teacher Dipankar was also running but I had no cellphone and would never find him amid the many hundreds of runners just for the 25 K, not to mention the thousands there for other races. Walking into my particular "holding area", I stood in awe and admiration of the "elite runners" warming up with short sprints. They appeared like veritable gazelles, fleet of foot and running like the wind. My good running pace is 6 minutes and 30 seconds per kilometre, they must be at 4 minutes per kilometre only—or less! So much for comparison.

Due to all the waiting and water consumption, no sooner had the race started at 5:30 AM than I ran to the side with a few others to "release the waters", so to speak. Typically, after 2 – 3 kilometres, I found my pace. No dogs or buffaloes to look out for, instead it was only the unevenness of the road and the occasional gravel or small chuckhole. Calcutta has always treated me well, felt like home in a way, and so I ran comfortably and with a certain amount of joy in the "City of Joy". I looked at my watch to pace myself and realized I might actually be able to meet my "stretch goal" of 2 hours 43 minutes and enjoy the satisfaction of same time as three years prior. In a distance race, you reach a point where it is often the same bevy of fellow runners spread out over about 100 metres or so. You admire their pace and think they are all running with much less effort than you are! One never knows unless it is obvious—heavy respirations, grunts, flat feet, and flailing arms and legs.

The race takes you on a final loop near the Victoria Memorial instead of going straight to the finishing line. I was aware of this and had prepared myself for it mentally. I could make my target. No back pain, no great leg pain, not huffing and puffing too much, just a certain stiffness in the mid-section and lower back. Mind focused. With signs for 500 metres, 300 metres, then 200 metres to go, I ran as hard as I could towards the finishing line. 2 hours, 43 minutes—I made it! I slowed down, like a long distance train that has just entered Howrah station, its air brakes groaning and echoing throughout the station, announcing its tired arrival at destination. I kept walking. My friend's daughter Vishnupriya, who had done the 10 K race, saw me, smiled, said congratulations, and asked if I'd seen her father.

"Obliteration of thoughts"

Later, when Dipankar came in and the three of us posed for pictures, now squatting, now standing, I found I didn't have much to say! I felt stiff but not only that. The feeling of enjoyment and satisfaction was not really there, even though my friend heartily congratulated me on what he recognized as an achievement. Feeling a bit numb, I walked the 2 kilometres back to my flat. I texted the owner, but she would not grant a checkout later than 12 noon. After showering, I lay down on my bed for 35 minutes. I just needed to feel my back relax and extend, to feel the inflammation in my brain decompress, to get my mind together again. I then mechanically packed up.

I would go back to my favourite Artsy Coffee & Culture and pick up the Gitanjali again. But a noisy crowd was in the café and nothing from the Gitanjali resonated with me now. I ate and drank to my content. I had no thoughts, it felt like any thoughts had been obliterated. "Obliteration of thoughts" was the phrase that came to mind. I took a taxi to Dum Dum airport with that same feeling of numbness, something short of paralysis of thought and feeling. Where was the satisfaction? In the timing only! I texted a few people and got the customary "congratulations" back. I did not feel what I was "supposed to feel", but I had done well, considering my epic plight just 24 hours earlier, reduced to screaming in pain on the bed due to that lightning bolt that went through my upper body and laid me out like a battlefield casualty.

Back in Rajghat on Saturday, 21 December, aware that I had only a 3 week window before an even longer race, I started a slow jog with no clear intention as to how long I would go. I've always found that anything over 13 kilometres seems to breach some self-imposed limit, and the body adjusts not through self-conscious pain and struggle but through actual enjoyment, the so-called "runner's high." As long as you are not too focused on the watch and timing. I was not, and I was going slow, so I kept going and going, and it felt like a massage. I slow jogged for 3 hours exactly and hit 23 kilometres. It felt so good, so unexpectedly good! I texted friends, and we all felt I was ready for the next big race— the 20 miler in Chennai!

In such a positive frame of mind, my ego got the better of me. The school's Annual Sports Day was around the corner, with the 3,000 metre sprint to take place on 28 December. Having completed a 23 kilometre training run, I knew I needn't do anything else long distance and, in fact, I could "taper" down a week before the 5 January run. Also, this was my last year at school, and just as I'd run the 3,000 metre last year, as the only teacher running with the students, I thought why not do it again. But why? It is undoubtedly the pumped up feeling of hearing the kids cheer me on! "Sanjay sir, Sanjay sir" as I round Down Field in front of the crowd. In other words, a boost to the ego! Vanity!

As in the previous year, I first ran a strong 5 kilometres at dawn on my own. I was loose and felt ready. But I wasn't ready for a bit of comedy at my own expense. I had only available an underwear with poor elastic, so I had to take it. What happened is that no sooner had the race begun and I'd run about 100 metres than I felt my underwear slipping! I reached behind to pull it up, but it slipped again. I could not pull out of the race to the side of the track. Everyone would see me pulling up my pants—and to what effect? The underwear would just slip again! So I kept running and running, at fast pace, much faster than my long distance pace, and I felt my underwear go lower and lower, below my waist. I reassured myself that it simply would not go much lower, the elastic would stop it, there is no way it could go to my thighs or my knees or my ankles! Thinking on these lines, I had the sensation that I was running nangu pangu or naked in front of the crowd and I touched my shorts just to be sure! They were still there! I finished in 15 minutes and something, 5 minutes per kilometre, and sat down relieved that my pants hadn't fallen off! I sat down for a long time.

Then I cancelled my timekeeping duties of other events, went home, bathed, went to the Dining Hall, and lay down. I had a fever. And not only that. Something else was not right, something in my left leg, a tightness in the hamstring. I didn't know it then, but I'd strained my left hamstring, and this would impact my 32 kilometre race in Chennai in a way I'd never imagined or experienced before. And for what—vanity! An ego boost that would soon be forgotten, but for which the longer term physical effects and ensuing disappointment in performance I would have to live with, though it would dawn on me only later. Another lesson of running for the books. Never again! A friend had in fact warned me of just such a thing, to watch out for injury in a short race, especially at our "venerable age", he had said! I had listened but felt myself invulnerable. And now I was brought low, back to size—again!

I went to Chennai. I adjusted to the warmer and more humid climate with a few comfortable but short training runs to Adyar beach and back to my place of stay, Vasanta Vihar, the Krishnamurti Study Centre off Greenways Road. I would be running with friend, colleague, and veteran runner Siddhartha who was also staying at Vasanta Vihar. This put my mind at ease about reaching the starting line some distance away by Napier bridge. A 4 AM start meant aiming to reach by 3:30 AM and leaving our place by 3 PM and, for me, it meant waking at 2 AM to shower, eat some fruit, enjoy a coffee and just prepare myself without rush.

All the preparations went like clockwork, the race began in pitch dark, and I felt myself running at a good pace. All systems go! Wink, wink. We come onto the long East Coast Road and I am still doing ok. I now notice some of the half marathon runners running with us and think, "that was me last year, half marathon, really enjoyed it." And for a moment, I envy their energy because I am now at the point where I feel myself slowing down, especially after the half marathon mark of about 21 kilometres. I check myself, what is it I feel? Can I push myself? But no, it is something strange, it is as though the tightness in the left hamstring is pushing into the hip. It does not feel good to push it. I tell myself, ok, slow down but just get to 25 kilometres and see. Which I do—and then start walking. What a relief! The pain subsides, and so I keep walking for a good 8 minutes or so. Runners are quite spread out. A few others are also walking. I don't register a feeling of disappointment really, since I'd made it to 25 K and I'd told myself when I upgraded from the Half Marathon to the 20-Miler that I well might slow jog or even walk a bit. I had not run this far since April 2022 and my one and only Marathon in Annecy, France. Suffice to say, I make it to the finishing line, but I walk twice more before finishing the last 2 kilometres in reasonably good form. At least I don't feel wiped out like after the Tata 25 K in Kolkata.

What is it about running? Why push yourself so? It's not really the race, it's the training beforehand. You have to enjoy it—getting up early, meeting the dawn, running in a place you like at a pace you like, being alone with thoughts that come and go, watching the road, seeing something new that catches your attention, a dog, a buffalo, someone's eyes, and so on. And, as said, long training runs for me become like meditation, a fine sense of the body and mind in movement together, a comfortable flow of energy, a certain peace in steady movement, almost a homeostasis and equilibrium, the feeling that you can run forever, even though your body is in a process of inflammation. Then there is the satisfaction of keeping up with your training regimen and timing. More and more you feel ready. And you imagine the starting line and your fellow runners, in shorts and T-shirts or tank tops, wearing bibs, from various parts of a country, pumping their legs up and down, fit, ready, and anxious to test themselves. At my level, it is never to beat the person in front of me, unless it's the last 200 metres or so. It is just to measure up to my own personal expectations and to enjoy it at the same time. Meanwhile, one knows intimately that it is only the fact of other runners that you are running as well as you are. Without them, you would only be drifting along. And you go back within, and there is that intriguing observation of mind and body when pushed to the limit, as running can do.

Siddhartha and I got on a train to Bangalore that very afternoon and then a long taxi ride in the dark to the Valley School where again I would be staying at the Krishnamurti Study Centre. A bit of a hilly area and I found myself with very little strength or desire to run even after four days of rest. I took a plane back to Varanasi on 14 January, feeling hampered by my left hamstring and it finally dawns on me that it was Sports Day and the 3,000 metre race that brought it on, my biggest mistake. No sooner had it dawned on me than I begin to recover. My training runs, back in familiar territory and flat ground, go off smoothly and without a hitch. The leg feels fine again. It has taken nearly 4 weeks to recover.

Still, the drama of this year's running season is not over! Early one morning, while running back across the river Ganga on the Malaviya bridge at a good clip, I fail to appreciate something I've run by or over numerous times. It is four iron bars sticking out of the cement, about one inch high each, as the likely foundation points on which to build some other structure. Lo and behold, I stub my toe on one of the rods sticking up and suddenly I am horizontal and falling! One remembers that feeling of being off your feet, suspended in air, right before hitting the ground. My arm extends to protect myself but it can't stop my actual right brow striking the pavement.

I'm on the ground. It's dark. My glasses are somewhere. A guy on a scooter stops to offer assistance. I find my glasses behind me and bend them back into shape while sitting there. It takes over a minute. I stand up. Is this a sign to call it a morning and go back? I've run 4 kilometres. It is the Sunday before the last and final race of the season, the following Sunday, 2 February, back in Kolkata. No, I decide, I'll run some more and just take it easy. So I turn down into Namo ghat. I feel something on my eyebrow but pay no attention to it. Soon I am picking up the pace. I run further, through the village of Sarai Mohana, on a loop I know well, and back to school, a good 10 kilometres total. The guard at the gate looks at me and asks what happened? What do you mean, I say. He points to my brow. In the mirror at home, I see the dried blood. I clean it. At breakfast, a friend tells me it looks like two fangs, as though a naag, a cobra, has bitten you! I rather like that. Bitten by running, I am. Plus, the morning seemed to have a simple lesson—if you fall down in life, get up, keep going! After all, nothing wrong with my leg, which is the main thing.

Back in Kolkata with friend Dipankar, we gear up by enjoying the Kolkata Book Fair for long hours on the Saturday before the race. Books, running, reading, writing, trekking, walking, devotion, friends—all good for the soul. In the evening, at dinner, we talk about timing. I'd like to do 2 hours 20 minutes max, maybe 2 hours 15 minutes, but possibly 2 hours 12 minutes since that was a time I hit last year. I still have it in my mind to prove that I am still as fit as last year, even though 2 hours 12 minutes was my slowest of three half marathons last year, my fastest being 2 hours 4 minutes.

The race start is "only" 5:30 AM and it is "only" a half marathon so I get up at 3:30 AM "only" and we are out the door by 4:30 AM. Unfortunately, we walk a good deal since we cannot find a taxi to take us even though it is day of Saraswati puja and you would expect availability of taxis. Finally, we catch a ride with another runner. He is from Mumbai and visiting his parents in Kolkata. We make it to the starting line at Salt Lake Stadium in good time. No sooner does the race start than one runner takes a tumble. We gasp "are you ok" but run around her. She is soon up and running herself.

It is a foggy morning. I know the course from last year. I loved it, it gave me a wonderful feeling. It is an out and back and one can expect to see thousands of runners on the return, with all the 10 km racers at that time. Plus, there are full marathoners who have already started. One can admire the truly fleet of foot and their stamina to boot. I've taken my cellphone with me this time, just like on that marathon in Annecy years ago. It is in my left back pocket. It is troubling me and I get the foggy idea that it might re-aggravate my left hamstring, so I switch it to my right back pocket. No, not comfortable and it occurs to me it might hamper my right leg. It cannot go in a front pocket because it might fall out and the cargo pocket won't work because it will wobble around. So I carry it in my right hand in the ziplock bag in which I brought it. It is not only a foggy morning but humid also and soon the perspiration on my brow fogs up my glasses. I cannot see more than a few metres in front of me. Even though visibility is low anyway due to fog, and I'm in almost my own interior running world, I must take them off. I need to see where I am, where I'm going. Then I can't put them back on because they are not de-misting, it is too foggy. It is better running without them. So I hold my glasses in my left hand and mobile in my right hand. Every now and then, I switch hands. Who else is doing this? I do catch someone else with their glasses in their hand but no mobile. So there I am, more than half the race to go like this. It's absurd of course. Plenty of people would just stay at home. But runners do have a crazy streak in them.

Soon, the body takes on a life of its own. I just feel my body running away with me. It is not slowing down. It is driven on by the mind. I feel a load of sensations, here, there, everywhere. Heart pumping, legs pumping, everything pushing, throbbing. When I feel the mind drift and that natural slowing down of my pace, I tell myself, "work it out through the body." And I do, in no time, I've put that laggardness behind me and I'm back on pace. The mind is keenly aware of every stride, stride by stride I am pushing forward, pleasurably, energetically, in spite of what must have been a crazy old man's appearance, specs in one hand, glasses in another.

Keeping up! Kolkata Half Marathon, 2 February 2025

I look at my watch. I can make 2 hours 12 minutes. I come round a bend in good stride, down the straightaway and final 2 kilometres. I begin to pass slower runners. My entire body is moving strongly, powerfully, for my age and level of training. It feels like peak form. I can see the finishing line. I cross and slow to a walk, hands on my hips. I meet a fellow runner, tall and slender Mohammed from Bangalore, who had run barefoot and whose acquaintance I had only recently made when he came to the conference in Varanasi in November and was part of my walking group. I'm feeling surprisingly good. I feel the warmth of my body, something rising and falling, my heart, my lungs, my legs, my feet. The mist on my glasses fades. I put them back on. I remove my mobile from the zip lock bag. It is fine but my fingers are too sweaty to unlock it. I try several times, then manage to have someone snap a photo of me. I wait for Dipankar.

Unlike the Tata 25 K race in December, where I had experienced that "obliteration of thoughts", my mind feels so sharp, the senses so sharp. I have energy. I walk straight, the mind aware of everything, feeling perceptive, feeling joyful, elated, supremely satisfied. Having had only an apple at 4:25 AM, I now enjoy four little mini coffees and half of a cheese sandwich with other runners at a gathering area.

Back in our flat, I enjoy two hard-boiled eggs and two brown bread toasts with butter and two oranges. After Dipankar checks out, I walk to a favourite café I'd discovered on the Friday when I arrived. It is now 12 noon, and there I enjoy first what I'd been craving—strawberry cheesecake with Americano coffee. By 12:45 PM, I have advanced to a dish of baked fish, rice, and vegetables followed by a cortado coffee. I look inside and outside the beautiful quaint little café in a city that has always treated me so well and just revel a little more in that feeling of sharpness, strength, and satisfaction, contemplating all the crazy ups and downs of this running season. At 4 PM, I am at the airport and enjoy two bananas. On the plane, I enjoy two little Snickers bars. Isn't this over-doing it? Rewarding myself with food? I buy sweets for the kids and a teacher and his family in my hostel plus for a few teachers in another hostel. Back in Varanasi and my room in Rajghat at 7:30 PM, I go light on dinner, just an apple with Amul cheese slices, crackers, another orange, and two bourbon biscuits.

Such a good feeling! I'm not quite as fit as last year, if I go by timing. Yet I'm feeling on top of the world even more than last year. And I feel I've learned more about myself, about life even, thanks to the sport and pastime of distance running.

February 2025

Narrative: Leaving a Place

Today I must leave. By choice. The time has come to embrace another phase, another place.

But it's been almost 5 years. Varanasi – Rajghat – I can't appreciate you enough. With you, I experienced a renewal of body, mind, and soul. And with friends made here – and myriad places.

In the last month, from 9 February to 10 March, as I said my goodbyes. I managed to visit all my favourite places, though it is that bit of detail that would make sense more to a local than to most everyone who reads this:

- Cycling to Sarnath – Mulaganda Kuti Vihara in particular – the Buddha and the first 5 disciples

- Aadha Aadha café – and the walk via ghats and galis – just beyond Dasaswamedh ghat (steps by the river)

- Numerous runs across the Malaviya bridge at sunrise and down by Namo ghat, also by Sarai Mohanna and Kamauli

- Sunrise walks from Adi Keshav mandir to Namo ghat – and other early morning darkness and return walks to Gaay ghat or Paanchganga ghat

- A classic ghats, galis, mandirs walk (with students) starting from Laxmi Chai Wala down Kachouri Gali and the Brahmanal to Manikarnika, stopping at a personal favourite shivling in the crypt/*garba griha* at Manikarnikeshwar and a personal favourite temple, San Katha mandir

- Walk by ghats and galis (with friends and colleagues) to Auntie's café

- Boat ride (with friends) to Vaatika's pizzeria, where I've often enjoyed good food and dessert on special occasions in the company of students and friends over the years

- The long cycle ride (with friends) to the island, down winding village lanes and past misty fields at sunrise, all the way to the banks of the Ganga where the egrets, gulls, and other birds reflect like magic over the water

I lived simply again. No car, no house. All my living in one room in a hostel. And the adjoining bathroom (bucket baths – no shower), kitchen (only mini-fridge, electric kettle, and sink), and store room. Ceiling fans and windows - no cooler, no AC. Dust. I felt the outside temperature air at any time of day – no sealed living. Only the help of a space heater in winter. Co-existence with lizards, long-legged spiders, and ants. The water point for drinking water down the stairs and outside the hostel gate. Handwashing of undergarments while the dhobi/washerman washed my other clothes. Boys who lived downstairs and upstairs. All vegetarian food, no alcohol.

I leave with four suitcases and a backpack. One suitcase is books. My purpose was served as a Teacher of Geography, World and Indian History, Civics and Political Science plus enrichment classes like Introduction to Spanish and Global Awareness.

I so loved this place and the people here and in the surrounding area, where I was constantly greeted. At times, running in the villages, seeing village life, it felt like Peace Corps Mali days. And teaching, having fielded hundreds of dedicated Peace Corps Volunteers as teachers in far flung areas of Mozambique until recently, it felt like I too was like my Volunteers. Circle of life, circle of giving.

Rajghat, I will miss you. I will carry you with me.

10 March 2025

Sketch: "Go with an Empty Mind!"

It was November in Delhi and just after Diwali. He was packing his things in his bhua's home for the return trip to Rajghat when an thought occurred to him. He walked into his bhua's room.

"Bhua, something occurs to me."

"Tell me."

"You know the memoir I've been meaning to write…"

"Yes."

"Well, what if I write it before going to Japan? Because I will need to focus on giving my all to Japan, on total immersion like last time, this time even with language learning and work. I won't be able to do write the way I want at the same time."

"Meaning?"

"Well, I would miss the beginning of the school year in Japan, but I would get a job later. What other time will I find in my life like right then, a moment of transition. It means I would spend maybe two months in India after school finishes in Rajghat to dedicate myself to writing, it can be Gangtok like I was thinking before. And then my mind will be clear."

"Yes, go to Japan with an empty mind!"

"Yes!"

She understood and the phrase stuck with him.

Almost exactly four months later, he found himself in Gangtok. In one of those strange coincidences, on the first day, he met a young female Japanese tourist staying in the same hotel on the ridge. Light-hearted, she was traveling the world for a year. She told him about her journey in India. He had stayed in Hotel Pandim before and knew the hotel owner and his family. His son was now six years, two and a half years older than before. And "French madame" was staying there at the same time, the 88 year old retired airline stewardess, never married and with no children, who had been coming to Sikkim every year for the past 23 years. She was widely known for her ability to walk 30 or even 40 kilometres in a day to the villages on the other side of the valley. In times past, she also helped rehabilitate dormitories, kitchens, and washrooms of the more remote monasteries.

"I'm in love with silence", she exclaimed, which he found unusual and a bit daunting but it stuck with him. Silence was a quality of the hills and Gangtok, relative to the plains and Varanasi, where horns tooted even on vacant lanes. Relative silence, yet with conveniences and cafes, had drawn him here to write and reflect.

It wasn't long before he developed a routine. Every second or third morning, he went on a run around the ridge. He loved what was called the Bhanupath, that stretch of road below the old palace that led in the direction of the old residency, now called Raj Bhawan. The tall trees, the bamboo, the azaleas, and especially the ivy and ferns that covered the hillside seemed the most enchanting 100-200 meters of road he could think of in India. When he didn't run, he walked, often varying his walks to go down the hill and drink a quick small cup of chai in a clay kulher cup. Then he went upstairs for a coffee and breakfast, enjoying especially tomato cheese sandwich and corn flakes with a sliced banana.

At first, he would write in his room in the morning. Later, he would alternate between different cafes, such as The Coffee Shop on MG Road, Café Fiction below Rachna's Bookshop, and Zongri Café on Tibet Road. He also found "the best chai in Gangtok" at the simplest hole-in-the-wall café called Sam's Dumpling House run by the two friendliest, most charming, most hardworking women. Another place to re-energize was the lovely Café Bisauni just below the walkway with the flower-seller out front beneath the stairs. The most nourishing food dish he looked forward to was the Nepali thali at Nimtho's.

The gift of time, of uninterrupted time, of relative silence, and of a task in front of him. But a task of "no resistance." It had been brewing for long, this idea of a memoir, of putting down the most memorable moments in his life. In fact, he had already written so much, starting four years ago in Rajghat. He would write in his room, typically on a Sunday, going into some image on his run that morning – an image that triggered a memory, another place, event, people, set of circumstances. These "vignettes", haphazard as they were and how they came to him, became the basis of his memoir. He had written others more recently on vacation breaks in Kolkata, Chennai, and Bangalore, knowing of his plans to assemble, narrate, and write the full memoir after school ended. Before the trip to Japan. When his mind needed to be clear, empty, fresh. Renewed once more.

April 2025

Reflection: The Purpose of Memoir Revisited

"Art washes from the soul the dust of everyday life."
– Pablo Picasso, above the entrance to Artsy Café & Culture,
Kolkata

This memoir is nothing spectacular. It will not sell. It was never intended to sell.

People ask, why should I read it, I've seen so many, what makes it unique?

My answer is: nothing makes it unique then, except that it's my life. Do not expect any high points of philosophy or a worldview. Nor am I seeking to titillate with unreal and fanciful experiences.

I wrote for myself, to understand a few things with the perspective of age, experience, and whatever self-knowledge and insight I have acquired. Nor was the objective full disclosure, especially given sensitivities involved. But to see the essence, glimmers of some truth about yourselves or certain events – and let it be "emotional truth", especially for someone like me, who did not always acknowledge the emotions of what he was experiencing, even to himself let alone others.

On a different note, when I was younger, I would double the suffering. What was in the mind could not be let go. As a child, I remember I just needed a new day to start fresh. But as an adolescence and young adult, some species of gloom and melancholy could sit with me for days. Likely, I would rationalize it and justify it sub-consciously. I was right in feeling this way!

Not for nothing does Seneca say, "We suffer more in imagination than we do in reality." We compound our suffering with our thoughts – a mixture of self-pity, rationalization, and imagined slights, hurts, and revenge. When the mind finally slows down, we are lucky if we can wake up and see things differently, and take a different course of action, one which will "cut the suffering by half", which is how S. N. Goenka describes one of the aims of vipassana meditation. Not eliminate it, but cut it in half. For we, not our circumstances, are the authors of half our suffering. Freedom lies in how we respond to our circumstances, the gap between stimulus and response. Narrowed down, that is our space of action, and it pays to "mind the gap."

I have found that observing the sensations of the body helps trigger a mind-body connection, balancing both. The mind runs away with thoughts, branch to branch, the monkey mind in frenetic mental activity. The body too, without awareness brought by the mind, becomes dissolute, slack, a creature of sloth. The mind regenerates the body, the body regenerates the mind. Care and balance of both is needed.

In my younger days, with the conceit of a young spiritually inclined person is vulnerable to, thinking "I do not really care about material pleasures," I allowed myself the mistaken impression that the life of the senses, and the emotions along with it, counted for less. Less than what? Mind or spirit. What I perhaps didn't understand, in that value-biased perspective, is that mind itself, thought itself, is a sixth sense. More today than I remember in my youth, one hears the phrase "over-thinking." And one must learn when and what to believe and not believe about one's thoughts. Thinking is definitely not everything in spite of the primacy we give the term, often with reason, when we use such phrases as "critical thinking" and so on.

When you observe yourself, closely, in different states of consciousness, including dream states on occasion, then you realize the logic and illogic of the mind. You realize the near impossibility of knowing where "thoughts" originate, and that most of what we mean by "thought" is simply something that comes to mind and ought to be observed, allowed to pass, and not grasped, responded to, or taken seriously. What sticks, what remains, what is a pattern, on the other hand, can be reflected on, looked into. But most of what "we think" – or better said, "what comes to us", perhaps from a stream of consciousness that is beyond the individual self – is to be observed if at all, then let go and discarded, like the passing clouds.

When one is able to "let thoughts go", then in fact the other senses – sight, hearing, smell, taste, even touch – become much sharper. In what I have found worth remembering, this is what I experienced in vipassana but also when I was brought low by back trouble the day before a race. And it is what I experience regularly in the morning when my energy level is high, when I haven't read too much or talked too much, and "the world" is not too much with me. While we also experience this in places of beauty, it need not be. In fact, those who actually reside in mountains or by the beach or a river are prone to lose a "first feeling" for what others see as exceptionally beautiful surroundings. Meanwhile, a flower, a tree, a bird, a patch of sky, a certain sight, though it be in an urban area or surrounded by drab or even off-putting surroundings, can be perceived with the same feeling of beauty. In other words, beauty is everywhere, it's the eye of the beholder that matters.

This too is the symbolic meaning of the lotus, that even in the filthiest surroundings, beauty may still grow. It is also worth contemplating that a lotus blooms unseen, in remote places, but it blooms all the same, not for anyone else. It just blooms. Alone or among hundreds and thousands.